A CULTURAL AND LINGUISTIC EXCAVATION OF THE BIBLE

JEFF A. BENNER

A Cultural and Linguistic Excavation of the Bible
Cover design by Jeff A. Benner

Copyright © 2023 by Jeff A. Benner
Printed in the United States of America.

Virtualbookworm.com Publishing. P.O. Box 9949, College Station, TX 77842, US

Softcover ISBN: 978-1-63868-122-9
E-book ISBN: 978-1-63868-126-7

Library of Congress Control Number: 2023910358

TABLE OF CONTENTS

Acknowledgments   xi

Preface   xiii

Introduction   xvii

THE BIBLE AND ITS PEOPLE

The Bible   1

The Torah   5

The people of the Bible   12

Hebrew Culture   20

Hebrew Philosophy   28

THE HEBREW LANGUAGE AND ALPHABET

The Hebrew Language   39

The Hebrew Alphabet   52

Changes in the Hebrew Alphabet   92

The Hebrew Vocabulary   101

THE OLD TESTAMENT

History of the Hebrew Bible   145

Hebrew Poetry   157

The Bible and Other Semitic Languages   175

Biblical Interpretation   191

Word Studies   196

THE NEW TESTAMENT

The Intertestamental Period   223

The New Testament   227

The New Testament Culture   245

The Teachings of Yeshua   257

Conclusions   275

Timeline   277

Bibliography   283

Index   289

LIST OF ILLUSTRATIONS

Figure 1.   A tsiytsiyt   xix

Figure 2.   Floorplan of a Nomadic Tent.   24

Figure 3.   The Nomadic Tent   27

Figure 4.   The Hebrew word B-N   50

Figure 5.   The Hebrew word A-M   50

Figure 6.   The Hebrew word A-L   51

Figure 7.   A portion of the Aleppo Codex   54

Figure 8.   A portion of a text from a Phoenician inscription   55

Figure 9.   The *beyt* in Old Hebrew, Samaritan and Phoenician   55

Figure 10. Phoenician inscription discovered in Sidon.   56

Figure 11. Mesha Stele inscription   57

Figure 12. The Siloam Inscription   57

Figure 13. The Gezer Calendar   58

Figure 14. A Lachish Ostracon   58

Figure 15. An Ammonite inscription   59

Figure 16. The Tel Dan Inscription   59

Figure 17. "King of Israel" (top) and "house of David" (bottom)   60

Figure 18. The Greek Alphabet in ancient inscription   60

Figure 19. The first five letters of the Old Hebrew alphabet   61

Figure 20. The first five letters of the Old Greek alphabet   61

Figure 21. The Modern Greek alphabet   61

Figure 22. The Modern Latin alphabet   62

Figure 23. 5th century BC Hebrew (Aramaic) alphabet   62

Figure 24. The Modern Hebrew (Aramaic) alphabet   63

Figure 25. Ancient Serabit El-Khadim Inscription   64

Figure 26. Ancient Sinaitic letters: Ox, Hand, and Eye   65

Figure 27. The *L'Balt* inscription   66

Figure 28. The Wadi El-Hhol inscription   66

Figure 29. The name of God (YHWH) in Middle Hebrew   67

Figure 30. Text from a Modern Hebrew Bible   68

Figure 31. The ancient letter *peh* (mouth)   68

Figure 32. The ancient letter *ayin* (eye)   68

Figure 33. Evolution of the letter *Aleph*   70

Figure 34. Evolution of the letter *Beyt*   72

Figure 35. Evolution of the letter *Gimel*   73

Figure 36. Evolution of the letter *Dalet*   74

Figure 37. Evolution of the letter *Hey*   75

Figure 38. Evolution of the letter *Vav*   76

Figure 39. Evolution of the letter *Zayin*   77

Figure 40. Evolution of the letter *Hhet*   78

Figure 41. Evolution of the letter *Tet*   79

Figure 42. Evolution of the letter *Yud*   79

Figure 43. Evolution of the letter *Kaph*   80

Figure 44. Evolution of the letter *Lamed*   81

Figure 45. Evolution of the letter *Mem*   82

Figure 46. Evolution of the letter *Nun*   82

Figure 47. Evolution of the letter *Samehh*   83

Figure 48. Evolution of the letter *Ayin*   84

Figure 49. Evolution of the letter *Peh*   85

Figure 50. Evolution of the letter *Tsade*   85

Figure 51. Evolution of the letter *Quph*   86

Figure 52. Evolution of the letter *Resh*   87

Figure 53. Evolution of the letter *Shin*   88

Figure 54. Evolution of the letter tav   88

Figure 55. Evolution of the letter *ghayin*   89

Figure 56. The parent root *L-K* and its derivatives   109

Figure 57. Morphology of the Hebrew word *b's'ph'to'tey'kha*   112

Figure 58. The name of God (YHWH) on the Temple Ostraca   128

Figure 59. The spellings of YHWH in the Masoretic text.   131

Figure 60. Hebrew manuscript, 11th Century AD   145

Figure 61. Silver scroll discovered in Ketef Hinnom   146

Figure 62. The Nash Papyrus   146

Figure 63. A section of the Isaiah Scroll   148

Figure 64. A page from the Aleppo Codex   149

Figure 65. A portion of Psalm 145 from the Aleppo Codex   150

Figure 66. A portion of Psalm 145 from the Dead Sea Scrolls   151

Figure 67. A portion of an Aramaic Targum   152

Figure 68. A portion of the Greek Septuagint   153

Figure 69. A portion of the Latin Vulgate   153

Figure 70. An Ugarit Abecedary   177

Figure 71. Statue of Ibbit-Lim   181

Figure 72. A tablet from the Eblaite archives   182

Figure 73. A "circle" of nomadic tents.   211

Figure 74. Eliezer Ben-Yehuda, c. 1912   228

Figure 75. 4th century Greek Manuscript   229

Figure 76. 5th century Aramaic Manuscript   229

Figure 77. Letter by Simon Bar Kockba written in Hebrew   241

Figure 78. 2nd Temple period coins with Hebrew inscriptions   242

Figure 79. Dead Sea Scroll fragments written in *Paleo*-Hebrew   242

LIST OF TABLES

Table 1.   Alphabet Chart   91

Table 2.   Hebrew words with an ayin   93

Table 3.   Hebrew words with a *ghayin*   94

Table 4.   Hebrew names without a "g" sound   96

Table 5.   Hebrew names with a "g" sound   96

Table 6.   Hebrew words spelled with a *sin* and *samehh*   99

Table 7.   Child roots from the parent root בל   107

Table 8.   Child roots from the parent root פר   107

Table 9.   Adopted roots from the parent root בח   108

Table 10. The seven Hebrew verb forms   115

Table 11. Conjugations of the verb אבד   115

Table 12. Different spelling of Hebrew words   119

Table 13. The seven unique groups of sounds   120

Table 14. English words derived from Hebrew   122

Table 15. Hebrew names derived from Aram   125

Table 16. Hebrew names derived from Eber   126

Table 17. Hebrew names derived from Judah   127

Table 18. Hebrew letters compared to Ugarit   178

Table 19. Names found in Ebla tablets   185

Table 20. Hebrew and Eblaite words   186

Table 21. Hebrew words from the parent root חם   202

Table 22. Hebrew words in the New Testament   240

ACKNOWLEDGMENTS

The first person I need to thank is my wife, Denise. Many years of research and writing has gone into this work and because of this, you could call my wife a writer's widow. She picked up the slack by taking care of the house, the kids and just about everything else.

Two individuals, Dr. Larry Hirsch and Dr. William Bean, both of whom are no longer with us, are responsible for putting me on my path of biblical study. Their passion for truth and their teachings had a huge influence on me and my journey and I will always be grateful to them for their guidance and instruction.

Scott Curran and I were standing in my driveway one day, many years ago, and I was sharing some of the insights I had been learning about the Bible and its background. He told me that I should write a book. Thank you, Scott, for planting that little seed in me.

No book writes itself and even the author is not able to take full credit for the work as there are many others who have helped in the creation of that work. For this work, there are many beta readers and editors, too many to list here, that have assisted me with the development and editing of this work and I am grateful to each and every one of them.

There is, however, one individual who has devoted a significant amount of her time and energy in the editing of this manuscript. But not only this one, she has edited many of my works and through her guidance, suggestions and corrections she has improved my writing immensely and I can say that without her, I would not be the writer I am today. Thank you, Doris Dippel, for everything you have done.

And last, but certainly not least, I would like to acknowledge and thank you, my readers and your unwavering desire to learn new truths and insights.

The translations referenced in this work include:

Authorized Standard Version (ASV), *English Standard Version* (ESV), *King James Version* (KJV), *New American Standard Bible* (NASB), *New International Version* (NIV), Revised Mechanical Translation (RMT), *Revised Standard Version* (RSV), *Stone Edition of the Tanakh* (SET) and *Young's Literal Translation* (YLT).

PREFACE

That which was from the beginning, which we have
<u>heard</u>, which we have <u>seen</u> with our eyes, which
we looked upon and have <u>touched</u> with our hands,
concerning the word of life. (1 John 1:1, ESV)

Instead of reading the Bible with just our minds, we need to read it
with our senses, as well. That is, we need to see, hear, smell, taste and
touch it from the perspective of those who lived it. In other words, do
not experience the idea of "grace" as an abstract thought in the sense
of being favored. Instead, know it through the more concrete experience of Hebrew thought, which is like the experience of coming
home after being away for a long period of time, seeing your home
in the distance, hearing the voices of your family and smelling the
cooking fires.

For me, this journey began in 1992. For the first time in my life, I
had recently begun a very serious study of the Bible, inspired in part
because my new wife's church had some beliefs that were very different from my own. I can still remember sitting at the kitchen table
with my Bible, a Bible concordance and dictionary and my notepad,
doing a study on angels.

Using the Bible concordance, I discovered that the "messengers" Jacob sent to his brother in Genesis 32:3 was in-fact, the same "angels" he met with in Genesis 32:1. The concordance revealed that the Hebrew word behind "messenger" was the very same Hebrew word behind the word "angel"—*mal'akh*. This raised a few questions in my mind:

> *"Why would the translator use two different words for this one Hebrew word?"*

> *"Is the translator changing the original meaning of the passage?"*

> *"Where else has the translator been so inconsistent with his translations?"*

Unbeknownst to me at the time, this and other similar discoveries in my biblical studies laid the foundation for my *Ancient Hebrew Lexicon of the Bible*, published in 2005. I wrote it to bring to light the cultural and linguistic background of the words that form the Hebrew Bible.

The insights into the culture and language of the Bible that I learned while writing the lexicon spurred me on to doing my own translation, the culmination of which was *The Torah: A Mechanical Translation*[1], published in 2019. Also in 2019 I published my *Benner's Commentary on the Torah*.

---

[1] Accompanying this translation is the *Revised Mechanical Translation* (RMT), which is occasionally referenced in this work.

Now I invite you to continue this journey with me as we walk through *A Cultural and Linguistic Excavation of the Bible*, where we will dig deep into the history of the Bible, its people and their language, and uncover hidden truths that have been lost through centuries of mistranslations, misinterpretations and textual manipulation.

Jeff A. Benner

Magnolia, MS. USA
June 28, 2023

INTRODUCTION

We all are aware that behind the English translation of our Bibles are Hebrew, Aramaic and Greek words. But what many may not have considered is that behind those ancient words were cultures and philosophies vastly different from our own. The Biblical authors' perspectives on life and the world around them were steeped in their traditions, lifestyles, manners and thoughts. When reading and studying this ancient text, we cannot interject our cultural perspectives into the narrative without bringing about interpretations and conclusions far removed from the authors' intended meaning.

To illustrate the importance of this, let's examine a passage from the New Testament and interpret it from within its original cultural and linguistic contexts.

> *"Just then a woman who had been subject to bleeding for twelve years came up behind him and touched the <u>edge of his cloak</u>. She said to herself, 'If I only touch his cloak, <u>I will be healed</u>.' Jesus turned and saw her. 'Take heart, daughter,' he said, 'your faith has healed you.' And the woman was healed at that moment."* (Matthew 9:20-22, NIV)

Have you read a passage and found yourself asking questions that nobody else is asking?

> "Why is the text so specific that she needed to touch the *edge* of his garment?"

> "How did she know that she would be healed if she touched this *edge*?"

Questions like this deserve answers and oftentimes these answers can only be found in the culture and/or language behind the translations.

Let's begin with the "cloak" or, as some translations say, "garment." This would be the rectangular, poncho-like garment worn by all Jewish men. More on this a little later. Behind the English word "edge" is the Greek word κρασπεδον (*kraspedon*, Strong's[2] #G2899), which means "edge" or "border."

However, when we examine how this Greek word was used in the *Septuagint*, a Greek translation of the Old Testament and contemporary to the New Testament period, we find that it was used to translate the Hebrew word ציצית (*tsiytsiyt*, Strong's #H6734), which is usually translated as "fringe," such as can be seen in the following passage:

---

[2] James Strong's *The Exhaustive Concordance of the Bible*, besides being a concordance, includes a dictionary of every Hebrew and Greek word in the King James Version of the Bible and was first published in 1890. As part of this concordance and dictionary, Strong assigned a number to each Hebrew (identified with "H" before the number) and Greek (identified with "G" before the number) word of the Bible.

"[S]peak[3] to the sons of Yisra'eyl[4], and you will say to them, and they will make for themselves fringes (tsiytsiyt in Hebrew and kraspedon in Greek) upon the wings of their garments..." (Numbers 15:38, RMT)

The Hebrew word for "wing" is כנף (*K.N.Ph*, Strong's #H3671) and does mean "wing," such as the "wing" of a bird, but it can also mean "corner;" which in the context of this passage refers to the four corners of Hebrew males' garments. In the image below (Figure 1), we see an example of the *tsiytsiyt* or "fringe" tied to the "corner" of the garment.

Figure 1. A tsiytsiyt
(Image is in the Public Domain)

---

[3] One of the attributes of the RMT is that it does not use punctuation or upper-case letters In Its translation because these conventions did not exist in the Hebrew text. This translation attempts to mimic the Hebrew in every way possible. The only exceptions are the use of commas to identify different clauses that are evident in the Hebrew, and identification of names by using upper case for the first letter.

[4] In the RMT, names are transliterated from the Hebrew text (i.e. Yisra'eyl). Other translations take their transliteration of names from the Greek *Septuagint* (i.e. Israel).

We now know that the woman in the passage from Matthew was reaching for the "corner" of Yeshua's[5] garment where the *tsiytsiyt* would have been tied, but we still do not know *why* she reached for the corner. To answer this question, we turn to the Book of Malachi:

> *"But unto you that fear my name shall the Sun of*
> *righteousness arise with healing in his <u>wings</u>..."*
> (Malachi 4:2, KJV)

And now we are back to the word "wings," the Hebrew word being *kanaph*. As this word also means "corners," we now know the *why*; he, Yeshua, had healing in the "corners" of his garment.

But why would Yeshua be referred to as the *"sun of* righteousness?" When we do a little investigation into this word, we find our answer. The Hebrew word for "sun" is שמש (*shemesh*, Strong's #H8121). However, while not used in the Bible, this Hebrew word can mean "minister[6]." Now let's take another look at Malachi 4:2, but this time with new understanding:

> *"But unto you that fear my name shall the <u>minister</u>*
> *of righteousness arise with healing in his <u>corners</u>..."*

Before moving on, we need to take a closer look at the Hebrew word *tsiytsiyt*. As we have seen previously, this word is used for the "fringes" on the corners of the garments, but that is not what this

---

[5] The Hebrew name *Yehoshu'a* (Joshua) is written as *Yeshua* in the Aramaic. Both of these names are transliterated into Greek as *Iesous*, which is Anglicized as "Jesus."

[6] In the Bible we do find the Aramaic verb שמש (*shemash*, Strong's #H8120) which means "to minister." As Hebrew and Aramaic are sister languages, many of the words in their vocabularies are interchangeable.

word means literally. It specifically means "blossom[7]." In the same way that the function of the blossom is to produce fruit, the function of the *tsiytsiyt* is to remind the wearer that he is figuratively producing fruit, just as is stated in the verse that follows the command to wear the *tsiytsiyt*:

> *"And it shall be unto you for a fringe, that ye may look upon it, and remember all the commandments of the LORD, and do them..."* (Numbers 15:39, KJV)

In the above word study, we have experienced the importance of understanding the Bible from its original cultural and linguistic perspectives. In the pages that follow, we will continue to excavate the Bible, uncovering its many riches by digging into the meanings behind the words and phrases. Gear up and let's get started!

---

[7] The word *tsiytsiyt* is derived from the word ץיצ (*tsiyts*, Strong's #H6731), a literal blossom, and its cognate, *tsiytsiyt*, is a figurative blossom.

THE BIBLE
AND
ITS PEOPLE

THE BIBLE

THE OLD TESTAMENT

Most Christian denominations, including the Catholic and Protestant churches, recognize thirty-nine books in the Old Testament. These books are usually divided into four sections: The *Pentateuch*, the historical books, the poetic books and the prophetic books. Jews include the same thirty-nine books in their Bibles, but they divide them into three sections; *Torah* (teachings), *Nevi'im* (prophets) and *Ketuvim* (writings). The Jews refer to these three sections, their Bible, as the *Tanakh*, a word created by the first three letters of each of the three sections (*TaNaKh*).

THE APOCRYPHA

The Catholic Church includes another set of books in their Bible, generally seven in number, which are called the *Apocrypha*.[8] The Eastern Orthodox Church includes an additional five books in its

---

[8] A Greek word meaning "hidden."

Apocrypha. While most Protestants do not consider these apocryphal books as canon[9], many do consider them worthy of study for Biblical context.

We will examine several of the books of the *Apocrypha* when we go into more detail about the intertestamental period between the Old and New Testaments.

THE PSEUDEPIGRAPHA

There is another set of books, rarely accepted by Jews or Christians, called the *Pseudepigrapha*.[10] While there are very few groups that consider any of the books of the *Pseudepigrapha* as canon, like the books of the *Apocrypha*, they can help with Biblical context. For example, the *Book of Enoch* sheds light on the meaning of the scapegoat (*Azazel* in Hebrew) of Leviticus 16.

The following is a literal translation of Leviticus 16:7-10:

> *"[A]nd he will take the two hairy goats and he will make them stand to the face of YHWH[11], at the opening of the appointed tent, and Aharon will place upon the two hairy goats lots, one lot is for YHWH and one lot is for Azazeyl, and Aharon will bring near the hairy goat, which went up upon him the lot for YHWH, and he will do him as a failure, and*

---

[9] Books that are considered sacred and inspired and valid for the interpretation of one's religion.

[10] A Greek word meaning "false name" from the practice of attributing the authorship of a given work to a false author.

[11] The RMT uses YHWH to represent the four-letter name of God, often pronounced as *Jehovah* or *Yahweh*.

> *the hairy goat which went up upon him the lot for*
> *Azazeyl, he will stand living to the face of YHWH to*
> *make a covering upon him, to send him for Azazeyl*
> *unto the wilderness."* (RMT)

Each goat represents one type of person. The goat selected for YHWH represents the obedient servant who is committed to God; this one sacrifices his life to serve before YHWH. The other goat represents the haughty and proud who is free to live his life his own way, separate from YHWH, and is sent out into the wilderness.

While it would seem that the goat released into the wilderness has the better deal, this is not true; the goat sacrificed to YHWH is completely dedicated to YHWH, while the other is sent out into the wilderness, probably to die from starvation. Actually, the Jewish tradition says the goat was taken to a high place, a cliff, and thrown over it.

What exactly is *Azazel*? Three theories have credence: The first is that Azazel is a combination word meaning "goat" (*az*) and "shake" or "sent away" (*azel*), hence the translation in some Bibles of "scapegoat." The second is that it is the name of the place to which the goat was sent: a desert, solitary place, or a high place. The third is that Azazel is the name of an individual, angel or demon.

The latter is more reasonable, as the Hebrew says one of the goats is "to" YHWH, while the other is "to" *Azazel* (one who is the opposite of YHWH). The Hebrew translated as "to" could also be translated as "belonging to." One goat "belonged to YHWH" and the other "belonged to *Azazel*." The *Book of Enoch* sheds light on who Azazel was.

3

> *"And Azazel taught men to make swords, and knives, and shields, and breastplates, and made known to them the metals of the earth and the art of working them, and bracelets, and ornaments, and the use of antimony, and the beautifying of the eyelids, and all kinds of costly stones, and all coloring tinctures. And there arose much godlessness, and they committed fornication, and they were led astray, and became corrupt in all their ways."* (Enoch 8:1-3)

While Enoch, one of the extra-Biblical works, is not considered "canon" by most churches, one must embrace that they can be instrumental in explaining certain passages, customs, rituals and other aspects of the Old Testament.

THE NEW TESTAMENT

The New Testament consists of twenty-seven books and is usually divided into four sections: the Gospels, the Book of Acts of the Apostles, the Epistles[12] and the book of Revelation. The New Testament is the story of Yeshua and his Jewish disciples. While most Christians, both Catholics and Protestant, accept the entirety of the New Testament as canon, religious Jews reject it, as they do not recognize Yeshua as the Messiah. However, secular Jews do study the New Testament because it is one of the very few documents from that period that depict Jewish life in the first century AD.

---

[12] A Greek word meaning "letters."

THE TORAH

While we have already discussed the Old Testament, here we are going to look at one segment of the Old Testament, the *Torah*. The first five books of the Bible are Genesis, Exodus, Leviticus, Numbers and Deuteronomy, often called the *Pentateuch*[13] by Christians and the *Torah*[14] by Jews. For the Jews, the names of these five books derive from the first Hebrew or first principal word of each book. Thus, the name of the first book (Genesis in Christian Bibles) is *b'reshiyt*, which is the first word in the book and means "in the beginning." The names of the other four books are *Shemot* (names), *Vai'yiqra* (and he said), *B'midbar* (in the wilderness) and *Devariym* (words).

Both Christians and Jews attribute the authorship of these five books to Moses, but this is strictly a tradition, as nowhere in these five books is the author identified. In fact, there is evidence that

---

[13] A Greek word meaning "five books."

[14] A Hebrew word meaning "teachings," but also used as a name for the first five book of the Bible.

there were multiple authors, a theory known as the Documentary Hypothesis.

To illustrate multiple authorship, let's look at some examples:

PASSAGES WRITTEN BY SOMEONE OTHER THAN MOSES

THE BURIAL OF MOSES

> *"And Moses was an hundred and twenty years old when he died: his eye was not dim, nor his natural force abated. And the children of Israel wept for Moses in the plains of Moab thirty days: so the days of weeping and mourning for Moses were ended. And Joshua the son of Nun was full of the spirit of wisdom; for Moses had laid his hands upon him: and the children of Israel hearkened unto him, and did as the LORD commanded Moses. And there arose not a prophet since in Israel like unto Moses, whom the LORD knew face to face, in all the signs and the wonders, which the LORD sent him to do in the land of Egypt to Pharaoh, and to all his servants, and to all his land, and in all that mighty hand, and in all the great terror which Moses shewed in the sight of all Israel."* (Deuteronomy 34:7-12, KJV)

Obviously, Moses could not have written this account; therefore, we know that this portion was written by someone else. Is it not then possible that other portions may have been written by someone other than Moses, as well?

BEFORE THE KINGS OF ISRAEL

> *"And these are the kings that reigned in the land of Edom, before there reigned any king over the children of Israel."* (Genesis 36:31, KJV)

During the lifetime of Moses, no king reigned over Israel. The author of this passage wrote about the kings of Israel from the viewpoint that they were facts of history. Apparently, the author of this passage lived during or after the time of the kings of Israel.

RACHEL BURIED NEAR BETHLEHEM

> *"And Rachel died, and was buried in the way to Ephrath, which is Bethlehem."* (Genesis 35:19, KJV)

As the city of Ephrath was not known as "Bethlehem" until after the death of Moses, the phrase *"which is Bethlehem,"* was obviously written by someone other than Moses.

Granted, we have spoken to just a couple of passages, but if these passages in the *Torah* were written by someone other than Moses, there could just as easily be three or four or a hundred others.

DUPLICATE PASSAGES OF ONE EVENT BY SEPARATE AUTHORS

ISRAEL AT MOUNT SINAI

> *"When the people saw the thunder and lightning and heard the trumpet and saw the mountain in smoke, they trembled with fear. They stayed at a distance."* (Exodus 20:18, NIV)

> *"Then Moses led the people out of the camp to meet with God, and they stood at the foot of the mountain. Mount Sinai was covered with smoke, because the LORD descended on it in fire. The smoke billowed up from it like smoke from a furnace, the whole mountain trembled violently."* (Exodus 19:17-18, NIV)

In the Exodus 20 passage, Israel sees the thunder and lightning and stays at a distance from the mountain. But, in the Exodus 19 description, they go up to the mountain and see smoke and fire. It appears that while different authors wrote these two narratives, they were combined into one story by one known as a "redactor." This person took the various stories known at the time and attempted to integrate them into a single account. For this reason, we see many of the same stories repeated at different times. So, while it is commonly understood that these are two different stories that occurred at two different times, they may be the same story written by two different authors and combined into one by the redactor.

Another account of Israel's experience at the mountain occurs in the book of Deuteronomy, where one passage says that Israel did not want to hear the voice of God speak to them, while another states that he did speak to them:

> *"For this is what you asked of the LORD your God*
> *at Horeb on the day of the assembly when you said,*
> *'Let us not hear the voice of the LORD our God*
> *nor see this great fire anymore, or we will die.'"*
> (Deuteronomy 18:16, NIV)

> *"The LORD spoke to you [Israel] face to face out of*
> *the fire on the mountain."* (Deuteronomy 5:4, NIV)

Notice that the Deuteronomy 18 passage identifies the mountain as Horeb and not Sinai. Apparently, this mountain is addressed by two different names, depending on the author of the passage.

CONFLICTING PASSAGES BY SEPARATE AUTHORS

MAKING KNOWN THE NAME YHWH

> *"[A]nd Avram said to the king of Sedom, I rose up*
> *my hand to YHWH, the mighty one of Elyon, pur-*
> *chaser of skies and land."* (Genesis 14:22, RMT)

> *"[A]nd I appeared to Avraham, to Yits'hhaq, and to*
> *Ya'aqov with the mighty one of Shaddai, and my title is*
> *YHWH, I was not known to them,"* (Exodus 6:3, RMT)

In the Genesis passage, Abraham invokes the name YHWH, but according to the Exodus quote, God had not revealed his name, YHWH, to Abraham.

A GUIDE THROUGH THE WILDERNESS

> *"The LORD your God who goes before you... who went before you in the way to seek you out a place to pitch your tents, in fire by night and in the cloud by day, to show you by what way you should go."* (Deuteronomy 1:30, 33, ESV)

> *"And he said,'Please do not leave us, for you know where we should camp in the wilderness, and you will serve as eyes for us.'"* (Numbers 10:31, ESV)

In the Deuteronomy passage, Moses tells the people that God will be their guide through the wilderness, showing them which way to go and where to camp. However, in the Numbers passage, Moses beseeches his father-in-law, Hobab, to go with Israel to show them where to go and where to camp in the wilderness, as he was familiar with the area.

Though not included in the quoted passages, we have two different names for Moses' father-in-law. In some passages he is called Jethro while in other passages he is called Hobab.

STYLES OF WRITING

We all speak and write differently, and styles of writing can be compared to determine the authors of different texts. For example, one person might say, "*I talked to mom,*" while another person would say, "*I spoke to my mother.*" We can easily see that these two phrases are from two different people.

We frequently see these same variations in writing style within the text of the *Torah*. In Numbers 21:16 we read אמר יהוה למשה (*amar yhwh l'mosheh*), which means "*YHWH said to Moses*," but in Exodus 4:30 we find the phrase דבר יהוה אל משה (*diber yhwh el mosheh*), which means "*YHWH spoke unto Moses*." These differences in writing style are found throughout the *Torah*. We can even see the writing of one person throughout the text intermixed with the writing style of another person, a result of the redactor's splicing together separate accounts into one.

THE AUTHORS OF THE CREATION NARRATIVES

Genesis chapter 1:1 through 2:3 uses the word *Elohiym* for the name of God, but in Genesis 2:4 through 4:26, the name YHWH is used. According to the Documentary Hypothesis, the first section was written by an author who uses the word *Elohiym*. Therefore, he is called the "Elohist source." The second section was written by an author who uses the word YHWH and is therefore called the "Yahwist source." Thus, in total, there are believed to be five authors of the *Torah*: The Elohist source, the Yahwist source, the Deuteronomist source (the one who wrote the book of Deuteronomy), the Priestly source (the author of much of Leviticus and Numbers), and finally, the redactor (the one who assembled the four sources into one document and inserted text when necessary to make the narrative flow).

Now that we've walked through an overview of the Bible, its versions and authors, we begin to drill down to take a closer look at the people who lived during the times of the documents we call the Bible.

THE PEOPLE OF
THE BIBLE

THE OLD TESTAMENT

In the Old Testament we have four different people groups discussed or described: natives, strangers, immigrants and foreigners.

Attempting to differentiate between these different people groups can be difficult at times, as the translators are not very consistent in how they translate the Hebrew names of these different people groups. For example, in the KJV the Hebrew word *ger*, which we will examine closer below, is translated as "alien," "foreigner," "immigrant," "sojourner" and "stranger." Another word that we will look at momentarily is the Hebrew word *nakhriy*, which the KJV translates as "alien," "foreigner" and "stranger."

NATIVES

The natives (sometimes translated as "home-born") are those who were born to one of the twelve tribes of Israel. The Hebrew word for a native is אזרח (*ezrahh*, Strong's #H0249). This word comes from the verbal root[15] זרח (*Z.R.Hh*, Strong's #H2224), which means to "come up" or "come out of." So, an *ezrahh* is one who has "come out of" Israel.

> *"All that are <u>home-born</u> shall do these things after this manner, in offering an offering made by fire, of a sweet savor unto Jehovah."* (Numbers 15:13, ASV)

STRANGERS

The Hebrew verb זור (*Z.W.R*, Strong's #H2114) means "to be separated out." The participle form of this verb means a "stranger," one who is "separated out." This word is frequently used in the Bible for someone who is not from one's own tribe.

> *"If brothers dwell together, and one of them dies and has no son, the wife of the dead shall not be married outside the family to a <u>stranger</u>; her husband's brother shall go in to her, and take her as his wife, and perform the duty of a husband's brother to her."* (Deuteronomy 25:5, RSV)

---

[15] The Hebrew language is a system of root words from which nouns and verbs are derived and will be discussed in more detail later.

IMMIGRANTS

The Hebrew word for an immigrant is גר (*ger*, Strong's #H1616), derived from the verb גור (*G.W.R*, Strong's #H1481), which means to "dwell with" or "dwell among." An immigrant is one who was not a native-born Israeli, but lived with the natives. According to the *Torah*, the immigrants were to live according to the same customs and laws as the natives did.

> *"One law shall be to him that is home-born, and unto the* [immigrant] *(גר) that* [dwells with] *(גור) you."* (Exodus 12:49, ASV)

FOREIGNERS

A foreigner was one born in a foreign land, but unlike an immigrant, was not bound to the customs and laws of the native or immigrant.

> *"Unto a <u>foreigner</u> thou mayest lend upon interest; but unto thy brother thou shalt not lend upon interest."* (Deuteronomy 23:20, ASV)

Two Hebrew words designate a foreigner: נכרי (*nakhriy*, Strong's #H5237) and נכר (*nekhar*, Strong's #H5236). Both of these words are derived from the root נכר (*N.K.R*, Strong's #H5234) meaning "to be recognizable," probably because a foreigner was easily recognizable by their very different costume, mannerisms and language.

THE NEW TESTAMENT

In the New Testament we find four different people groups: nations, Hellenists, Jews and proselytes. Unfortunately, due to misinterpretations and mistranslations of the text, much misunderstanding exists concerning the identity of these different people groups.

NATIONS

The Greek word εθνος (*ethnos*, Strong's #G1484) literally means "nation." This word is used in the 2,000-year-old Greek *Septuagint* to translate the Hebrew word גוי (*goy*, Strong's #H1471), which also means "nation." A nation is any group of people living and working under one rule. Many different nations are mentioned in the Bible including the Canaanites, Egyptians, Moabites, Arameans, and others. But more importantly, even Israel is called a "nation."

> *"And I will make of thee (Israel) a great nation (goy)..."* (Genesis 12:2, KJV)

> *"... and of good report among all the nation (ethnos) of the Jews..."* (Acts 10:22, KJV)

Translating the Greek word *ethnos* in the New Testament as "gentile," which it usually is, is problematic. While the word "gentile" does mean "one who belongs to a tribe or clan," it has come to universally mean a "non-Jew." But as we have seen, the Hebrew word *goy* and the Greek word *ethnos* do not mean a non-Jew; they mean "one who belongs to a tribe or clan."

15

Who are the *ethnon* (nations - plural of *ethnos*) mentioned in the New Testament?

The "ten lost tribes" from the northern "nation" of Israel were taken into captivity by the Assyrians in the eighth century BC. It is believed by many that these "ten lost tribes" are "lost," but this is not exactly true, at least not in the sense most people assume.

> *"And there was one Anna, a prophetess, the daughter of Phanuel, of the tribe of Asher..."* (Luke 2:36, RSV)

The tribe of Asher is one of the "ten lost tribes," but as we can see, Anna, from the tribe of Asher, was not "lost." The "lost" tribes were not "lost" in the sense of being "missing," but in the sense of walking away from the teachings of YHWH. Even Yeshua mentioned that his mission was to reach the "lost" tribes and commissions his disciples to do the same.

> *"But he [Yeshua] answered and said, 'I am not sent but unto the lost sheep of the house of Israel.'"* (Matthew 15:24, KJV)

> *"But go rather to the lost sheep of the house of Israel."* (Matthew 10:6, KJV)

Even James mentioned that he was a servant to the "twelve tribes," which would include the "ten lost tribes."

> *"James, a servant of God and of the Lord Jesus Christ, to the twelve tribes which are scattered abroad, greeting."* (James 1:1, KJV)

When Paul preached to the various "nations" in the Book of Acts, he was doing what Yeshua commanded by preaching to the "lost" tribes, the lost *goy/ethnos* of Israel.

HELLENISTS

The Greek word Ελλην (*Hellen*, Strong's #G1672) means a "Greek." Derived from this word comes the word Ελληνιστης (*Hellenistes*, Strong's #G1675), a Hellenist, which means "Greek-like[16]." This word is used in the New Testament for Jews who had adopted the Greek culture and language:

> *"But there were some of them, men of Cyprus and Cyrene, who on coming to Antioch spoke to the Hellenists also, preaching the Lord Jesus."* (Acts 11:20, ESV)

While the Greek word *Hellenistes* is usually translated as "Greek" or "gentile," neither of these groups was "Greek-like." A Greek was a Greek, and a gentile was neither a Greek nor Greek-like.

It is often attested that Paul's mission was to the "gentiles" (meaning "non-Jews"). However, if we examine Paul's missions carefully, we find that every time he came to a city, he always entered the synagogue on the Sabbath (see Acts 13:5, 14, 14:1, 17:2, 10, 17, 18:4, 19, 26, 19:8). As was his custom (see Acts 14:1, 17:2), he went there to preach the gospel to the Jews and Hellenists (see Acts 14:1, 17:12,

---

[16] *The Analytical Greek Lexicon* (page 133) defines the word *hellenistes* as: to imitate the Greeks, one who uses the language and follows the customs of the Greeks; in N.T. a Jew by blood, but a native of a Greek-speaking country.

19:10). Paul did have a few interactions with non-Jews, but these were always impromptu meetings and not part of his mission (Acts 14:11, 16:32, 17:18).

How then, are we to understand Paul when he states the following?

> *"...I am the apostle of the Gentiles."* (Romans 11:13, KJV)

As we saw above, the Greek word *ethnon* (the plural form of *ethnos*) means "nations" and is often used for the lost "nations" or "tribes" or Israel. Just as Yeshua and James said that they were servants to these lost tribes, Paul is simply making it clear that he was following in their footsteps, just as he stated in 1 Corinthians:

> *"Be imitators of me, as I am of Christ."* (1 Corinthians 11:1, ESV)

JEWS

The Jews, in contrast to the Hellenists, were those Jews that remained faithful to the teachings of the *Torah* and their Hebrew heritage, but had rejected the Greek culture and language.

PROSELYTES

Mentioned only four times in the New Testament are the "proselytes" (Matthew 23:15, Acts 2:11, 6:5 and 13:43). The word "proselyte" is a transliteration of the Greek word προσηλυτος (*proselutos*, Strong's #G4339), which means a "stranger." These were non-Jews, whom today we would call "gentiles" that had joined Israel and followed YHWH and his teachings.

> *"...both Jews and <u>proselytes</u>, Cretans and Arabians—we hear them telling in our own tongues the mighty works of God."* (Acts 2:11, ESV)

HEBREW CULTURE

THE HEBREWS' NOMADIC LIFESTYLE

Many Biblical characters, such as Abraham, Isaac, Jacob, Moses, David and others, lived a nomadic lifestyle. They were nomads who lived in tents, traveled from location to location searching for water and pastures for their livestock.

THE WILDERNESS

The nomad's home was the wilderness, often arid, but with an occasional oasis, river, water basin and pasture. The nomad was as much at home in the wilderness as we are acclimated to our environment. He also knew the area in which he traveled well, including where all the water sources were, where pastures were located at different times of the year and all the landmarks that directed him on his travels.

Rain was the essential element for the nomad. Without it, he and his family, his flocks and herds could not survive. The tribe's chief was responsible for ensuring that they were at the right place at the right seasons. The rains could be local, providing water and pasture, but might also be very distant. These distant rains flooded the rivers, causing them to overflow and water the floodplains of the rivers within their areas of travel.

FAMILY

The nomadic family consisted of the *beyt* (house, family), *mishpechah* (clan) and *matteh* (tribe). The family was comprised of the parents, children and maybe grandparents. The clan included the extended family: grandparents, aunts, uncles, cousins and more, all residing in one camp, with as many as 50 to 100 tents laid out in a circular pattern. Any fewer, and it would have been difficult to protect the family, while more would have made it difficult to feed everyone. When the clan became too large to be supported by one area, it would split into two clans (see Genesis 13). All the clans (those descended from one ancestor) may have covered hundreds of square miles and made up the larger tribe. A Biblical example of this tribal structure would be the house of Moses, of the clan of Levi, of the tribe of Israel.

POSSESSIONS

Nomads lived a very simple life, and because of their constant travels, they could not carry a significant number of possessions. Instead, the nomad's wealth was measured by the size of his flocks and herds, which supplied him with most of his needs, including milk, meat, skin, hair for tents, horns for trumpets, bladders for liquid containers and much more.

His cooking supplies and equipment consisted of bags made of skins for carrying food reserves like grains and dried fruits, a few utensils such as spoons, knives and bowls and a grinding mill for making flour from various grains. He also carried some harvesting tools such as sickles and mattocks to gather crops when available. For defense, he also had weapons such as a bow and arrow. Many of his weapons served dual purposes. For instance, the tent poles, which were sharpened at one end to drive into the ground, also served as spears.

FOODS

The nomad's diet consisted of a variety of foods including bread, fruits (when available), milk, cheese and meat. Grains, such as barley and wheat, were gathered and ground into flour, mixed with water and placed on hot rocks to make bread. They enjoyed fruits like grapes, pomegranates, olives and dates when they were available. These were often dried for later use and sometimes mixed with flour for a cake-type bread. Milk from the sheep and goats was used to make cheese. Animals from the flock were occasionally butchered, especially for special events like the arrival of a guest or the birth of a baby.

MEDICINES

Many foods were also used for medicinal purposes. For example, honey was eaten for stomach and intestinal problems and applied to wounds as an antiseptic. The fat of animals was made into soap for bathing and washing.

SOCIAL ACTIVITIES

The men would often gather, usually during mealtimes, to discuss past events, needs, locations and other details of operating the camp. The women would meet together to prepare foods, make clothing and make tent repairs. Storytelling was probably one of the most important forms of entertainment. The older members of the clan would tell stories of the clan's history to the children to pass on the experiences of the tribe and clans to the next generation.

One of the major responsibilities of the clan was to provide hospitality to anyone who came to them, regardless of whether the visitors were members of a related clan or even an enemy from another tribe. In both cases, it was the clan's responsibility to provide food, shelter and protection for the visitor as long as they were within the camp.

RELIGION

The religion of the Hebrew nomads was very different from our understanding of religion. The entirety of the lifestyle of the nomad was his religion. As his very existence was dependent upon rain, he understood that his life was in God's hands at all times. The nomad saw the power, justice, love and mercy of God in all things. All of his activities, such as eating, making shelter or working, were seen as a service to God. In essence, his life was one continuing prayer to God.

THE GOAT HAIR TENT OF THE NOMADS

The nomad's most important possession was their tent, which was made of spun goat hair and supported with poles and ropes.

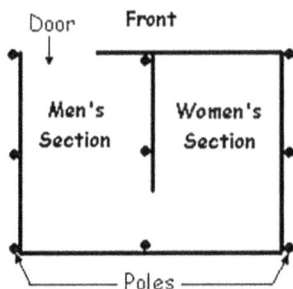

Figure 2. Floorplan of a Nomadic Tent.
(Image created by the author)

The tent was divided into two parts (see Figure 2). The main section behind the tent door was the men's section. The other section was the women's with a wall dividing the two parts. The only males allowed into the women's section were the father of the tent and children.

Later, we will cover the history of the Hebrew alphabet, but for this discussion we will be examining two Hebrew letters, the letters *beyt* and *dalet*. In the Modern Hebrew alphabet, these letters are written as ב and ד, respectively. However, in ancient times, these letters were written with pictures, ﬡ and ﬡ. Notice the similarity to the image of the tent above with the pictographic Hebrew letter ﬡ (*beyt*), meaning "home." This letter represents the tent's floorplan, the "home" of the nomadic Hebrews.

The entrance to the tent was covered by a curtain that hung down from the top of the entrance. The Hebrew word *dal* means "hang down" and is the root for the word *dalet,* meaning "door." This word is also the name of another Hebrew letter, ﬡ (*dalet*), representing the tent door. The tent's door was the most important part of the tent, not because of its appearance, but for its function as the entrance into the tent:

> *"...he [Abraham] sat at the door of his tent in the heat of the day."* (Genesis 18:1, ESV)

In the Hebrew culture, the family's father was responsible for the organizing of the duties and responsibilities of the family "business." In some ways, he was like a "king," who had the authority over the family. The door of the tent could be equated with the throne of a king. Therefore, the father would often sit at his door much as a king would sit on his throne. All family legal matters were performed at the tent door. From there he watched over his household, as well as watching for passing travelers.

> *"Dark am I....dark like the tents of Kedar, like the tent curtains of Solomon."* (Song of Solomon 1:5, NIV)

Tents were constructed of black goat hair. The hair was spun into strands woven together forming panels approximately two feet wide and the length of the tent. Over time, the panels would bleach from exposure to the sun and periodically needed to be replaced. Very little was discarded, as much work was invested in creating all their materials. This included the tent panels, which when they no longer functioned properly as a part of the roof, would be removed and recycled into walls or mats.

Another Hebrew letter derived from the tent itself is the letter ㅂ (*hhet*[17]), meaning "wall." This letter in the ancient pictographic script is a picture of a tent wall.

---

[17] The author of this work prefers the transliteration *hh* for the letter *samehh* instead of *ch*, the standard transliteration, because *ch* is too often pronounced like the *ch* in "church," rather than the guttural *h* sound that it actually represents.

The size of the tent depended on the size and wealth of the family. As the family grew, additional panels were added to increase the size of the tent. This is alluded to in the following passage:

> *"Enlarge the place of your tent, stretch your tent curtains wide, do not hold back; lengthen your cords, strengthen your stakes."* (Isaiah 54:2, NIV)

HEAT

A tent provided shade from the sun. During the intense heat of the day, the walls of the tent could be lifted to allow the breeze to pass through the tent.

COLD

The black tent absorbed heat, warming the tent during cold nights. A fire could also be built just inside the door for warmth.

RAIN

While the woven goat hair fabric of the roof had pinholes of light that appeared like stars at night, the hair fibers swelled when wet, making it waterproof. Just as the stars disappear when it rains, so too, did the "stars" on the tent roof. Because of this, the Hebrews saw the night sky as God's tent over his family.

> *"…He stretches out the heavens like a canopy, and spreads them out like a tent to live in."* (Isaiah 40:22, NIV)

WIND

The tent had a low profile to allow the wind to pass over the tent easily. Strong ropes, secured by pegs driven into the ground, supported the poles that held up the tent.

In many ways, the goat hair tent of the Near Eastern nomads was unique and ideally suited for the desert regions in which they lived.

Figure 3. The Nomadic Tent
(Image is in the Public Domain)

HEBREW PHILOSOPHY

A HISTORY OF PHILOSOPHY FROM
A LINGUIST'S PERSPECTIVE

Philosophy is the study of knowledge and linguistics is the study of language. While these two branches of science are very different, they do have overlapping components. The language of a people and the philosophy of those who speak that language are strongly connected.

In this world, there are two major branches of philosophy, Eastern and Western, but for our purposes and for reasons that will be made clear shortly, we will call these two branches of philosophy "simple" and "complex." The difference between the two is that "simple philosophy" studies and investigates the "known" world, while "complex philosophy" studies and investigates the "unknown world." One who lives with a "simple" philosophy looks at an ocean and sees an endless expanse of water. They see the ocean as a barrier and never attempt to investigate it. On the other end of the spectrum, one who lives with a "complex" philosophy looks at the same ocean and wonders what lies beyond it and spends an exorbitant amount of time, energy, and resources to answer the question about what is on the other side of the water. Every culture around the world falls within a spectrum of these two philosophies.

Have you ever wondered why the indigenous in America, who had just as much time and as many resources as Europeans at their disposal, were building small boats with stone axes, while the culture from which Christopher Columbus came was building large sea-going vessels made with great timbers, iron and massive sails? Thus, when Christopher Columbus arrived in the Americas, he came from a culture having a very complex philosophy and discovered a culture with a very simple one.

Only a few cultures with a very simple philosophy still exist today. They are found deep in the jungles of the Amazon and Africa or on isolated islands. Besides these rare and isolated cultures, the remaining world has more sophisticated philosophies with varying degrees of complexity. Yet, it has not always been so.

The author proposes the theory that "simple" philosophy is a natural form of philosophy innate in all people. The more "complex" forms of philosophy can only be learned. For the greater extent of the world's history, all cultures followed a simpler philosophy until the Greeks arose and began to formulate more complex philosophies. The sciences could be developed only through these more complex forms of philosophy. While a person with a simple form of philosophy looks at a rock and asks, "What can I do with this rock?" A person with a more complex philosophy asks, "What happens if I melt this rock and combine it with another rock?"

When a culture functioning with a more complex philosophy meets a culture with a simpler philosophy, the more complex philosophy always dominates, eventually erasing the other culture's simpler philosophy. Sometimes this comes about through simple assimilation, but most often it occurs through force or even violence. Throughout history, we see this happen over and over again. One example is when the Jews were dominated by the Greek and then Roman cultures. As a result, much of Jewish simple philosophy was influenced by them. When the Romans invaded northern Europe, they replaced the simple philosophy of those cultures with their more complex one. Later, when the Europeans came to America, we see this same transition of philosophy was forced on the Native Americans. At some point in the future, the remaining isolated and uncontacted peoples worldwide ultimately will be dominated by our modern complex philosophical worldview, completely erasing any trace of the more simple and natural philosophy we are born into.

The Hebrew Bible was written in a culture that had a very simple philosophy. Therefore, we must approach our interpretation of the Bible from a simple viewpoint to correctly understand it. However, if we project a more complex form of philosophy onto the text, we come away with an interpretation that the writer did not intend.

Modern stone age peoples that still exist in small pockets around the globe have a simple philosophy very similar to that of the Ancient Hebrews of the Bible. An example to illustrate this is the conventions used to describe directions. In the Ancient Hebrew language, there are two words for "south." The first is *yamin*, which means "to the right[18]." The other is *negev*, which means "desert[19]." Similarly, in the primitive *Pirahã* tribe of the Amazon, linguist Daniel Everett[20] discovered that their directions were identified as "toward the river," "toward the middle of the jungle," or other similar absolute directions.

Mr. Everett also states that the *Pirahã* refer to themselves as the "straight ones," while outsiders are called the "crooked ones." Similar concrete expressions can be found in the Hebrew language, as well, but linguists have translated them out by replacing their concrete terms with abstract ones that are more familiar to our culture and language. Take, for example, the King James translation of Proverbs 14:2 which reads:

> *"He that walketh in his <u>uprightness</u> feareth the LORD: but he that is <u>perverse</u> in his ways despiseth him."*

However, when this is translated literally from the Hebrew, it reads:

> *"One who will walk <u>straight</u> will revere YHWH, but the one who makes his path <u>crooked</u> is worthless."*
> (RMT)

By studying the culture, lifestyle, and language of people who live by a simpler philosophy, we can better understand the Ancient Hebrews.

---

[18] The Hebrews oriented their compass directions to the east, the place of the rising sun, while we orient our compass directions to the north.

[19] The southern desert region of Israel is called the Negev.

[20] Everett, Daniel. "Losing Religion to the Amazonian *Pirahã* Tribe." Lecture at The Long Now Foundation, San Francisco, 2009.

We can also study the modern-day Bedouin who lives a lifestyle very similar to that of Abraham over 4,000 years ago.

Donald P. Cole spent a year living with the Bedouins and documented his research into their culture with his book *Nomads of the Nomads.* As one interesting observation, he noted that the tents of the Bedouin were not the property of the men, but of the wives[21], which may be due to the fact that the women created the tents. This little revelation sheds light on a problematic word in the Hebrew Bible:

In three verses, Genesis 9:21, 12:8 and 35:21, we find the Hebrew word אָהֳלֹה (*ahaloh*), which does not conform to standard Biblical Hebrew morphology. In each case and in every translation consulted, this word is translated as "his tent." The problem is that the Hebrew word for "his tent" is אָהֳלוֹ (*ahalo*), such as seen in Genesis 31:25. However, the Hebrew word for "her tent" is אָהֳלָה (*ahalah*). If we remove the *nikkudot*[22], which are not part of the original text, we find that the Hebrew word for "his tent" is אהלו and the Hebrew word for "her tent" is אהלה. And "her tent," אהלה, is the word found in the three verses noted above. When the Masoretes came to the word אהלה, meaning "her tent," they added the *hholam* vowel with the "*o*" sound, to force the pronunciation *ahalo*, to imply this word meant "his tent."

In Genesis 9:21, Noah was not sleeping off his drunken stupor in "his tent," because he did not own a tent. He was sleeping in "her tent," the tent owned by his wife.

---

[21] (Cole, 1975, p. 64)

[22] These are the dots and dashes that were added above and below the Hebrew letters by the Masoretes to represent the vowel sounds, which are mostly missing in Biblical Hebrew.

Another clarification is found in Genesis 24:67 that reads:

> *"And Isaac brought her into his mother Sarah's tent..."* (KJV)

Based on this passage, many have assumed that Sarah had her own tent apart from her husband Abraham's. But based on what we have learned from the Bedouin culture, we now know that Abraham did not have a tent; only his wife Sarah did.

This is a good place to note that while we are able to reconstruct some of the culture of the Ancient Hebrews, such as we have done here, much of their culture has been lost to us and this should be kept in mind as we study and interpret the text.

ABSTRACT VS. CONCRETE THOUGHT

As we previously examined, throughout the world there are two major branches of philosophy, Western and Eastern. Western philosophy had its beginnings in the 6th century BC in Greece with such philosophers as Socrates, Plato and Aristotle. Eastern philosophy has its roots in the ancient past and was the philosophy of all ancient cultures of the Far East (including China and Japan), Middle East (including India and Babylon) and Near East (including Syria and Israel).

While there are many differences between the Western and Eastern schools of thought, one of the major differences is their use of abstracts and concretes.

Just as with artwork, words can also be created in the concrete or the abstract. A concrete word, idea or concept is something that the five senses can perceive. It can be seen, heard, smelled, tasted or touched. An abstract is something theoretical that the five senses cannot perceive.

As the Bible was written from an Eastern philosophical perspective of concreteness, we must recognize that we cannot correctly interpret it through our more abstract Western philosophy. To do so yields meanings and interpretations that may not be those of the original authors.

Thorleif Boman's monumental work, *Hebrew Thought Compared with Greek*, states:

> *"The thinking of the Old Testament is primitive and hence can be compared only with the thinking of other primitive peoples and not with thinking as advanced as Plato's or Bergson's."*[23]

In his book *Manners and Customs of the Bible*, Victor H. Matthews explains how the culture of the Hebrews can be studied:

> *"One of the joys of studying the Bible is attempting to reconstruct the manners and customs of the peoples of ancient times. The gulf of thousands of years can be bridged, at least in part, by insights into their everyday life. These can be garnered through the close examination of the biblical narratives and*

---

[23] (Boman, 1960)

through the use of comparative written and physical
remains from other ancient civilizations."[24]

George Adam Smith stated that:

> *"...the Hebrews were mainly a doing and feeling*
> *people. Thus, their language has few abstract terms.*
> *Rather, Hebrew may be called primarily a language*
> *of the senses. The words originally expressed con-*
> *crete or material things and movements or actions*
> *which struck the senses or started the emotions.*
> *Only secondarily and in metaphor could they be*
> *used to denote abstract or metaphysical ideas."*[25]

APPEARANCE VS. FUNCTIONAL DESCRIPTION

Modern Western philosophy describes objects in relation to their appearance, while Ancient Eastern philosophy describes an object in relation to its function.

A stag and an oak are two very different objects and our Western minds would never describe them in the same way. The Hebrew word for both of these objects is איל (*ayil*) because the functional description of these two objects is identical in the Ancient Hebrew mind. The Hebraic definition of *ayil* is "a strong leader." Therefore, the same Hebrew word is used for both.

A stag is one of the most powerful animals of the forest and is seen as "a strong leader" among the other animals of the forest. The oak

---

[24] (Matthews, 1991)

[25] (Smith, 1944, p.10)

tree's wood is very hard compared to other trees, such as the pine, which is soft. Thus, the oak is seen as a "strong leader" among the trees of the forest.

Compare the two different translations of Psalm 29:9:

> *The voice of the LORD makes the <u>deer</u> give birth...* (ESV)

> *The voice of the LORD twists the <u>oaks</u>...* (NIV)

In one translation, the Hebrew word *ayil* is translated as "deer," while in the other, it is translated as "oak." Both of these are acceptable translations of the Hebrew word, but because we modern Western thinkers think only of the characterization of the "deer" or "oak," we miss the truer meaning intended by the author, which is as follows:

> *"The voice of the LORD makes a <u>strong leader</u> turn."*

A modern Western thinker describes a pencil by its appearance, such as, "Yellow, eight inches long, pointed at one end and blunt at the other." An ancient Eastern thinker would describe it according to its function: "I write with it." Notice that the Westerner uses adjectives that are noun modifiers and are rarely found in Biblical Hebrew. In contrast, the Easterner uses a verb, "write," and verbs are used prolifically in the Bible. They are action, function words.

THE
HEBREW
LANGUAGE
AND
ALPHABET

THE HEBREW LANGUAGE

Now that we have a solid comprehension of the different parts of the Bible, the people of the Bible, their culture and their philosophy, we turn our attention to the Hebrew language of the Bible, investigating the origins of the language and how it was intertwined with the people themselves in their practices and daily lives.

THE LANGUAGE AND CULTURE CONNECTION

In what has become known as the Whorf Hypothesis, Benjamin Lee Whorf stated that, *"language is not simply a way of voicing ideas, but is the very thing which shapes those ideas."*[26] An example of this is how one perceives time. In our Modern Western culture, we view time in the sense of the past, present and future, a fixed and measurable progression of time.

---

[26] (Clifford et al., 2016, p. 34)

Other cultures, such as the Hopi Indians of North America, do not share this same perspective of time. To the Hopis, there is what "is" (manifested) and what "is not yet" (unmanifested). Interestingly, the Ancient Hebrews had a similar view of time. Like the Hopi language, the Ancient Hebrew language does not use past, present and future tenses for verbs. Instead, it uses two tenses, one for a completed action (manifested) and one for an incomplete action (unmanifested).

An individual whose native language is Hopi views time from the Hopi perspective, but if he is required to adopt English, he learns the English perspective of time. During the late 1800s, the United States forced Native Americans to adopt the English language. When a Hopi no longer functioned within his native language, his original cultural perspectives, such as time, were lost and replaced with the Modern Western perspective, thereby destroying a part of their culture forever. This destruction of the language and culture is not unique to the Hopi, but happened countless times as the dominant Western culture replaced the culture of simpler peoples, including the Hebrews' language and culture.

In the Introduction, we learned that from a Hebraic point of view, the word *tsiytsiyt* carried with it a cultural perspective that connected the blossoms of a tree with the performance of a commandment.

When the Hebrews, more specifically the Jews, were expelled from the land of Israel after the Bar Kokhba revolt in 136 AD, the Hebrew people adopted the language of the people around them. Frequently that language was Greek for their everyday use. From that point on, Greek became the influential language in their lives, and dominated and determined their mental viewpoint about words and ideas.

The Hebrew word *tsiytsiyt*, meaning "blossom," became the Greek word κρασπεδον, meaning "a decorative fringe or thread" and the connection between a blossom and observing God's commands is now lost.

In 1948, Israel became a Jewish state, and, with that, Hebrew once again became the everyday language of the Jewish people. However, while the language has been resurrected, the original cultural perspective of that language disappeared long ago, though the Western influence on Hebrew survived. Therefore, in the mind of Modern Orthodox Jews a *tsiytsiyt* is still a decorative fringe and no longer functionally related to a blossom and the fruit of obedience.

This same sort of change can be seen throughout the Hebrew language, as is documented in the author's lexicon, *The Ancient Hebrew Lexicon of the Bible*. For example, the Hebrew word תורה (*torah*), which in the original Hebrew language meant a "teaching," now means "doctrine" in the Modern Hebrew language ." A כוהן (*kohen*) in the original language meant the "base" of the community, but in the Modern Hebrew language it means a "religious priest." The word קדוש (*qadosh*), which originally meant "special," now in the modern language means "holy."

THE MISSING 'ART' IN HEBREW LINGUISTICS

In 1810, William Gesenius published his *Hebrew Lexicon* and his *Hebrew Grammar* in 1813. By examining, comparing, and documenting the relationships and meanings of Hebrew words in the Hebrew Bible, Gesenius is credited with being the first to approach the Hebrew language of the Bible using a scientific perspective.

Gesenius' work has been edited and revised many times. While other authors have duplicated and modified his work, any further advancements in Hebrew philology have seemed to stagnate since its introduction over 200 years ago. It's almost as if Gesenius' work has come to be considered the final authority on Hebrew philology. Students of the Hebrew language that adhere to his framework of interpretation are often unwilling to venture beyond the accepted limits of study.

For too long, the Hebrew language of the Bible has been examined from a purely scientific perspective. The University of Nottingham website's article, *Art Versus Science,* asks the question, *"Are [the arts and sciences] really as distinct as we seem to assume? And if they are, what is the distinction? Do we have a clear definition of each that allows us to see their separation? There is no universal agreement on these questions."* The article goes on to explain that *"science requires creative thinking,"* which is an art, and that artists *"must also learn a technique, sometimes as rigorous and precise as found in any science."*[27]

This work endeavors to add an "artistic" approach by viewing the Hebrew language more like a painting or a dance, full of animation, interpretation and imagination, rather than studying it like an inanimate rock. It is from that perspective that we shall now look at Hebrew word structure.

TWO-LETTER ROOT WORDS

In his research into the ancient Hebrew language, the author of this work hypothesized that all three-letter Hebrew root words were derived from two-letter Hebrew roots. Over a period of ten years, he

---

[27] (Mumford, 2012)

set out to test this hypothesis, publishing his results in the *Ancient Hebrew Lexicon of the Bible* in 2005. In this lexicon, he connected many three-letter root words with what he believes to be their two-letter roots.

While the *Ancient Hebrew Lexicon of the Bible* has been accepted and used by many individuals, Biblical scholars ignore and criticize it because it does not conform to accepted and proven Hebrew philology. Their attitude raises the question:

> *"Why are scholars so resistant to investigating new approaches to Biblical Hebrew studies?"*

The following anecdote demonstrates why some professionals may be reluctant to consider new truths:

In a small way, the author of this work was involved with the pre-production of the movie documentary *Patterns of Evidence: The Exodus*. The producer of the film told him a very interesting and eye-opening story. The movie makers had interviewed a famous Biblical scholar and presented their extraordinary evidence concerning the exodus of the Israelites from Egypt. While being interviewed on-camera, the scholar responded with a somber countenance and stated that the evidence was interesting, but not conclusive. However, once the camera was turned off, his expression immediately changed to one of excitement, and he commented that this evidence could change knowledge of Biblical history in a profound way.

Why would this scholar ignore the evidence on camera, yet show great enthusiasm when the camera was turned off? The answer is straightforward. He could not be perceived as accepting these radical changes to the paradigm of Biblical history, for it would negatively affect his reputation as a Biblical scholar if he thought outside of the box. This kind of intellectual institutionalization prevents the development and process of scientific research and stifles any growth in the field.

Therefore, if Biblical linguists are unwilling to push the envelope into new research and word studies through the "art" of *a posteriori* reasoning and logic, it remains for people like this author and others of like mind to promote these advancements.

PICTOGRAPHIC HEBREW

Another aspect of the Hebrew language ignored by Biblical scholars is the proposal that the Hebrew letters have meanings based on their original pictographs.

For instance, we know that the Hebrew word for "father" is אב (*av*). It is also a fact that the origins of the Hebrew alphabet are the ancient pictographic script and that the Hebrew word for "father" would have been written with two "pictures"—ﬡﬢ. The first picture, from right to left, is of an "ox-head" and is the Hebrew letter *aleph*, a Hebrew word meaning "ox." The second is of a "house" and is the Hebrew letter *beyt*, a Hebrew word meaning "house." It is at this point the "science" of linguistics ends and the "art" of linguistics begins.

Hebrew words may have multiple meanings. For instance, the Hebrew word *aleph* may mean: "ox" (a strong animal), "chief" (a strong person), or "thousand" (a strong number). The Hebrew word *beyt* may mean, "house" (the actual house, or those of the house, such as in "the house of David") or "family." What happens when we take the meanings of the Hebrew words *aleph* (strong one) and *Beyt* (family), and apply them to the word אב (*av*)? Surprisingly, we get "strong one of the family," a very logical definition for a "father." At this point, this reasoning is nothing more than a hypothesis. Still, if this methodology can be repeated with other Hebrew words, which the author has done in the *Ancient Hebrew Lexicon of the Bible*, the hypothesis becomes a theory based on *a posteriori* logic. RATHER THAN ATTEMPTING TO PROVE OR DISPROVE THIS THEORY, MOST BIBLICAL SCHOLARS IGNORE IT BECAUSE IT DOES NOT CONFORM TO ACCEPTED HEBREW LINGUISTICS.

Opponents of this philological theory also argue that because the *Paleo*-Hebrew letters had evolved out of the original pictographic script and no longer resembled the original "pictures," their meanings were lost. But there is evidence that suggests that the Biblical writers who used the *Paleo*-Hebrew script still knew and understood the definitions of each letter. We can see an example of this in the following passage:

> *"And you, son of man, sons of your people, the ones speaking with you by the walls and in the doors of the houses, and speak <u>one</u> on <u>one</u>, each to his brother saying, 'Please come and listen to what is the word that is going out from YHWH.'"* (Ezekiel 33:30, RMT)

Note that the word "one" appears twice. The first one is the Hebrew word חד (*hhad*) and the second one is אחד (*ehhad*), which is derived from חד (*hhad*), but both words mean the same thing— "one." In the ancient pictographic script, the word חד (*hhad*) would be written as

דּה. The first letter, ה, is a picture of a "wall," and the second letter, ד, is a picture of a "door." Did the author who wrote this passage know that the meaning of these pictures was a "wall" and a "door?" Some Hebrew scholars say "no," but some think otherwise. Reread the verse above. Did you see it? "*...by the <u>walls</u> and in the <u>doors</u>...*"

Is this just a coincidence? Possibly, but other examples can be found in the Hebrew Bible.

Psalm 34 is an acrostic[28]. The 3rd verse begins with the 3rd letter of the Hebrew alphabet, the *gimel*, which in the ancient pictographic script was a picture of a foot (✓) and was associated with the idea of "gathering <u>together</u>." We will look into the meanings of these letters in more detail later.

> "*Oh, magnify the LORD with me, and let us exalt his name <u>together</u>!*" (Psalm 34:3, ESV)

The 5th verse begins with the 5th letter, the letter *hey*, which is a picture of a man with his arms raised and <u>looking</u> at something great in the distance (ℂ).

> "*Those who <u>look</u> to him are radiant, and their faces shall never be ashamed.*" (Psalm 34:5, ESV)

The 11th verse begins with the 12th letter[29], the *lamed*, which in the ancient pictographic script was a picture of a shepherd staff (∠). As

---

[28] A biblical acrostic is where each line or verse begins with the next letter of the alphabet. An example in English would be; Apples are delicious, berries are colorful, cherries are bright, and so on.

[29] The 6th letter of the Hebrew alphabet, the vav, is missing from this acrostic, causing the number of the verse to be off by one with the number of the letter.

the staff was used to direct the sheep, this letter is associated with the ideas of authority and <u>teaching</u>.

> *"Come, O children, listen to me; I will <u>teach</u> you the*
> *fear of the LORD."* (Psalm 34:11, ESV)

The 15th verse begins with the 16th letter, the *ayin*, which was a picture of an <u>eye</u>.

> *"The <u>eyes</u> of the LORD are toward the righteous*
> *and his ears toward their cry."* (Psalm 34:15, ESV)

The 17th verse begins with the 18th letter, the *tsade*, which was a picture of a trail leading to a stronghold and carries with it the idea of <u>deliverance</u>.

> *"When the righteous cry for help, the LORD hears*
> *and <u>delivers</u> them out of all their troubles."* (Psalm
> 34:17, ESV)

WORD DEFINITIONS

Most of what we know about the Biblical Hebrew language comes from the Hebrew Bible itself. Definitions are derived through the context of how these words are used in the Bible. The more a word is used, the better we can define it according to the multiple contexts in which it is employed. Conversely, the fewer times a word is used in the Hebrew Bible, the less context we have to assist with its definition, and the less precise that definition can be.

As they are found in Gesenius' *Lexicon,* the definition of Biblical Hebrew words has almost completely stagnated since he completed his work, and anyone who attempts to redefine Hebrew words is accused of "rewriting the Bible" or "creating secret knowledge."

To further illustrate the stifling of scholarship, in Gesenius' *Lexicon* the Hebrew verb ארר (*A.R.R*) means "to curse." This verb is related to the verb רור (*R.W.R*), which is defined as "to flow." From this verb comes the noun ריר (*R.Y.R*), which is defined as "spittle" or "drool." This is about the extent of Biblical Hebrew scholarship as related to these words and is where the defining of Hebrew words has stagnated.

After reading the works of other Hebrew scholars who propose that the Hebrew language of the Bible had a more concrete rather than an abstract vocabulary, the author hypothesized that a more concrete definition of ארר (*A.R.R*) would be "to spit" rather than the abstract "to curse." If this is true, then we can conclude that within the culture of the Hebrew people of the Bible they would "curse" another by "spitting" on them. But when Hebrew linguistics are studied only through the two-hundred-year-old accepted definitions from Gesenius, such interpretations are impossible and prevent linguists from advancing any further in their understanding of the Hebrew language of the Bible and its more definite meanings.

We must also remember that over the past 200 years many advancements and discoveries have been made in the fields of archaeology, anthropology and philology that have had an impact on how we understand the language of the Bible and the culture of its people. In a later section, we will see some examples of this when we investigate how recent discoveries of texts in related Semitic languages have shed some light on the Hebrew language of the Bible.

AN ALTERNATE APPROACH TO HEBREW LINGUISTICS

When we look at the words that comprise this sentence, we acknowledge that each letter represents a sound. In the same way, a word is a compilation of these letters and represents a concept. For instance, the letter F represents the "f" sound, the letter L the "l" sound, and the letter Y the "y" or "i" sound. When these letters are put together, they form the word "FLY," which conveys either the concept of a species of flying insect or the act of soaring in the air.

What if, in ancient times, writing was the opposite, and the letters represented a concept, and the word described a sound? This would be similar to how we use acronyms such as FYI, FBI and NBC. In each of these, it is the letter that conveys the concept, such as "Federal," "Bureau" and "Investigation," and the word FBI only represents sounds. We can take this one step further and actually pronounce the acronym, such as S.C.U.B.A (Self Contained Underwater Breathing Apparatus), which we pronounce as a word: "scuba."

We see something very similar in the Ancient Hebrew language, as with the word אָב, which we examined above. Each letter represented a concept (ox and house), but the two letters combined create a new concept, a Hebrew word meaning "father," and a new sound—*av*.

Figure 4. The Hebrew word B-N
(Image created by the author)

The Hebrew word בן (*ben*) is spelled *beyt-nun* (see Figure 4). In the original pictographic script, the letter *beyt*, as we mentioned, is an image of the home. In its original pictographic script, the letter *nun*, a Hebrew word meaning "continue," is an image of a "seed." It represents the idea of "continuing," as the seed continues the next generation. When these two letters are combined, we have the "home continues" and describes a "son," the one who continues the home. Such is how a simple philosophy viewed life.

Figure 5. The Hebrew word A-M
(Image created by the author)

The Hebrew word אם (*eym*) is spelled *aleph-mem* (see Figure 5). In the original pictographic script, the letter *aleph* is the ox head representing "strength." The Hebrew letter מ (*mem*), a word meaning "water" in Hebrew, is an image of "water." When combined, these two letters mean "strong water," which is "glue" and is the Hebrew word for "mother," the one who is the "glue" of the family, the one who holds the family together.

Figure 6. The Hebrew word A-L
(Image created by the author)

The Hebrew word אל (el) is spelled *aleph-lamed* (see Figure 6). The *aleph*, the picture of an ox, represents "strength," and the *lamed* is a picture of a shepherd staff representing "authority." These letters form the Hebrew word *el* meaning the "strong authority" and is the Hebrew word for "God."

THE HEBREW ALPHABET

OLD HEBREW AND THE SAMARITAN ALPHABET

To correctly discuss the Hebrew alphabet as it exists today, its foundation must be unearthed to appreciate why it is such a unique basis for the Hebrew language. History suggests that the Hebrew letters we use today are not the same Hebrew letters used in antiquity. So, we shall begin at the beginning and uncover their origins and sources. In 1854, Thomas Hartwell wrote:

> *"The present Hebrew Characters, or Letters, are twenty-two in number, and of a square form: but the antiquity of these letters is a point that has been most severely contested by many learned men."*

Hartwell continues:

"But the most decisive confirmation of this point is to be found in Ancient Hebrew coins, which were struck before the [Babylonian] captivity, and even engraven on all of them are manifestly the same with the modern Samaritan."[30]

According to their own confession, the Samaritans were the descendants of the northern tribes of Israel who were not sent into Assyrian captivity in 722 BC, but remained and continuously resided in the land of Israel.

Research indicates Torah Scrolls of the Samaritans used an alphabet that was very different from the alphabet used in Jewish *Torah* Scrolls. According to Samaritans and Hebrew scholars, the Samaritan alphabet is deemed to be the original "Old Hebrew" alphabet.

Even as far back as 1691, this connection between the Samaritan and the Old Hebrew alphabets was made by Henry Dodwell:

"[The Samaritans] still preserve [the Pentateuch] in the Old Hebrew characters."[31]

Humphrey Prideaux correspondingly wrote in 1799:

"And these five books [of the Samaritans] still have among them, written in the old Hebrew or Phoenician character, which was in use among them before the Babylonish captivity, and in which

---

[30] (Hartwell, 1840, p. 190)
[31] (Dodwell, 1691, p. 118)

53

> *both these and all other scriptures were written, till*
> *Ezra transcribed them into that of the Chaldeans.*"[32]

This same theory is presented in the 1831 edition of the *Encyclopedia Americana*:

> *"During the Babylonish captivity, they received*
> *from the Chaldees the square character in common*
> *use; and in the time of Ezra, the old Hebrew manu-*
> *scripts were copied in Chaldee characters.*"[33]

The Hebrew *Torah* (*Pentateuch*[34]) was initially written with an alphabet like that of the Samaritans. However, after the exile in Babylon, it was transcribed with the Chaldean square alphabet, which was still employed 1,000 years ago for the *Aleppo* Codex (see Figure 7) and is still used in Modern Hebrew today.

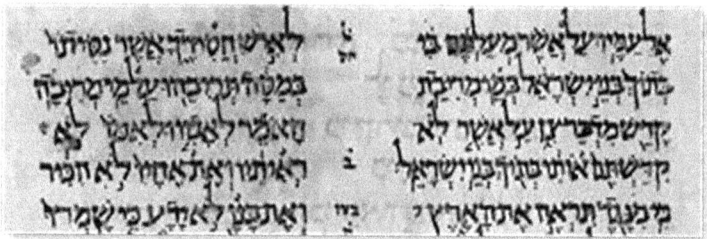

Figure 7. A portion of the Aleppo Codex
(Image is in the Public Domain)

---

[32] (Prideaux, 1719, p. 431)

[33] (*Encyclopedia Americana*, Hebrew Language and Literature, 1831, p. 212)

[34] The Greek name for the *Torah* and means "five books."

OLD HEBREW AND THE PHOENICIAN ALPHABET

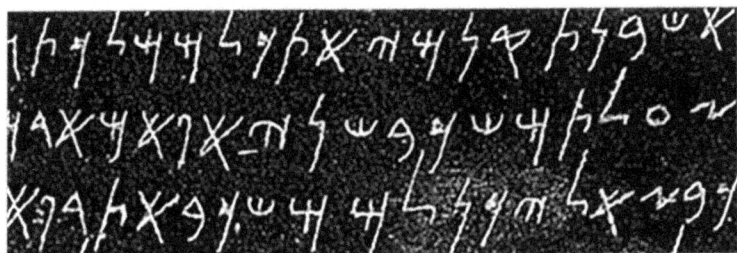

Figure 8. A portion of a text from a Phoenician inscription
(Image is in the Public Domain)

While Prideaux noted that the Old Hebrew alphabet was the same as the Samaritan alphabet, he also pointed out that it was identical to the Phoenician alphabet (see Figure 8). Phoenicians, who lived north of the land of Israel between the 16th and 3rd centuries BC, were centered around the Biblical cities of Sidon and Tyre in modern day Lebanon.

Figure 9. The *beyt* in Old Hebrew, Samaritan and Phoenician
(Images in the Public Domain)

When we compare the letters of the Old Hebrew, Samaritan and Phoenician alphabets, we see similarities, such as when we compare the letter *beyt* (see Figure 9).

The 1831 edition of the *Encyclopedia Americana* also makes this connection between the Hebrew, Samaritan, and Phoenician alphabets:

> *"[The Hebrews'] written characters were the*
> *same as the Phoenician, to which the letters of the*
> *Samaritan manuscripts approach the nearest."*[35]

While the origins of the Old Hebrew alphabet were widely accepted, this theory was based on a limited amount of evidence, as the *Foreign Quarterly Review* points out:

> *"What is left [of Phoenician] consists of a few in-*
> *scriptions and coins..."*[36]

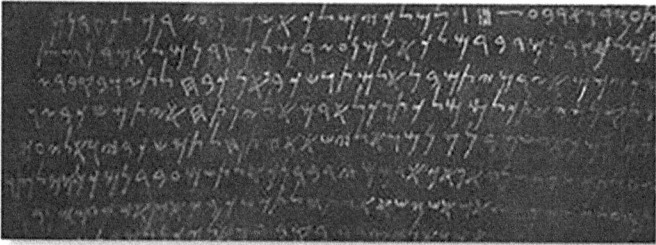

Figure 10. Phoenician inscription discovered in Sidon.
(Image is in the Public Domain)

The first significant discovery connecting the Phoenician alphabet and its associated language with Hebrew occurred in 1855 when Turkish laborers accidentally uncovered an ancient sarcophagus in the Phoenician city of Sidon. The sarcophagus had a lengthy inscription written in the Phoenician alphabet and language, which was found to be identical to Hebrew with just a few exceptions. [37]

---

[35] (*The Encyclopedia Americana,* Hebrew Language and Literature, 1831, p. 212)
[36] Ibid., page 445
[37] (*The Foreign Quarterly Review,* Phoenician Inscriptions, 1838, p. 446)

OLD HEBREW DISCOVERIES

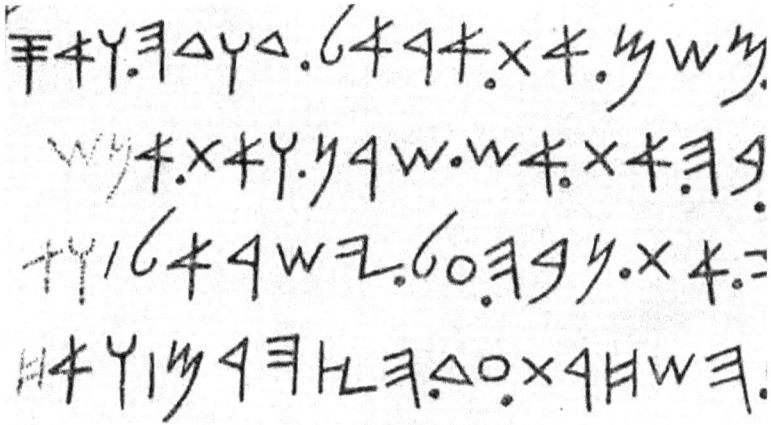

Figure 11. Mesha Stele inscription
(Image is in the Public Domain)

The Mesha Stele (Figure 11), also called the Moabite Stone, was discovered in 1868 in the Biblical city of Dibon, capital of the Moabites. The inscription was written with the same letters as the Phoenician, Old Hebrew and Samaritan. Thus, it was discovered that the Moabite language was also the same as Hebrew with some minor variations.

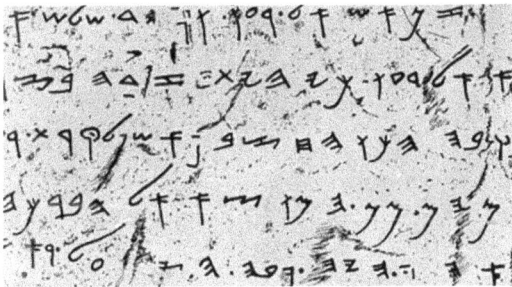

Figure 12. The Siloam Inscription
(Image is in the Public Domain)

The Siloam Inscription (Figure 12), discovered in 1880, is written on the wall of Hezekiah's tunnel which connects the Gihon spring to the Pool of Siloam in East Jerusalem. This Hebrew inscription was written in the same style as the Phoenician and Moabite inscriptions.

Figure 13. The Gezer Calendar
(Image is in the Public Domain)

In 1908, during the excavation of the city of Gezer 30 miles from Jerusalem, a limestone tablet was discovered with a Hebrew inscription written in the Old Hebrew alphabet (Figure 13).

Figure 14. A Lachish Ostracon
(Image is in the Public Domain)

In 1935, eighteen ostraca (broken pottery fragments) were discovered in the ancient city of Lachish, in Israel, with writing that used the Old Hebrew alphabet (Figure 14).

Figure 15. An Ammonite inscription
(Image is in the Public Domain)

In 1966, an inscription was discovered with an Ammonite inscription in Amman, Jordan. The alphabet and language were also similar to both the Phoenician and Old Hebrew (Figure 15).

Figure 16. The Tel Dan Inscription
(Image is in the Public Domain)

The Tel Dan Stele, discovered in northern Israel in 1993, is an Aramaic inscription using the same script as Old Hebrew (Figure 16).

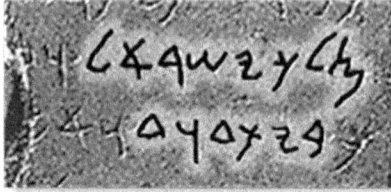

Figure 17. "King of Israel" (top) and "house of David" (bottom)
(Image created by the author)

This inscription also revealed another amazing fact. The inscription includes the phrase מלך ישראל (*melek yisrael*) meaning "king of Israel" and the line below it reads בית דוד (*beyt david*) meaning "house of David" (see Figure 17). These phrases are extra-Biblical evidence that confirm not only the existence of the nation of Israel, but also king David.

OLD HEBREW TO GREEK AND ARAMAIC

Figure 18. The Greek Alphabet in ancient inscription
(Image is in the Public Domain)

The Old Hebrew alphabet, also called *Paleo*-Hebrew, was adopted by the Greeks around the 12th century BC.

Figure 19. The first five letters of the Old Hebrew alphabet
(Image created by the author)

The first five letters of the Hebrew alphabet are *aleph*, *beyt*, *gimel*, *dalet* and *hey* (see Figure 19). The Greeks adopted these same letters to become the *alpha*, *beta*, *gamma*, *delta* and *epsilon* (meaning "simple E").

Figure 20. The first five letters of the Old Greek alphabet
(Image created by the author)

While Hebrew is typically written from right to left, Greek was written from left to right and the letters' orientation was reversed (see Figure 20).

Figure 21. The Modern Greek alphabet
(Image created by the author)

Over the centuries, these ancient Greek letters evolved into their Modern Greek forms (see Figure 21).

Figure 22. The Modern Latin alphabet
(Image created by the author)

The alphabet typically used by English speaking people is Latin in origin, and, because the Romans adopted the Greek alphabet, we can see the *Paleo*-Hebrew letters in our Modern English alphabet (see Figure 22).

THE ARAMAIC ALPHABET

As we summarized above, all Semitic peoples including the Arameans used the *Paleo*-Hebrew alphabet. Arameans are commonly referred to as the Chaldeans, and their *Aramaic* alphabet evolved independent of the Hebrew alphabet.

Figure 23. 5th century BC Hebrew (Aramaic) alphabet
(Image created by the author)

By the 5th century BC, the time of the Israelites' captivity in Aramea (Babylon or Chaldea), the Aramaic letters no longer resembled the Old Hebrew it had borrowed. This Aramaic "square" script is what Israel adopted during their captivity (see Figure 23).

א ב ג ד ה ו

Figure 24. The Modern Hebrew (Aramaic) alphabet
(Image created by the author)

This old Aramaic alphabet, then adopted by the Israelites, continued to evolve into the modern letters we are familiar with today, but are no longer called "Aramaic," but instead, "Hebrew" (see Figure 24).

ALPHABET ORIGINS

By the end of the 19th century AD, the transformation and translation of the *Paleo*-Hebrew alphabet was well-established. The remaining mystery was to discover the origin of this alphabet, as mentioned in *A Compendius and Complete Hebrew and Chaldee Lexicon to the Old Testament*, published in 1886:

> *"א (aleph), The first letter in the Hebrew alphabet...*
> *Its name אלף (aleph) is from אלף (eleph) meaning a*
> *yoke-beast, ox or heifer; and its oldest figure prob-*
> *ably pictured a bovine head."*[38]

The 1922 *New Larned History for Ready Reference, Reading and Research*[39], in its entry for the letter "A," also denotes the suspected origins of the Hebrew alphabet:

---

[38] (Davies & Mitchel, 1886, p. 1)
[39] (Larned, J. N., 1922)

> *"A, the initial letter of the English and almost all*
> *other alphabets... The Phoenicians called the letter*
> *"aleph" seemingly because of the resemblance of*
> *the character to the head of an ox. Although nothing*
> *is known with any degree of certainty concerning*
> *the ultimate origin of this letter."*[40]

The editors of the *New Larned History* did not know that this mystery had been already solved just a few years earlier by Sir William Flinders Petrie.

THE ANCIENT SEMITIC ALPHABET

In 1905, a discovery in the Sinai Peninsula changed the world's acknowledgement of the origins of this Semitic alphabet.

Figure 25. Ancient Serabit El-Khadim Inscription
(Image is in the Public Domain)

Flinders Petrie, a renowned Egyptologist and pioneer in modern archaeology, was performing an archaeological excavation at Serabit

---

[40] (Larned, 1922, p. 1)

el-Khadim, an ancient turquoise mine in the Sinai Peninsula. He discovered a number of inscriptions in and around the mines that resembled Egyptian hieroglyphs, but, due to the limited number of characters, concluded that it was an alphabet, which he later called *Proto*-Sinaitic.

Dr. Alan H. Gardiner, another renowned Egyptologist, studied these inscriptions in detail. He discovered that they consisted of a total of thirty-two symbols[41] and was easily able to identify this Sinaitic alphabet as Semitic.

Figure 26. Ancient Sinaitic letters: Ox, Hand, and Eye
(Image created by the author)

Dr. Gardiner found that the letters in these ancient Sinaitic inscriptions were pictures of the very names of the Hebrew letters. The image of an ox-head (left) was the letter *aleph*, a Hebrew word meaning "ox." The image of the hand (center) was the letter *yud*, a Hebrew word meaning "hand." And finally, the image of an eye (right) was the letter *ayin*, a Hebrew word meaning "eye."

By the relationships between the pictograph and the names of the Semitic letters, Dr. Gardiner proposed to prove that this was a precursor to the previously known Phoenician/Old Hebrew (*Paleo-Hebrew*) alphabet.

---

[41] Ibid., Page 225

Figure 27. The *L'Balt* inscription
(Image is in the Public Domain)

Once it was determined that the new script was Semitic, Dr. Gardiner was able to translate a portion of one inscription in 1916. This inscription (Figure 27) includes the letters *lamed, beyt, ayin, lamed* and *tav*, which form the Semitic word לבעלת (*l'balt*), meaning "to the lady."[42]

DATING THE SEMITIC ALPHABET

The inscriptions discovered in the past century and a half have been accurately dated through archeological advances. The original Semitic alphabet with its pictographic letters can be divided into three periods: Early, Middle and Late.

Figure 28. The Wadi El-Hhol inscription
(Image is in the Public Domain)

---

[42] (*The American Journal of Semitic Languages and Literatures*, 1919, p. 35)

The Early Semitic alphabet existed between the 20th and 12th centuries BC. However, note that the 20th century date is based on the oldest inscriptions found thus far, and future discoveries may push the date of the Semitic alphabet back even farther into history. The Wadi El-Hhol inscription (Figure 28) found in southern Egypt is the oldest Semitic inscription found, and dates to between the 19th reverse these and 20th centuries BC. The Sinaitic inscriptions from the Sinai Peninsula that we looked at previously, date to about the 15th century BC.

The Middle Semitic alphabet, also called *Paleo*-Hebrew, was in use between the 12th and 4th centuries BC. The Gezer calendar, Mesha Stele, Siloam inscription, the Lachish inscription and the Phoenician sarcophagus date to this period, as well. While the widespread use of this script ceased around the 4th century BC, it continued to be used in a limited capacity, such as on coins, into the 1st century AD.

The Late Semitic alphabet, the square Aramaic script, began to be used by the Hebrews in the 4th century BC during their Babylonian captivity, and its use continues to this day. Most of the scrolls from the Dead Sea Caves are written in the Late Semitic Script and date to between the 2nd and 1st centuries BC.

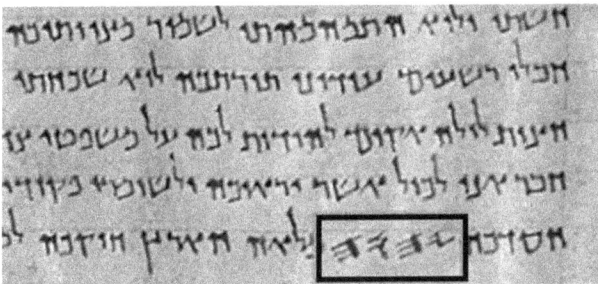

Figure 29. The name of God (YHWH) in Middle Hebrew
(Image is in the Public Domain)

However, among these scrolls, a few, such as the Leviticus scroll, were written with the Middle Semitic script. In addition, many of the scrolls written in the late Hebrew, wrote the name YHWH in the middle Hebrew (see Figure 29). The reason for this is unknown, but may possibly be because they saw the middle Hebrew script as "special" and therefore used it for the "special" name.

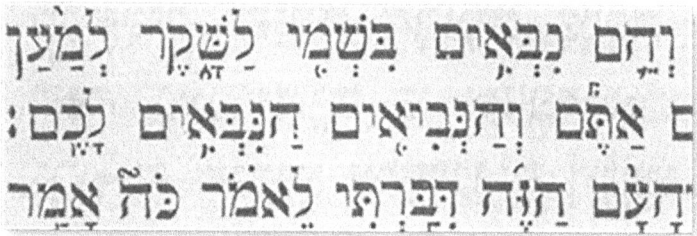

Figure 30. Text from a Modern Hebrew Bible
(Image is in the Public Domain)

The late Semitic script continued to be used for the works of the *Talmud*, the Masoretic Hebrew Bible and modern printed Bibles (Figure 30).

DETERMINING THE MEANINGS OF THE LETTERS

Figure 31. The ancient
letter *peh* (mouth)

Figure 32. The ancient
letter *ayin* (eye)

(Images created by the author)

As we discussed earlier, each Hebrew letter was initially written as a picture, a pictograph. For example, in the Modern Hebrew alphabet, the letter *peh* is written as פ, but in the ancient pictographic script it was a picture of a mouth (see Figure 31). The letter *ayin*, written as ע in Modern Hebrew, was originally a picture of an eye (see Figure 32).

How do we know that these pictures are of a mouth and eye? We touched on this earlier when we discovered that the names of Hebrew letters are also Hebrew words. The Hebrew word פה (*peh*) means "mouth" and the Hebrew word עין (*ayin*) means "eye."

> *"Yea, they opened their mouth (פה / peh) wide against me, and said, Aha, aha, our eye (עין / ayin) hath seen it."* (Psalm 35:21, KJV)

Each picture represents several different ideas and concepts. For example, in the case of the letter *peh*, the meanings of this letter are "mouth," "speaking" (as done with the mouth), and "edge" (from the lips being the edge of the mouth). How do we know that these are meanings of the letter *peh*? Because the Hebrew word פה (*peh*) also has these very same meanings.

> *"[A]nd the sons of Yisra'eyl did so and Yoseph gave to them carts by the <u>mouth</u> (word) of Paroh and he gave to them provisions for the road."* (Genesis 45:21, RMT)

> *"[A]nd Yehoshu'a weakened Amaleq and his people by the <u>mouth</u> (edge) of the sword,"* (Exodus 17:13, RMT)

Jeff A. Benner

In the same way, the Hebrew letter *ayin* has the meanings of "eye," "see" (the function of the eye) and "knowledge" (as gained from seeing). So, again, we can see that the Hebrew word עין (*ayin*) has these same meanings:

> *"[A]nd Aharon spoke all the words which YHWH spoke to Mosheh, and he did the signs to the <u>eyes</u>* (sight) *of the people..."* (Exodus 4:30, RMT)

> *"[A]nd it will come to pass, if from the <u>eyes</u>* (knowledge) *of the company she has been done for an error..."* (Numbers 15:24, RMT)

Reconstructing the Hebrew Alphabet

Now that we have an overview of the different phases of the Hebrew alphabet, now it is time to trace the evolution of every letter through each phase of development.

ALEPH

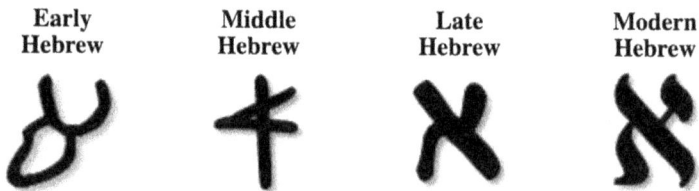

| Early Hebrew | Middle Hebrew | Late Hebrew | Modern Hebrew |

Figure 33. Evolution of the letter *Aleph*
(Image created by the author)

70

The original pictograph for this letter, ν, is a picture of an ox head representing strength and power evidenced in the work performed by the animal.

The name for this letter in Hebrew is *aleph* and corresponds to the Greek name *alpha* and the Arabic[43] name *aleph*. *Aleph* is not only the name of the letter, but is also a Hebrew word that can mean "oxen," "yoke" or "learn," each of which is closely related in meaning to the picture of an ox.

The original picture of an ox head evolved into a simpler form (χ), but still resembled the image of an ox head. This form of the letter was adopted by the Greeks, then later, by the Romans, eventually becoming our letter "A." This letter continued to evolve into ✝ in the Middle Hebrew, which, incidentally, is the origin of the number "1." This letter continued to progress in the Aramaic alphabet to become the Late Hebrew letter א. This form eventually became the modern Hebrew letter א. In Modern Hebrew, this letter represents the number 1, as it is the first letter of the alphabet.

In Modern Hebrew, this letter is silent. However, it most likely had an original pronunciation of an "*a*." Supporting this theory, the Greek letter *alpha*, derived from the *aleph*, represents the "*a*" sound to this day.

---

[43] The Arabic alphabet, which has a common origin with Hebrew, oftentimes offers us clues into the ancient form of the alphabet because it followed a different evolutionary path than did Hebrew.

BEYT

Early Hebrew	Middle Hebrew	Late Hebrew	Modern Hebrew
ט	9	ע	ב

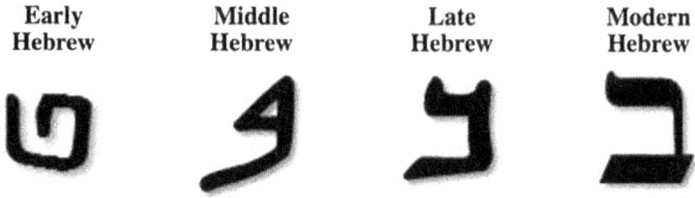

Figure 34. Evolution of the letter *Beyt*
(Image created by the author)

The ancient pictograph ט is representative of the Hebrew's home, their house or tent. The Hebrew and Arabic name for this letter is *beyt*, which is also a Hebrew word that means "house" or "home." The name is also preserved in the Greek name for this letter, *beta*.

The Early Hebrew form of this letter evolved into 9 in the Middle Hebrew and then into the Greek letter *beta* (β), our letter "b" and the number "2."

The Middle Hebrew continued to evolve into the Late Hebrew ע and then into the Modern Hebrew ב. In Modern Hebrew, this letter, the second letter, represents the number 2.

This letter is pronounced with a "b[44]," just as it is in the Greek, Latin and Arabic alphabets.

---

[44] Some Hebrew letters have two sounds, one a stop (a sound that abruptly ends, such as "*p*") and the other a spirant (a sound that continues, such as "*ph*"). In the case of the letter *beyt*, the stop is a "*b*" and the spirant is a "*bh*" ("*v*").

GIMEL

Early Hebrew	Middle Hebrew	Late Hebrew	Modern Hebrew

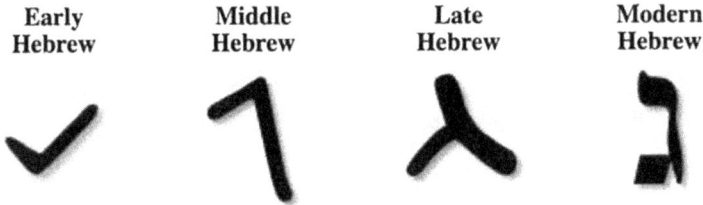

Figure 35. Evolution of the letter *Gimel*
(Image created by the author)

The pictograph for this letter is ✓. The Modern Hebrew name for this letter is *gimel*. However, the Greek name, *gamma*, and the Arabic name, *geem*, may be preserving a more ancient name of *gam*.

The Hebrew word *gam* means "to gather together," such as when a group of animals "gather" at a water hole to drink. Related to the Hebrew word *gam* are the nouns *a'gam*, meaning "watering hole," *agmu* meaning "reeds," and the verb *G.M.A* meaning "to drink." The image of the original pictograph is a picture of a foot, based on the idea of walking to gather together.

The Early Hebrew form evolved into ٦ in Middle Hebrew, also becoming the Greek Γ (*gamma*), as well as the Latin "C" and "G."

This letter continued to evolve, developing into ⋏ in the Late Hebrew. This form of the letter became the number 3 as well as the Modern Hebrew ג. In Modern Hebrew, this letter represents the number 3.

The Hebrew, Greek and Arabic alphabets all agree that this letter has a "*g*" sound.

DALET

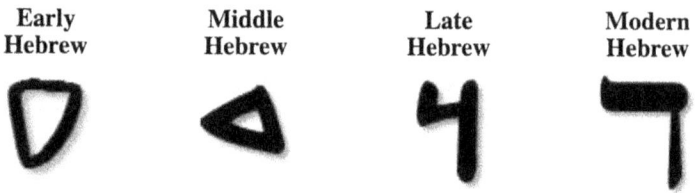

Early Hebrew	Middle Hebrew	Late Hebrew	Modern Hebrew

Figure 36. Evolution of the letter *Dalet*
(Image created by the author)

The original pictograph for this letter is ▽ and is an image of a tent door. The Modern Hebrew name for this letter is *dalet*, a Hebrew word meaning "door," and is similar to the Greek name *delta*. The Arabic name, however, is *dal*, which is also a Hebrew word meaning "door," and may be the original name for this letter.

The Early Hebrew pictograph evolved into the Middle Hebrew letter ◁, the origin of the Greek letter Δ (*delta*), the Latin D and the number 4.

The Middle Hebrew evolved into the Late form ৭, becoming the Modern Hebrew ד. In Modern Hebrew, this letter represents the number 4.

The Hebrew, Greek and Arabic alphabets all agree that this letter has a "*d*" sound.

HEY

| Early Hebrew | Middle Hebrew | Late Hebrew | Modern Hebrew |

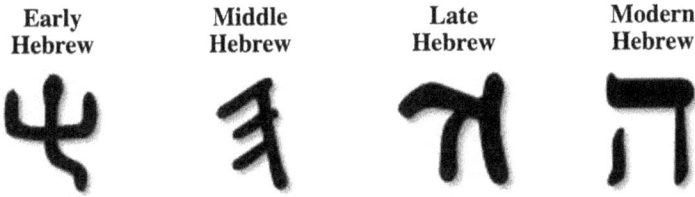

Figure 37. Evolution of the letter *Hey*
(Image created by the author)

The original pictograph for this letter is a picture of a man standing with his arms raised —ᕴ. The name of this letter is *hey*, a Hebrew word meaning "behold," such as what one would say when looking at a great sight. The Early form evolved into the Middle Hebrew ᖪ by rotating the letter 90 degrees to the left.

This form of the letter was adopted by the Greeks and the Romans to become the letter E[45] as well as the number 5.

This letter then evolved into ᴎ in the late Hebrew, which later developed into the Modern Hebrew ה. In Modern Hebrew, this letter represents the number 5.

This letter is used as a consonant with an "*h*" sound. Prior to the introduction of the *nikkud*, it may have also been used as a vowel with an "*e*" sound. Supporting this theory, the Greek name for this letter is *epsilon*, meaning "simple e," and has an "*e*" sound.

---

[45] Note that the three horizontal lines are facing to the left in the Middle Hebrew, but to the right in the Greek. This is due to the direction of writing. Hebrew is written from right to left and, therefore, the letters face toward the left. Greek is written from left to right and therefore the letters face toward the right.

VAV

Early Hebrew	Middle Hebrew	Late Hebrew	Modern Hebrew
Y	𝓡	﹀	﹀

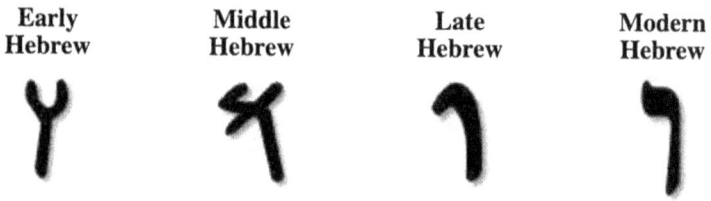

Figure 38. Evolution of the letter *Vav*
(Image created by the author)

The original pictograph used in the Early Hebrew alphabet is Y, a picture of a tent peg.

The Modern Hebrew name for this letter is *vav*, a word meaning "peg" or "hook."

While this letter has a "*v*" sound in Modern Hebrew, evidence suggests that in ancient times it had a "*w*" sound. Four Hebrew letters, which we have mentioned and will discuss in more detail later, doubled as consonants and vowels; *aleph*, *hey*, *vav*, and *yud*. Each of these letters can be used as a consonant or a vowel. For instance, the letter *hey*, as a consonant, is pronounced "*h*," but when used as a vowel in ancient times, it was probably pronounced "*eh*." The *yud*, as a consonant, is pronounced "*y*," but as a vowel, "*iy*." Logically, we can conclude that since the vowel sound for the letter *vav* is "*ow*" or "*uw*," then the consonantal pronunciation would be "*w*," and not "*v*." In addition, in the Arabic alphabet, this letter has a "*w*" sound.

The Early Hebrew form evolved into Y in Middle Hebrew. In the Ancient Greek alphabet, this letter was called *wau* and was also pronounced "*w*." This letter fell out of use around the 5th century

BC, but not before it became part of the Latin alphabet, becoming the letter "F."

This letter became ו in Late Hebrew and is the origin of the number "9"[46] and ו in Modern Hebrew. In Modern Hebrew, however, this letter represents the number 6.

ZAYIN

Early Hebrew	Middle Hebrew	Late Hebrew	Modern Hebrew

Figure 39. Evolution of the letter *Zayin*
(Image created by the author)

The ancient pictograph for this letter, ⟋, is some type of agricultural implement, possibly a mattock or plow.

This form of the letter became the Greek *zeta* (Z) and the Latin "Z" and the number "7."

The original form of this letter remained much unchanged through the Middle Hebrew period, but evolved into ı in Late Hebrew, eventually becoming ז in Modern Hebrew. In Modern Hebrew, this letter represents the number 7.

---

[46] As the letter *tet* became the number 6, we can speculate that at some point in the past, the *vav* and *tet* letters were reversed. The letter *tet* was in the 6th position of the Hebrew alphabet and the letter *vav* in the 9th.

This letter's pronunciation is "*z*" as attested by the Hebrew, Arabic and Greek alphabets.

HHET

Early Hebrew	Middle Hebrew	Late Hebrew	Modern Hebrew

Figure 40. Evolution of the letter *Hhet*
(Image created by the author)

The ancient pictograph is a picture of a "tent wall." This letter evolved slightly into H in Middle Hebrew and became the Latin letter "H" and our modern number "8." This letter continued to evolve into in the Late Hebrew and ח in Modern Hebrew. In Modern Hebrew, this letter represents the number 8.

The Modern Hebrew name for this letter is *hhet* and is a Hebrew word meaning "string." As "string" does not appear to have any connection to the picture of this letter, we can look to another Hebrew word, *hhets*, which means a "wall." Therefore, *hhets* may be the original name for this letter.

The sound of this letter in ancient and modern times is a guttural "*hh*[47]."

---

[47] This pronunciation is like the "*ch*" in the name Bach.

TET

Early Hebrew	Middle Hebrew	Late Hebrew	Modern Hebrew

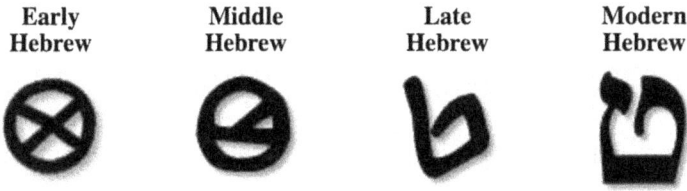

Figure 41. Evolution of the letter *Tet*
(Image created by the author)

The original pictograph for this letter is ⊗, a container made of wicker or clay. The name for this Hebrew letter is *tet*, meaning "mud" or "clay," materials that were commonly used to make baskets. In the Greek alphabet, the name of this letter is *theta*, with a *"th"* pronunciation and may be the original pronunciation of the Hebrew letter.

The Early Hebrew letter remained unchanged into the Middle Hebrew script, but became ט in Late Hebrew. The Late Hebrew letter became the Greek letter *theta* (Θ), the Modern Hebrew ט and our number 6. In Modern Hebrew, this letter represents the number 9.

YUD

Early Hebrew	Middle Hebrew	Late Hebrew	Modern Hebrew

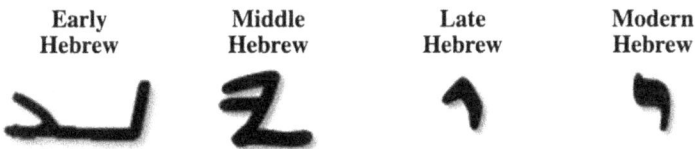

Figure 42. Evolution of the letter *Yud*
(Image created by the author)

The original pictograph of this letter is ﹏, an arm and hand and is called a *yud*, a Hebrew word meaning "hand."

The pictograph became ⟨ in Middle Hebrew and is the origin of the letters "I" and "J." The letter continued to evolve into the simpler form ⟩ in Late Hebrew, becoming ⟩ in Modern Hebrew, and also represents the number 10.

The pronunciation of this letter is a "*y*" as a consonant, but as a vowel, it is pronounced "*iy*."

KAPH

Early Hebrew	Middle Hebrew	Late Hebrew	Modern Hebrew
𝕎	𝒴	૫	כ

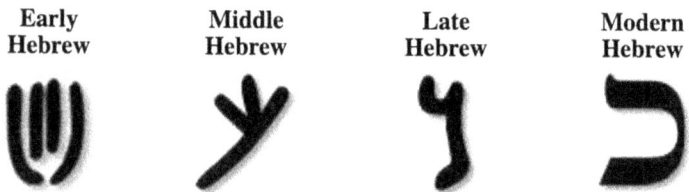

Figure 43. Evolution of the letter *Kaph*
(Image created by the author)

The Ancient form of this letter is 𝕎, the open palm of a hand.

The Hebrew name for this letter is *kaph*, a Hebrew word meaning "palm." This letter is pronounced as a "*k*" when used as a stop and a "*kh*[48]" when used as spirant.

The Early Hebrew form evolved into 𝒴 in Middle Hebrew and is the origin of the letter "K." This letter continued to evolve into ૫ in Late Hebrew, becoming the Modern Hebrew כ and the ך (final *kaph*). In Modern Hebrew, this letter represents the number 20.

---

[48] A guttural sound made at the back of the throat, similar to the letter *hhet*.

LAMED

Early Hebrew	Middle Hebrew	Late Hebrew	Modern Hebrew

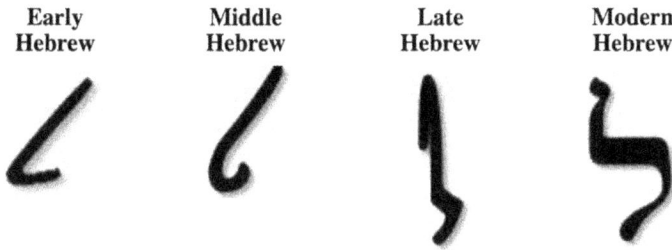

Figure 44. Evolution of the letter *Lamed*
(Image created by the author)

The Early Hebrew pictograph is ∠, a staff, such as may have been used by a shepherd or herder. The letter remained virtually unchanged through Middle Hebrew and became the Greek *lamda* (Λ) and the Latin, "L." In Late Hebrew this letter evolved into ˻ and later became ל in Modern Hebrew. It also represents the number 30.

The Modern Hebrew name for this letter is *lamed*. While this name is not a Hebrew word found in the Bible, the related word *mal'mad* is found and means a "staff."

The Arabic name is *lam*, which may be the more ancient name for this letter. The pronunciation of this letter is "*l*."

MEM

Early Hebrew	Middle Hebrew	Late Hebrew	Modern Hebrew
ᴍ	ל	ק	מ

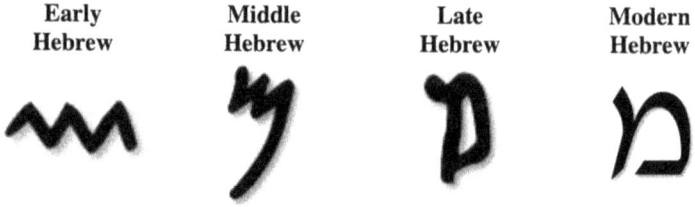

Figure 45. Evolution of the letter *Mem*
(Image created by the author)

The Early Hebrew pictograph for this letter is ᴍ, a picture of waves of water.

The Modern Hebrew name for this letter is *mem*, most likely from the word *mayim* meaning "water," and has an "m" sound.

The Early Hebrew evolved into ל in Middle Hebrew and is the origin of the letter "M."

The Middle form continued to evolve into מ in the Late Hebrew, which further evolved into the מ and ם (final *mem*) in Modern Hebrew. In Modern Hebrew, this letter represents the number 40.

NUN

Early Hebrew	Middle Hebrew	Late Hebrew	Modern Hebrew
ᔪ	ל	ג	נ

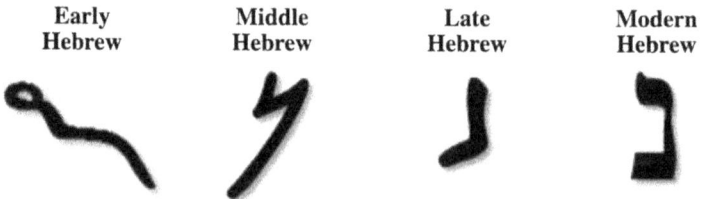

Figure 46. Evolution of the letter *Nun*
(Image created by the author)

The ancient pictograph ᴎ is a picture of a seed sprout representing the idea of continuing to a new generation.

The Hebrew name for this letter is *nun*, a Hebrew word meaning to "continue," "offspring" and "heir" and has an "*n*" sound.

The Early Hebrew evolved into ⟨ in the Middle Hebrew and is the origin of the letter "N." The Middle Hebrew continued to evolve into ⟨ in Late Hebrew and became the ⟨ and ⟨ (final *nun*) in Modern Hebrew. In Modern Hebrew, this letter represents the number 50.

SAMEHH

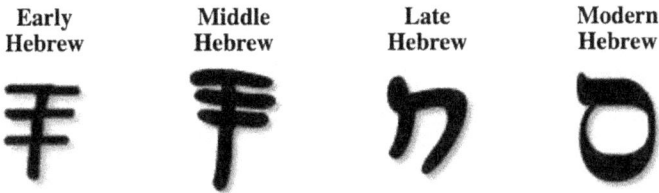

| Early Hebrew | Middle Hebrew | Late Hebrew | Modern Hebrew |

Figure 47. Evolution of the letter *Samehh*
(Image created by the author)

The original pictograph ₮, is a picture of a "thorn." The Modern Hebrew name for this letter is *samehh*, but, as will be demonstrated later, the original name was most likely *sin*, a Hebrew word meaning "thorn."

The Early Hebrew evolved very little in Middle Hebrew and is the origin of the Greek letter *ksi* (Ξ) and the Latin "X." This letter continued to evolve into ⟨ in Late Hebrew and then ⟨ in Modern Hebrew. In Modern Hebrew, this letter represents the number 60.

This letter is pronounced with an "*s*." However, in Greek this letter is pronounced "*ks*."

AYIN

Early Hebrew	Middle Hebrew	Late Hebrew	Modern Hebrew

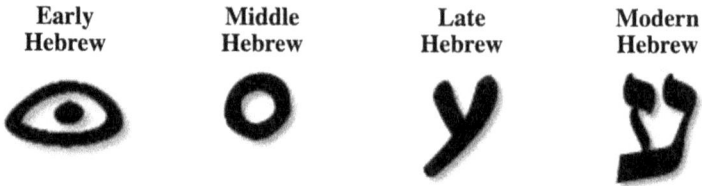

Figure 48. Evolution of the letter *Ayin*
(Image created by the author)

The ancient picture for this letter is ⊙ and is a picture of an eye. The name of this letter is *ayin*, a Hebrew word meaning "eye."

The Early form evolved into the simpler form o in middle Hebrew. In the Greek alphabet and later, the Latin alphabet, this Hebrew letter became the letter "O." This is also the origin of the number "0." In Late Hebrew this letter became y, which did not change in the Modern Hebrew period. In Modern Hebrew, this letter represents the number 70.

In Modern Hebrew, this letter is silent, but this may not have been the case in ancient times. However, reconstructing the original pronunciation of this letter is problematic. There is evidence to suggest that it originally had some sort of "g" sound, but, as we shall see later, that would be the missing twenty-third Hebrew letter, the *ghayin*. When this letter became part of the original Greek alphabet, it was pronounced "o[49]," suggesting that the Hebrew *ayin* may have been pronounced after the same manner.

---

[49] This Greek letter is called *omicron* (O), meaning "small o," in contrast to the Greek letter *omega* (Ω), meaning "great o."

PEH

Early Hebrew	Middle Hebrew	Late Hebrew	Modern Hebrew

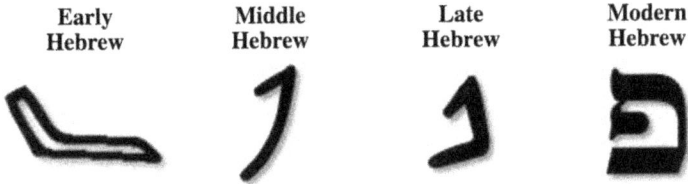

Figure 49. Evolution of the letter *Peh*
(Image created by the author)

The Hebrew word *pey* means a "mouth" and the ancient pictograph is a picture of a mouth—. This letter has two sounds, "*p*" as a stop and "*ph*" (f) as a spirant.

The Early Hebrew evolved into 7 in Middle Hebrew and is the origin of the Greek *Pi* (Π) and the Latin P. The letter continued to evolve into ב in Late Hebrew and פ and ף (final *pey*) in Modern Hebrew. In Modern Hebrew, this letter represents the number 80.

Tsade

Early Hebrew	Middle Hebrew	Late Hebrew	Modern Hebrew

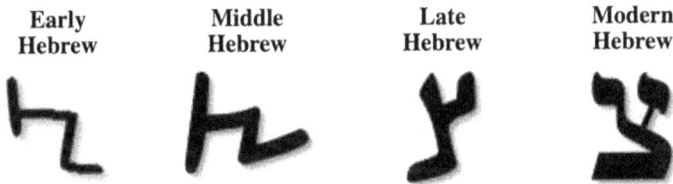

Figure 50. Evolution of the letter *Tsade*
(Image created by the author)

The pictograph appears to be a picture of a trail leading up to a destination, such as a stronghold.

The early pictograph, ⊢, changed very little in Middle Hebrew, but slightly in Late Hebrew becoming ⅄. From the Late Hebrew comes the Modern Hebrew צ and ץ (final *tsade*). The archaic Greek letter *san* (Ϻ) was derived from the Hebrew *tsade*, but was dropped from the Greek alphabet long ago. In Modern Hebrew, this letter represents the number 90.

The modern name for this letter is *tsade*, with a "*ts*" sound. The Hebrew word *tsad* means "side," but is also related to the idea of a stronghold, which is often built on the "side" of a mountain.

QUPH

Early Hebrew	Middle Hebrew	Late Hebrew	Modern Hebrew

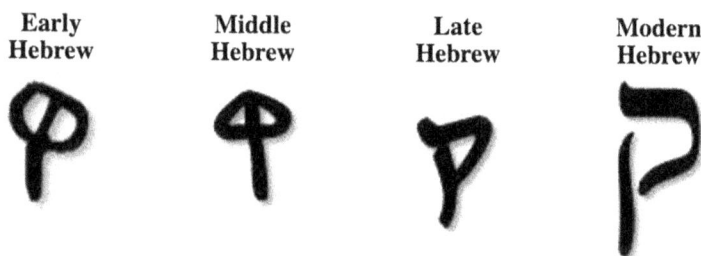

Figure 51. Evolution of the letter *Quph*
(Image created by the author)

The oldest known pictograph for this letter is ϙ, but what this pictograph represents is uncertain. The name of this letter is *quph*, a word found twice in the Bible (1 Kings 10:22 and 2 Chronicles 9:21), but it is not a Hebrew word; it is a word of foreign origin meaning "ape." If *quph* is a Hebrew word, albeit, not found in the Bible, we may be able to recreate its meaning based on the meanings of other Hebrew words related to it. Several verbs are derived out of the two-letter root word *quph*: *N.Q.P* means "to encircle," *Q.P.A* means "to congeal,"

Q.P.D means "to gather up" and *Q.P.Ts* means "to shut." All of these meanings are related to a sunrise or sunset where the light "congeals" or is "gathered up" at the horizon. If the pictograph is turned 90 degrees, like many of these letters, it could be the image of the sun at the horizon.

Of all the Hebrew letters in the alphabet, this one changed the least over the millennia. Even the Latin letter Q, which is derived from the Hebrew letter, still looks much the same as it did over 4,000 years ago.

Hebrew, Greek, Arabic and Latin agree that this letter's pronunciation is "q." In Modern Hebrew, this letter represents the number 100.

RESH

Early Hebrew	Middle Hebrew	Late Hebrew	Modern Hebrew

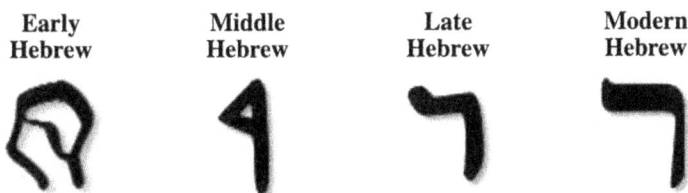

Figure 52. Evolution of the letter *Resh*
(Image created by the author)

The ancient picture for this letter is ℞, the head of a man. The Hebrew name for this letter is *resh*, a word meaning "head." This form of the letter was simplified in the Middle Hebrew becoming ٩. This form, in turn, became the Modern Hebrew ר, the Greek *rho* (P) and the Latin R. In each instance, this letter is pronounced with an "r." In Modern Hebrew, this letter represents the number 200.

SHIN

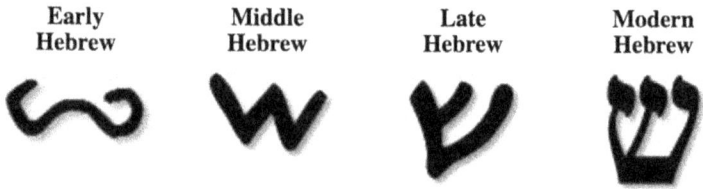

Figure 53. Evolution of the letter *Shin*
(Image created by the author)

The Ancient picture for this letter is ∽, picture of the two front teeth. The Modern Hebrew name for this letter is *shin*, a Hebrew word meaning tooth, and is pronounced "sh."

The early pictograph evolved into w in the Middle Hebrew, which became the Greek letter *sigma* (Σ) and the Latin S. The Middle Hebrew continued to evolve into ע in Late Hebrew and remained the same in Modern Hebrew. In Modern Hebrew, this letter represents the number 300.

TAV

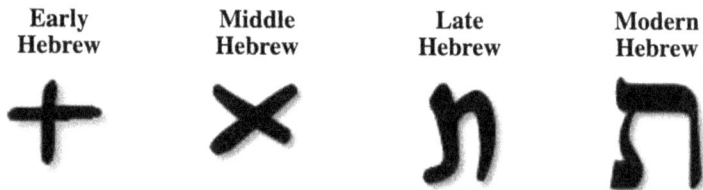

Figure 54. Evolution of the letter tav
(Image created by the author)

The Early Hebrew pictograph ✝, is a type of "mark," probably of two sticks crossed to mark a place. The Modern Hebrew, Arabic and

Greek names for this letter is *tav* (or *taw*), a Hebrew word meaning, "mark." Hebrew, Greek and Arabic agree that this letter is pronounced "*t*." Just like the letter *quph*, this letter has changed very little and is the origin of Latin letter "T."

The original pictograph evolved slightly into ✕ in Middle Hebrew and continued to evolve into ת in Late Hebrew. This form changed very little as the Late Hebrew alphabet evolved into Modern Hebrew. In Modern Hebrew, this letter represents the number 400.

GHAYIN

Early Hebrew	Middle Hebrew	Late Hebrew	Modern Hebrew
	N/A	N/A	N/A

Figure 55. Evolution of the letter *ghayin*
(Image created by the author)

In a moment, we will discuss the evidence for the existence of this letter, but for now, we will only be reconstructing the letter.

This letter did exist in the Ugarit alphabet (⋈) and does exist in the Arabic alphabet (غ) to this day and is called a *ghayin*.

As this letter does not exist in the Greek or Latin alphabets, we are left with very little evidence for the original pictograph of this letter. The closest candidate is, a twisted rope, which is found in some ancient Semitic inscriptions. If this pictograph is accurate, it may be related to the Hebrew word *ghah* meaning "twisted." Which also means that the original name may have been *ghah*.

This letter was lost to the Hebrew alphabet some time before the Bible was written, as by that time, the *ghayin* had been absorbed into the letter *ayin*.

We know that this letter had a sort of "*g*" sound like it did in Ugarit and does in Arabic. When Hebrew names that include the Hebrew letter *ayin* are transliterated into Greek, we sometimes find the letter *ayin* being transliterated with the Greek letter *gamma*.

THE ALPHABET

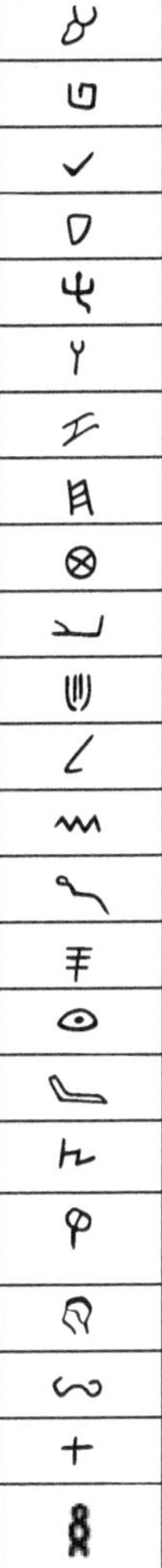

Name	Early	Middle	Late	Modern	Greek	Latin
Aleph	𐤀	✝	א	א	A	A
Beyt	ᗡ	𐤁	⅃	ב	B	B
Gimel	✓	1	⅄	ג	Γ	C
Dalet	▽	◄	勹	ד	Δ	D
Hey	५	�₹	九	ה	E	E
Vav	Y	Y	﹀	ו	F[50]	F
Zayin	ℐ	⊒	﹜	ז	Z	Z
Hhet	ⱱ	ⱨ	п	ח	H	H
Tet	⊗	⊖	ⴱ	ט	Θ	n/a
Yud	⌣	ⱬ	◌	י	I	I
Kaph	⑭	ⱴ	ᒐ	כ	K	K
Lamed	∠	⅃	⎰	ל	Λ	L
Mem	⋌⋌	ⁿᵍ	ⴉ	מ	M	M
Nun	⌐	ⁿ	⅃	נ	N	N
Samehh	⩲	⩲	𐤌	ס	Ξ	X
Ayin	◉	◦	ⴘ	ע	O	O
Peh	⌐	⅃	⅃	פ	Π	P
Tsade	⊢	⊢	ⴘ	צ	⋀[51]	n/a
Quph	⦿	⦿	ⴘ	ק	⦿[52]	Q
Resh	⦿	⊣	⅂	ר	P	R
Shin	⌁	ⱳ	ⴘ	ש	Σ	S
Tav	+	×	ⴉ	ת	T	T
Ghayin	ⱷ	n/a	n/a	n/a	n/a	n/a

Table 1. Alphabet Chart

---

[50] Archaic Greek letter.

[51] Archaic Greek letter.

[52] Archaic Greek letter.

CHANGES IN THE HEBREW ALPHABET

THE MISSING LETTER GHAYIN

While the Modern Hebrew alphabet consists of twenty-two letters, evidence suggests that there were additional letters in the original Semitic and Old Hebrew alphabets. One of the ancient Semitic languages of Canaan was Ugarit. This ancient language is almost identical to the Hebrew language of the Bible, but instead of having twenty-two letters, it has twenty-eight. A significant difference between Ugarit and Hebrew is the additional letter *ghayin* (𐎙), which does not exist in Biblical or Modern Hebrew. At some point in the ancient past, the letter *ghayin* disappeared and was replaced with the letter *ayin* (ע ,𐎓 in the Modern Hebrew). The evidence to be presented suggests that the letter *ghayin* originally existed within the Hebrew text of the Bible.

ONE WORD - TWO MEANINGS

The strongest evidence for the missing *ghayin* can be found in the two different meanings of one Hebrew word. For example, the Hebrew word רע (*ra*) can mean "friend" or "bad." In the ancient past, this was two Hebrew words with different spellings. One would have been the Hebrew word ⊙𐤏, written as רע in the Modern Hebrew alphabet and identified in Strong's Dictionary as #H7453, and meant "friend." The other Hebrew word would have been 𐤀𐤏, also written as רע in the modern Hebrew alphabet, but identified in Strong's Dictionary as #H7451, and meant "bad." Below are a few other examples of Hebrew words spelled with the *ayin* that have more than one meaning:

Hebrew	Ayin	Ghayin
עול	infant (#H5764)	wicked (#H5766)
יעל	profit (#H3276)	goat (#H3277)
ענה	heed (#H6030)	afflict (#H6031)
עיף	weary (#H5888)	darkness (#H5890)
עור	skin (#H5785)	blind (#H5786)
עיר	colt (#H5895)	city (#H5892)
שער	hair (#H8163)	storm (#H8175)
ערב	weave (#H6148)	dark (#H6150)
ערום	naked (#H6174)	crafty (#H6175)
ערף	neck (#H6202)	drop (#H6201)

Table 2. Hebrew words with an ayin

While one word having two meanings may not seem strange to us since the English language is filled with words with more than one meaning, this is a rare occurrence in Hebrew. When it does occur, it suggests that they were originally two different words.

If the letter *ayin* represents two ancient letters, how can we determine which letter was originally used in a given word? For example, was the Hebrew word סעה (*sah'ah*, Strong's #H5584) originally spelled with an *ayin* or a *ghayin*? When we compare the meanings of the words in the table above, we notice that the words in the far-right column are all related to darkness (dark, storm, clouds, rain, blind) and allegorically as wickedness (wicked, goat, city, bad, crafty). As the Hebrew word סעה means "storm" that is related to the idea of "darkness," we can conclude it was initially spelled with a *ghayin*, a picture of a twisted rope (𐤏) in the original pictograph and meaning "twisted," a concrete idea that is often equated with wickedness in Hebrew. In Table 3 below are a few other words that were most likely written with a *ghayin*:

עב	cloud
עוב	cloud
עוה	perverse
עות	crooked
עז	goat
עקל	crooked
עקש	crooked

Table 3. Hebrew words with a *ghayin*

MODERN AND HISTORICAL EVIDENCE OF LETTER CHANGES

This shift from the *ghayin* to the *ayin* is not unique with ancient or even Modern Hebrew words. Over time words and their roots evolve. To demonstrate this concept, let's look at an English word and its evolution. The words, "napkin" and "apron" are derived from the word "map." In ancient times, maps were written on sheets of fabric called "maps." As words evolve, letter sounds shift and one of the common shifts in letters is from an "m" to an "n" and vice versa. The word "napkin," a sheet of fabric, is the word "map" (with a shift from an "m" to an "n"), with the suffix "kin" added to it. The old English word "napron" is a sheet of fabric tied around the body. This is, again, the word "map" with the suffix "ron" added to it. As time went by, "a napron" became "an apron."[53]

This same shift of letters can also be seen in the evolution of many Hebrew words. In the Biblical Hebrew language, we have the ancient two-letter root זב (*zav*), meaning "yellow." From this root, two three-letter roots are derived, זהב (*zahav*, Strong's #H2091) meaning "gold" and זוב (*zuv*, Strong's #H2101) meaning "pus," both being yellow in color. Another Hebrew word, צהב (*tsahav*, Strong's #H6669), also has the meaning of "yellow," but has no connection to the ancient two-letter root צב (*tsav*, Strong's #H6632), which means a "wall." From this evidence, we can conclude that צהב (*tsahav*) is an evolved, or defective, form of the root זהב, as the צ (*ts*) and ז (*z*) sounds are very similar.

GREEK TRANSLITERATIONS OF THE GHAYIN

When the Hebrew Bible was translated into Greek (the *Septuagint*) over 2000 years ago, the scribes transliterated Hebrew names into Greek. An example of transliteration of a name into another language can be seen in the Hebrew name אדם, which, when transliterated into Latin letters, becomes "Adam."

---

[53] (Harper, n.d., apron)

When we examine Hebrew names containing the Hebrew letter *ayin*, we find two different transliterating methods. Table 4 contains Hebrew names where the *ayin* is not transliterated. The Hebrew letter *ayin* is silent and is represented by an apostrophe in the English transliteration. These names were originally spelled with the letter *ayin*. Table 5 contains Hebrew names where the *ayin* is transliterated with the Greek letter *Gamma* (Γ, γ), which has a "g" sound. These names were originally spelled with the letter *ghayin*.

Hebrew	Greek	English
בעל (ba'al)	Βααλ (*Baal*)	Ba'al
בלעם (bil'am)	Βαλααμ (*Balaam*)	Bala'am
עשתרות ('ashtarot)	Ασταρωθ (*Astaroth*)	'Ashtaroth

Table 4. Hebrew names without a "g" sound

Hebrew	Greek	English
עמרה ('amorah)	Γομορραν (*gomorras*)	Gomorrah
עזה ('azzah)	Γαζαν (*gazan*)	Gaza
פעור (pe'or)	Φογορ (*pogor*)	Peor

Table 5. Hebrew names with a "g" sound

ARABIC AND THE GHAYIN

Arabic, also a Semitic language like Hebrew, has retained both the *ayin* and *ghayin* as separate letters. The Arabic letter ع represents the *ayin*, while the غ represents the *ghayin*. The ancient Ugarit language also distinguishes between the *ayin*, written as ◁ , and the *ghayin*, written as ▷◁.

EDWARD HOROWITZ

The following is an excerpt from Edward Horowitz's book *How the Hebrew Language Grew*, by KTAV publishing:

> *"Ancient Hebrew had two different ע sounds. These sounds were represented in our alphabet by the letter ע. One was a harsh, heavy ע. This is now lost, and no longer used in Hebrew. The other was a soft, mild ע. When the Greek Jews translated the Bible into Greek, they had to transliterate Hebrew names having the harsh ע in it. They used the Greek letter gamma for it - so you can just imagine how hard a sound it must have been. This ע has even come all the way down to English. The Hebrew place names עמרה and עזה, both of which have this strong ע, were transliterated into Greek as Gommora and Gaza. Didn't the odd forms of these place names in English ever puzzle you? In medieval times there was exported from Gaza a thin fabric which was naturally named "gauze" after the city of its origin.*
>
> *Incidentally, Arabic a close sister language of Hebrew, still pronounces these two עs differently, and what's more writes them differently.*
>
> *This simple piece of knowledge about the existence of two different עs, should clear up a great many puzzling different meanings that you will often find in a root that has an ע in it."*[54]

---

[54] (Horowitz, 1960)

What does all this mean to the study of the Hebrew language? In studying the Ancient Hebrew language and alphabet, we must begin exploring the language at its simplest written level, the letters. Each letter is a picture that represents a meaning. When the letters are combined to form roots, each letter supplies a definition to the root. By studying the various words derived from any given root, we can begin to reconstruct the original root language of Hebrew. To be as accurate as possible, we need to be sure that we are using the correct words, roots and letters.

Now that the twenty-third letter (the *ghayin*) of the Hebrew alphabet has been found, we must ask if there are others that were lost? The answer is most likely "yes." Edward Horowitz claims that there are two *hhets* (ח), two *shins* (ש), two *zayins* (ז) and three *tsades* (צ) bringing the total count of Hebrew letters to twenty-eight. Interestingly, the Arabic alphabet contains twenty-eight letters, and the ancient Ugarit alphabet has thirty, but this includes two additional variations of the letter *aleph*, bringing us back to twenty-eight letters.

THE SHIN, SIN AND SAMEHH

In the Modern Hebrew alphabet, the letter *shin* (ש) represents two different sounds, a "*sh*" and an "*s*." To differentiate between these two sounds, a dot is placed above the *shin* in different locations. For the "*sh*" sound, the dot is placed on the right (שׁ) and is called a *shin* and for the "*s*" sound it is placed on the left (שׂ) and called a *sin*.

In most cases, words spelled with the *sin* are more closely related in meaning to words spelled with the *samehh* (ס). In addition, Hebrew words spelled with the *sin* are written with the *samehh* in other

Semitic languages, as well. As an example, in the Masoretic text, you will find the name ישראל (*yisra'el* / Israel). This name was most likely spelled initially as יסראל, which interestingly is the same spelling of Israel in the Aramaic translations of the Old Testament.

In the Hebrew Bible, several Hebrew words written with the שׂ (*sin*) are also written with a ס (*samehh*), which is demonstrated in Table 6 below.

With שׂ	With ס	Pronunciation	Definition
נשׂא	נסא	*nasa*	Lift up
שׂור	סור	*sur*	Remove
שׂכך	סכך	*sakak*	Cover
שׂוט	סוט	*sut*	Turn aside
שׂט	סט	*set*	Rebel
ששׂה	שסה	*shasah*	Plunder

Table 6. Hebrew words spelled with a *sin* and *samehh*

From this, we may conclude that in ancient times, the *samehh* and *sin* were one letter, but at some point, this letter was split into two. In some cases, the letter was changed to a *shin* and those that remained as they were became the *samehh*.

THE VAV AND YUD

Until 1947, the oldest manuscript of the Hebrew Bible was the Codex *Leningrad*, which dates to around 1,000 AD. With the discovery of the Dead Sea Scrolls in 1947, we now have manuscripts that are 1000 years older than the Codex *Leningrad*. Though the Hebrew texts from the Dead Sea Scrolls are about 2000 years old and the Hebrew text from the Codex *Leningrad* is about 1000 years old, they are

remarkably similar. However, there are some differences, such as in
how the texts use vowels. Throughout the Codex *Leningrad,* vowel
sounds are represented by the *nikkudot* (*nikkud* in the singular),
a series of dots and dashes that were placed above and below the
Hebrew letters. For instance, in the Masoretic text, the name "David"
is written as דָּוִד (*dawid*). The dot, called the *hhireq,* written below
the ו, represents the "i" sound. However, in the Dead Sea Scrolls, the
name "David" is written as דויד, where the letter י (*yud*) represents
the "i" sound.

From the vast number of manuscripts unearthed in the Dead Sea
Caves, translators found that the letters *waw* and *yud* (and to a lesser
extent the letters *hey* and *aleph*) were widely used as vowel-letters.
Exactly when and why they were removed from the text and replaced
with the *nikkudot* appears to be a mystery.

THE HEBREW VOCABULARY

HEBREW ROOT WORDS

Like a tree with its roots, trunk, branches and leaves, the Hebrew language is a system of roots and words, where one word and its meaning are the foundation for several other words whose spelling and meaning are related to that single root.

In the Biblical Hebrew language, root words are neither nouns or verbs, but instead a foundation for creating nouns and verbs. For instance, the root מלך (*M.L.K*), which we will look at in more detail in a moment, is the foundation of the noun מלך (*melekh*), meaning "king," as well as the verb מלך (*M.L.K*[55]), meaning "to reign."

In our English language, nouns are inanimate objects: A person, place or thing. Verbs are words of action. Biblical Hebrew is a little different,

---

[55] The verb, like the root word, is written without the vowels, as the verb must first be conjugated to determine which vowels will be placed within the verb. For instance, the verb *MaLaK* means "he reigns," while *aMaLaK* means "I reign."

as all words, nouns and verbs are words of action. A noun is "someone or something of the action," while a verb is the "the action of someone or something." We can demonstrate this with the root מלך (*M.L.K*), where the literal meaning of the noun is "the one who reigns," the king, and the meaning of the verb is "the reign of the king."

Other nouns are created out of this root by adding other letters. By adding the letter ה (*H*) to the end of the root, the word מלכה (*malkah*) is formed, which is a female ruler, a "queen." By adding a ו (*U*) to this feminine noun, the word מלוכה (*malukhah*) is formed meaning "royalty." By adding the letters ות (*UT*) to the end of the root, the noun מלכות (*malkut*) is formed, meaning the area ruled by the ruler, the "kingdom."

By studying the relationship between words and their roots, we can better understand the meanings of these words within their original context. Let's take three English words found in English translations of the Hebrew Bible: "maiden," "eternity," and "secret." These three words appear to be completely unrelated. But, let us examine the Hebrew words behind these translations: עלמה (*almah*), עולם (*olam*) and תעלמה (*te'almah*).

Each of these words shares the same three letters: ע (*ayin*), ל (*lamed*) and מ (*mem*)[56]. These words are related, as they come from the same root עלם (*Ah-L-M*). Rather than perceiving them as being different and independent words, we need to recognize that their meanings are connected. By interpreting these words in the context of their root relationship we can uncover their original meanings.

---

[56] The letter "*mem*" has two forms, ם when it appears at the end of a word, and מ when it appears anywhere else in a word.

The root עלם (*Ah-L-M*) literally means "beyond the horizon," that haziness of distance that is difficult to see clearly. By extension, it means to be out of sight, hidden from view. עלמה (*almah*) is the young woman that is hidden away (protected) in the home. עולם (*olam*) is a place or time that is in the far distance and is hidden to us. תעלמה (*te'almah*) is something that is hidden away, or secret.

Besides finding the common meaning in different words of the same root, we can also distinguish different meanings of words that come from different roots. For instance, there are two Hebrew words translated as "moon." One is ירח (*yere'ahh*, Strong's #H3394), which comes from a root meaning "to follow a pre-scribed path" and is, therefore, used for the moon's orbit as it follows a prescribed path in the night sky. The other is לבנה (*lavanah*, Strong's #H3842), which comes from a root meaning "to be white" and is, therefore, used for its bright appearance. To translate both of these nouns as "moon," which they do, the translators do a dis-service to the reader, as the author chose one word over the other for a specific purpose.

The examples cited above have illustrated that we ought not ignore the Hebraic definitions of the words in the Bible. When we do, we miss much of what the text is attempting to tell us and make wrong assumptions about their meaning. But there is even more to uncover, so let's dig deeper.

PARENT ROOTS

All Hebrew linguists recognize that most Hebrew words are derived from a three-letter root word. However, some linguists have suggested that these three-letter roots are derived from the more ancient two-letter roots, which we will refer to as a parent roots from this point on.

Rabbi Matityahu Clark in his book *Etymological Dictionary of Biblical Hebrew* records and organizes Rabbi Samson Raphael Hirsch's commentaries of the Bible which relate to the Hebrew language. Rabbi Clark stated:

> *"The second major analytical tool in the Hirsch system we will call Gradational Variants. This involves five special consonants: א (aleph), ה (hey), ו (waw), י (yud) and נ (nun). These consonants play a special role with respect to roots whose third consonant is identical with the second...The new root form does not change the basic meaning of the original root, but adds some nuances of meaning."*[57]

Rabbi Clark then provides many examples of these "Gradational Variants," including: the three-letter root צרר (*tsarar*), which means "forcing," "constraining" and "oppressing." As Rabbi Hirsch pointed out, the second and third consonants are identical, the letter ר (*resh*). The Gradational Variants of צרר (*tsarar*) are: נצר (*natsar*)—guarding or protecting; יצר (*yatsar*)—forming or creating; צור (*tsur*)—fencing or enclosing. All of these "gradational variants" have two letters in common, the *tsade* and the *resh*, the parent root צר.

Let us look at another example. The three-letter root רדד (*radad*) means a "flattening down" or "submitting totally." The Gradational Variants are: רדה (*radah*)—ruling over or having dominion over; ירד

---

[57] (Clark & Hirsch, 1999, p. 295)

(*yarad*)—going down; רוד (*rud*)—humbling. In this case, the parent root is רד, spelled *resh-dalet*.

William Gesenius, considered one of the greatest Hebrew scholars of all time, wrote in his book *Gesenius' Hebrew Grammar*:

> *"A large number of triliteral stems really point to a biliteral base, which may be properly called a root, since it forms the starting-point for several triliteral modifications of the same fundamental idea."*[58]

Gesenius then cites the following example: The biliteral[59] root כר (*K-R*) is the root of כרר (*K-R-R*), אכר (*A-K-R*), כור (*K-W-R*) and כרה (*K-R-H*), each being related to the idea of "digging."

Another example he provides is the biliteral root דך (*D-K*), the root of דכא (*D-K-A*), דכך (*D-K-K*), דוך (*D-W-K*) and דכה (*D-K-H*), each being related to the idea of "striking" or "breaking."

Edward Horowitz, whose work we cited earlier, observes in *How the Hebrew Language Grew*:

> *"Scholars are fairly convinced that back of these three lettered roots lie old primitive two-lettered syllables. These two-lettered syllables represent some simple primitive action or thing. It does seem quite clear that there existed a bi-literal or two-letter base for many, if not most, of our three lettered roots."*[60]

---

[58] (Gesenius, 1893, p. 100)

[59] Or, what we are calling "parent roots."

[60] (Horowitz, 1960, p. 299)

Horowitz then provides the following three-letter roots: גוז (*G-W-Z*), גזר (*G-Z-R*), גזע (*G-Z-A*), גזז (*G-Z-Z*) and גזה (*G-Z-H*), each meaning "to cut," and all coming from the parent root גז (*GZ*). Horowitz noted:

> *"Do not be surprised if so many of these comparatively few two-lettered roots mean to cut, to split, to slit, or slice. After all, everything that primitive man did in the way of making a living for himself and his family in some way or other involved a cutting action."*

CHILD ROOTS

Of the twenty-two letters of the Semitic alphabet, four originally doubled as a consonant and a vowel. Called "weak" consonants, the four are the א (*A*), ה (*H and E*), ו (*W, O, and U*) and י (*Y and I*). The remaining eighteen consonants are termed "strong consonants."

A child root is formed by adding one of the weak consonants to the front, middle or end of a parent root. All the child roots formed from one parent root will be directly and closely related in meaning to the parent root.

From the parent root אל (*el*), meaning "God," but more Hebraically meaning "strength and authority," comes the child root איל (*ayil*), meaning a "buck," the strong one of the flocks. From the parent root בן (*ben*), meaning "son," comes the child root בנה (*banah*), meaning "to build," through the idea that the sons build a house, literally and figuratively. From the parent root לך (*lakh*), meaning "walk," comes the child root הלך (*halakh*), meaning a "journey."

In Table 7 below are the child roots formed from the parent root בל (*BaL*) meaning "flow."

אבל	*ABaL*	wilt: a flowing away of life
הבל	*HaBaL*	empty: flowing out of contents
בהל	*BaHaL*	panic: a flowing of the insides
בלה	*BaLaH*	aged: a flowing away of youth
בול	*BUL*	flood: a heavy flowing of water
יבל	*YaBaL*	stream: a flowing of water

Table 7. Child roots from the parent root בל

ADOPTED ROOTS

While child roots add a weak consonant to a parent root, an adopted root is a three consonant root consisting of three strong consonants.

The following adopted roots were formed by adding another strong consonant to the parent root פר (*PaR*), meaning "break."

פרח	*PaRaCh*	break forth
פרך	*PaRaK*	break apart
פרס	*PaRaS*	break in pieces
פרק	*PaRaQ*	break off
פרץ	*PaRaTs*	break open

Table 8. Child roots from the parent root פר

RECONSTRUCTION OF ROOTS

By comparing the various aspects of a parent root, the original meaning of the parent can be determined. For example, the two child roots

מקק (*M.Q.Q*) meaning "to rot" and מוק (*M.W.Q*) meaning "to stink" are formed out of the parent root מק. These two ideas are connected, in that something that rots begins to stink. When we examine the ancient pictographic letters of this parent root, we find the original meaning. The מ is a picture of water (〰) and the ק is a picture of the sun at the horizon (𐤒), representing the gathering or condensing of light. When we combine the meaning of these two letters, we have "water condensed." When the water of a pond condenses, or "dries up," the vegetation and fish that lived in that water die and begin to rot and stink. We now have a picture that helps us better understand the meaning and context of these words. One additional piece to complete the puzzle is the adopted root צמק (*Ts.M.Q*), meaning "dry."

Many times, adopted roots alone can help reconstruct the meaning of a parent root. The original meaning of the parent root בח (*bahh*), which is not found in the Biblical text, is difficult to determine, as the only known word derived from it is the word אבחה (*av'hhah*, Strong's #H0019), meaning the "point" of a sword or knife. However, when we examine the definitions of the various adopted roots that are related to this word, a commonality begins to form between each of them.

טבח	*TaBaHh*	Slaughter
זבח	*ZaBaHh*	Slaughter
בחר	*BaHhaR*	Choose[61]
בחן	*BaHhaN*	Test[62]
בכר	*BaK[63]aR*	Firstborn[64]

Table 9. Adopted roots from the parent root בח

[61] Through the idea of choosing a sacrifice.
[62] Through the idea of testing for the choicest.
[63] The letter ח (Hh) has been exchanged for the similar sounding כ (K).
[64] The firstborn of the flock is chosen for sacrifice.

Based on these adopted roots, we cannot precisely define the meaning of the parent root בח (*bahh*), but can conclude that it has a meaning closely related to the concept of "slaughtering."

THE ROOT SYSTEM OF HEBREW WORDS

Hebrew words are derived from a system of root words (parent, child and adopted roots), as demonstrated in the graphic below:

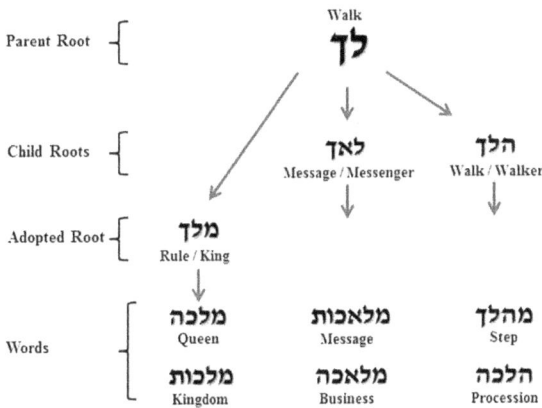

Figure 56. The parent root *L-K* and its derivatives
(Image created by the author)

Derived from the parent root לך (*L.K*)[65] are two child roots, הלך (*H.L.K*) and לאך (*L.A.K*), and one adopted root, מלך (*M.L.K*). The child הלך is formed by adding the letter ה (*H*) to the beginning of the parent. The child לאך is formed by adding the letter א (*A*) in the middle of the root. And the adopted, by adding the letter מ (*M*) to the beginning (see Figure 56).

---

[65] The letter kaph is written as ך when at the end of a word and as כ anywhere else in the word.

HEBREW WORDS

NOUN DERIVATIVES

The most common nouns found in the Bible are derived directly from the two-letter parent roots and the three-letter child and adopted roots. Other nouns, called "derivatives," are formed by adding specific letters in specific places within the root. For example, the noun derivative מפתח (*maph'tach*), meaning a "key," is formed by adding the letter מ (*m*) to the front of the root פתח (*P.T.Hh*), which we earlier saw meant "open." The most common letters added to a root to form a noun derivative are the letters מ (*m*) or ת (*t*), which are placed in front of the root, and י (*i*) or ו (*o* or *u*), which are placed inside the root.

FEMININE DERIVATIVES

All languages assign gender (masculine, feminine, neuter) to nouns. In Hebrew, all nouns are either masculine or feminine. In most cases, one simply "knows" whether it is masculine or feminine. For instance, the word עץ (*eyts*), meaning "tree," is a masculine noun and עת (*eyt*), meaning "appointed time," is a feminine noun. But in some cases, a feminine noun is *derived* out of a masculine noun by adding ה (*ah*), ת (*et*) or ית (*iyt*) to the end of the noun. For instance, the feminine noun עצה (*eytsah*), meaning "council," is derived from the masculine noun עץ (*eyts*) by adding the letter ה (*ah*) to the end of the word.

PLURAL NOUNS

Feminine nouns are made plural by adding the suffix ות (*ot*) and masculine nouns are made plural by adding the suffix ים (*iym*). However, in some cases, masculine nouns, usually very ancient words, use the ות (*ot*) suffix. For example, the Hebrew words אב (*av* - father) and אור (*or* - light) are masculine words, but are written as אבות (*avot*) and אורות (*'orot*) in the plural.

GRAMMATICAL TOOLS

The Hebrew language uses nouns for other functions within the sentence, that include adjectives, adverbs, prepositions, conjunctions, and more. As one example, the noun עקב (*eqev*) is a noun meaning the "heel" of the foot, but it can also be used as a particle and is translated as "because," in the sense of *what has been said* is on the "heel" of *what is about to be said.*

MORPHOLOGY OF HEBREW WORDS

Morphology is the study of how words are formed and is a crucial subject in Hebrew linguistics. Hebrew words often contain several affixes (i.e., prefixes, suffixes and infixes). For example, in Psalm 45:3[66] we find the word בשפתותיך (*b's'ph'to'tey'kha*), a word with a complex morphology.

> *"You are more beautiful than the sons of the human,*
> *beauty is poured down <u>with your lips</u>, therefore,*
> *Elohiym respected you for a distant time."* (RMT)

---

[66] Verse 2 in Christian Bibles. In Hebrew Bibles, the introductory passage to many of the Psalms is the first verse and the actual Psalm begins with verse 2. However, in Christian Bibles, the introductory passage and the beginning of the Psalm are combined in verse 1. Therefore, in many of the Psalms, the verses in the Christian Bible will be one verse off from the Hebrew Bible.

Jeff A. Benner

Besides the noun itself, this word includes a prefix and three suffixes as is demonstrated below.

Figure 57. Morphology of the Hebrew word _b's'ph'to'tey'kha_
(Image created by the author)

THE NOUN

In the image above (Figure 57), the Hebrew noun is the word שפה (S.P.H) and means "lip." If you notice, only the first two letters of the root of this word, the ש and פ, appear in the word above. As previously mentioned, many feminine nouns, such as this one, end with the letter ה (h). When a suffix is added to such a word as this, the ה (h) changes to a ת (t). So, in this case, the word שפה (S.P.H) is written as שפת (S.P.T).

Prefix

The letter ב (b) is a prefix that usually means "in," but can also mean "with." So, בשפה (b'saphah) means "with a lip."

Suffix #1

This feminine noun includes the feminine plural suffix ות (ot)—בשפתות (b'saphtot) and means "with lips."

112

Suffix #2

The letter ׳ (*ey*) is added to identify this noun as being in the construct state—בשפתותי (*b'saphtotey*) and means "with lips of..."

Suffix #3

The final letter in the word, ך (*kha*), is the second person, masculine, singular pronoun (you). So, the word בשפתותיך (*b's'ph'to'tey'kha*) means "with lips of you" or "with your lips."

HEBREW VERBS

Because the Hebrew language is action-oriented, rather than descriptive, it is prolific with verbs. Conjugating a Hebrew verb in a sentence identifies the person (1st, 2nd or 3rd), number (singular or plural), gender (masculine or feminine), tense (perfect or imperfect), mood (simple, causative or intensive) and voice (active, passive or reflexive). Understanding these different aspects of a verb, while not essential for proper Biblical interpretation, is extremely helpful when learning how to translate the Hebrew text.

TENSE

The Modern Hebrew language, just as with the English language, has three verb tenses, each related to time: past, present and future. However Biblical Hebrew has only two verb tenses: perfect and imperfect, and these two tenses are related to action. The perfect tense is a completed action and, in most cases, when translated into English, is represented with an English verb in the past tense (i.e.

he cut). The imperfect tense is an incomplete action and is usually represented with an English verb in the present (he cuts) or future tense (he will cut) when translated into English

When a Hebrew verb is prefixed with the letter *vav* it means "and," but it also reverses the tense of the verb. For example, the verb אמר (*amar*), is in the perfect tense (completed action) and means "he said." When this verb is written as ואמר (*v'amar*), it means "and he will say." The tense is changed from the perfect to the imperfect.

VOICE

Each verb also includes one of three voices: active, passive or reflexive. The active voice identifies the action of the verb as coming from the subject (he cut). In the passive voice, the action is placed on the verb's subject (he was cut). In the reflexive voice, the verb's action is toward the subject (he cut himself).

MOOD

Each verb also includes mood, of which there are three: simple, intensive or causative. The simple mood is the simple action of the verb (he cut). The intensive mood implies force or emphasis on the verb (he slashed or hacked). The causative mood expresses causation to the verb (he caused a cut).

The voice and mood of a verb are identified by seven different names, as shown Table 10 below:

Form	Mood	Voice	Example
Pa'al (Qal)	Simple	Active	He cut
Niphal	Simple	Passive	He was cut
Piel	Intensive	Active	He slashed
Pual	Intensive	Passive	He was slashed
Hiphil	Causative	Active	He made cut
Hophal	Causative	Passive	He was made cut
Hitpael	Intensive	Reflexive	He slashed himself

Table 10. The seven Hebrew verb forms

Table 11 below are a few examples of the conjugated verb אבד (*ABD*), meaning "to perish":

Verse	Exodus 10:7	Leviticus 23:30	Numbers 16:33	Numbers 33:52
Hebrew	אָבְדָה	וְהַאֲבַדְתִּי	וַיֹּאבְדוּ	וְאִבַּדְתֶּם
Transliteration	*av'dah*	*v'ha'vad'tiy*	*vai'yov'du*	*v'iy'bad'tem*
Person	3rd	1st	3rd	2nd
Number	Singular	Singular	Plural	plural
Gender	Feminine	Common	Masculine	Masculine
Tense	Perfect	Imperfect	Imperfect	Imperfect
Voice	Simple	Causative	Simple	Intensive
Mood	Active	Active	Active	Active
Translation	she perished	and I will cause to perish[67]	and they perished	and you will utterly destroy

Table 11. Conjugations of the verb אבד

---

[67] Which could also be translated as, "and I will destroy."

115

PRONUNCIATION OF HEBREW WORDS

Some of the topics below have been mentioned previously. Here we will look at these topics in greater detail to help the reader pronounce the Hebrew words without relying on the *nikkud* as found in Modern Hebrew Bibles, lexicons and dictionaries.

SPIRANTS AND STOPS

Three Hebrew letters, *beyt*, *kaph* and *peh*, have more than one pronunciation: one is called a "spirant" and the other a "stop." A spirant is a letter whose sound can be prolonged. Some examples of this from the English language are the "v," "z," "f" and "sh." A stop is a letter whose sound ends abruptly, such as the "b," "p," "d" and "t."

A few Hebrew letters have a different pronunciation depending on their position within the word. The letter ב (*beyt*) will usually be pronounced as a stop (*b*), unless it follows a vowel, in which case it is pronounced as a spirant (*v*). Let's look at the words בר (meaning "grain") and רב (meaning "abundant") as examples. Both of these words have the same letters, *resh* (ר), which has an "*r*" sound and *beyt* (ב), which can have a "*b*" or "*v*" sound. In the word רב, the letter *beyt* is at the end of the syllable and follows the implied vowel "a," so is pronounced as a spirant, "*v*." The word רב, therefore, is pronounced *rav*. In the word בר, the letter *beyt* is pronounced as a stop, "*b*" as it does not follow a vowel[68] and is, therefore pronounced *bar*.

---

[68] Unless the preceding word ends with a vowel, in which case, it will be pronounced as a spirant.

VOWELS

Four Hebrew letters double as consonants and vowels. These are the
א (*aleph*), ה (*hey*), ו (*vav*) and י (*yud*). As a consonant, the *aleph* is
a glottal stop (silent pause) and as a vowel it is pronounced "*ah*" or
"*eh*." The *hey* is an "*h*" as a consonant or an "*eh*" as a vowel. The
vav is a "*w*" as a consonant or an "*ow*" or "*uw*" as a vowel. The *yud*
is a "*y*" as a consonant or an "*iy*" as a vowel.

Besides these four vowels, there is another type of vowel, the implied
vowel. This means that the vowel is not written, but is necessary to
pronounce the word[69]. Again, using the word בר (meaning "grain")
as an example, we learned it includes the consonants "*B*" and "*R*."
By themselves, these two letters cannot be pronounced, as a vowel
is required between them. In many cases, the implied vowel will be
an "*a*" or an "*e*." In this case, the implied vowel[70] is the "*a*," and the
word בר is pronounced "*BaR*."

SYLLABLES

Hebrew has two types of syllables, open and closed. A closed syllable
includes a consonant-vowel-consonant combination, while an open
syllable has a vowel-consonant combination. The vowel may be one
of the four consonant/vowel letters, usually the *yud* (*I*) or the *waw* (*O*
or *U*) or an implied vowel. In most cases, the final syllable of a word
will be a closed syllable. The word ברית (*b'riyt*), meaning "covenant,"

---

[69] The *nikkudot* were created by the Masoretes to stand in for these "implied vowels."
[70] As the implied vowels were never written, our only recourse is to use the vowel
sounds that have traditionally been assigned to Hebrew words as recorded in the
Masoretic texts.

has two syllables. The first is ב, an open syllable pronounced *"be,"* and the second is רית, a closed syllable pronounced *"riyt."*

Generally, a word with three consonants will be divided as Cv-CvC (Consonant – vowel – Consonant – vowel – Consonant). A word with four consonants will be divided as Cv-Cv-CvC or CvC-CvC. When a word includes five consonants the breakdown is usually Cv-Cv-Cv-CvC or CvC-Cv-CvC.

If the word includes one of the four consonant/vowel letters, its position will determine if it is used as a consonant or as a vowel. Generally, when the consonant/vowel is placed at the beginning of a syllable or the end of a closed syllable, it will take on the consonantal sound. When it is in the middle of a closed syllable or the end of an open syllable, it will take on the vowel sound.

MASORETIC VOWELS

About one thousand years ago, a group of Jewish scholars called Masoretes, created the *nikkudot* and placed them above and below the Hebrew letters to represent vowel sounds. As mentioned previously, when the Dead Sea Scrolls were discovered, they revealed that the four Hebrew letters, א (*aleph*), ה (*hey*), ו (*vav*) and י (*yud*), were frequently used as vowels. In the Masoretic texts, such as the *Leningrad* Codex, many of these vowels are missing and replaced with the *nikkudot*. In Table 12 below are some examples of Hebrew spellings of some Hebrew words in the Masoretic text compared to how they are written in the Dead Sea Scrolls:

Verse	English	Masoretic	Dead Sea Scroll
Isaiah 2:2	All	כָּל	כול
Isaiah 2:3	God of Jacob	אֱלֹהֵי יַעֲקֹב	אלוהי יעקוב
Isaiah 2:4	And not	וְלֹא	ולוא

Table 12. Different spelling of Hebrew words

HEBREW WORDS FOUND IN ENGLISH WORDS

Etymology, the study of word origins, is a fascinating area of language study. We use thousands of words throughout our life, never stopping to ponder their origins or relationships to other words. Words can often be traced back through time and other languages to discover their origins and original meanings. Our purpose here is to show a common relationship between Hebrew and English words and their definitions. This area of study is what has come to be called "Edenics[71]."

All languages are based on a root system where a common set of letters can be found in different words of similar meaning. For example, the English words FoLiage, FLora and FLower have a similar meaning and are derived from an ancient FL root which probably meant something like "plant[72]."

The Hebrew word for "fruit" is פרי (*periy*), derived from the parent root פר (*PR*). Many English words for different types of fruit come from this *PR* Hebrew root, including: PeaR, aPRicot, PRune and PeRsimmon.

---

[71] This terminology was created by Isaac Mozeson, the author of *The Word: The Dictionary that Reveals the Hebrew Source of English* and founder of the study of Edenics.

[72] This word itself may be derived from the FL root by exchanging the "p" for the "f."

Over time, words evolve as they transfer from one language or culture to another. One type of evolutionary change is the reversal of letters, such as found in the word gRaPe, another fruit word from the *PR* root. An additional evolutionary change is the exchange of one letter sound for a similarly sounding letter. For example, a typical exchange of sounds is the L sound for the R sound, as we can see in the fruit words apPLe and PLum. Another standard letter change is the P to B or F, giving us BeRry and the word FRuit, both being evolved forms of the PR root.

The Hebrew word for "grain," which we previously examined, is בר (*BR - bar*). In English, we have the words BaRley (a type of grain), BaRn (a place for storing grain) and BeeR (made from grains).

Of all the sounds that the human voice can create there are seven unique groups of sounds. Any one sound in one group can easily be changed for another sound within the same group over time:

Type	English	Hebrew
Vowels (breath sounds)	a e i o u	א ה ו י
Labials (lip sounds)	b f p v w	ב ו פ
Gutturals (throat sounds)	hard-c g h j k x y	ג ה ח כ ע ק
Liquids (tongue sounds)	l r	ל ר
Nasals (nose sounds)	m n	מ נ
Dentals (tooth sounds)	d t	ד ט צ ת
Whistling fricatives (whistle sounds)	soft-c s z sh th	ז ס ש

Table 13. The seven unique groups of sounds

The principles of etymology noted above are called "Grimm's[73] Law." By applying Grimm's Law to some words, we can see many English words related to Hebrew words.

---

[73] The same brothers who wrote *Grimm's Fairy Tales*.

The Hebrew word חז (*hhaz*) means "to gaze." If we replace the Hebrew letter ח (*hh*), a guttural, with the English letter "G," also a guttural, and replace the Hebrew letter ז (*z*), a whistling fricative, with the English letter "Z," also a whistling fricative, we have the word "to gaze," which is the meaning of the word חז.

The Hebrew word דרך (*derek*) means "road." If we replace the Hebrew letter ד (*d*), a dental, with the English letter "T," also a dental, we have the words "track," "truck" and "trace," all English words related to a road.

Below are a few more examples of Hebrew words, their pronunciations and translations. You will notice that the English translations of these Hebrew words have an almost identical meaning as the Hebrew:

Hebrew	Pronunciation	Translation
איש	*iysh*	each
אצר	*atsar*	store
ארץ	*erets*	earth
בבל	*babel*	babble
בוש	*bush*	bashful
בר	*bar*	barley
גמל	*gamel*	camel
הוא	*hu*	he
הלך	*halak*	walk
הר	*har*	hill
חיטא	*hhiyta*	wheat
טל	*tal*	tall
ילל	*yalal*	howl

ילל	*yalal*	yell
יש	*yesh*	yes
כפר	*kaphar*	cover
לק	*laq*	lick
מג	*mag*	magic
מוק	*moq*	mock
נוד	*nod*	nod
נפל	*naphal*	fall
סך	*sak*	shack
ספר	*sepher*	cipher
סק	*saq*	sack
עבר	*ever*	over
עול	*evil*	evil
עורב	*orev*	raven
עין	*ayin*	eye
פר	*par*	bull
פרר	*parar*	break
צד	*tsad*	side
ציון	*tsion*	sign
צף	*tsaph*	spy
צרר	*tsa'rar*	sore
קאל	*qa'al*	call
קב	*qav*	cave
קרא	*qara*	call
שבע	*sheva*	seven
שית	*shiyt*	set
שמש	*shemesh*	sun
שש	*shesh*	six
תור	*tur*	tour

Table 14. English words derived from Hebrew

HEBREW NAMES

When studying Hebrew names in the Bible one must begin with an understanding of how names were formed in Hebrew. The name of a people, their land, and their language often begins with a patriarch, an individual considered to be the "father" of a people.

In Genesis 10:22, we see the name ארם (Aram). A male descendant of Aram is called an ארמי (*aramiy*) such as found in Genesis 25:20. Some translations, such as the RSV, translate this name as "Aramean." In contrast, other translations, such as the KJV and the ASV, use the name "Syrian," which comes from the Greek *Septuagint* and not the Hebrew Bible.

A female descendant of Aram is called an ארמיה (*aramiyah*), as can be seen in 1 Chronicles 7:14. Some translations, such as the KJV and ASV, translate this name as "Aramitess," while others, such as the RSV, translate it as "Aramean."

The descendants (plural) of Aram are called ארמים (*aramiym*), which is simply the plural form of ארמי (*aramiy*), and can be seen in 2 Kings 8:28. Some translations will translate this as "Arameans," while others will use "Syrians."

The land of the Arameans is called ארם (*Aram*), the same as the name of the patriarch, and can be found in Numbers 23:7. Some translations use Aram and Syria for the Hebrew ארם (*Aram*) interchangeably. For example, in the KJV the name ארם (*Aram*) is transliterated as "Aram" in Numbers 23:7, but is translated as "Syria" in 1 Kings 10:29. Other translations use "Syria" exclusively.

The language of the Arameans is called ארמית (*aramiyt*[74]), as appears in 2 Kings 18:26. This name is translated as "Aramaic" in some translations or as "Syrian" or "Syriac" in others.

When doing studies in the New Testament, it is helpful to know how the Greek language deals with each of these names. The best way to examine this is by referring to the Greek *Septuagint,* which in some cases uses very different methods for translating names.

The following tables detail each of the different forms of three different biblical names (Aram, Eber and Judah).

---

[74] This word literally means, "pertaining to the Arameans," which can include its language.

Table 15. Hebrew names derived from Aram

	Hebrew		Translation	Greek		Translation	OT Ref.	NT Ref.
Patriarch	אֲרָם	*aram*	Aram	Aram	*Aram*	Aram	Gen 10:22	Mt 1:3
Male Descendent	אֲרָמִי	*aramiy*	Aramite, Aramean	SuroV	*Suros*	Syrian	Gen 25:20	Lk 4:27
Female Descendent	אֲרָמִיָּה	*aramiyah*	Aramitess, Aramean	Sura	*Sura*	Syrian	1Ch 7:14	n/a
Descendants	אֲרָמִים	*aramiym*	Arameans	Suroi	*Suroi*	Syrians	2Ki 8:28	n/a
Land	אֲרָם	*aram*	Aram	Aram, SuriaV	*Aram, Surias*	Aram, Syria	Num 23:7	Lk 2:2
Language	אֲרָמִית	*aramiyt*	Aramean, Aramaic	Suristi	*Suristi*	Syrian, Syriac	2Ki 18:26	n/a

Jeff A. Benner

Table 16. Hebrew names derived from Eber

	Hebrew		Translation	Greek		Translation	OT Ref.	NT Ref.
Patriarch	עבר	*ever*	Eber	Eber	*Eber*	Eber	Gen 10:21	n/a
Male Descendent	עברי	*eevriy*	Hebrew	EbraioV	*Hebraios*	Hebrew	Gen 39:17	Phil 3:5
Female Descendent	עבריה	*eevriyah*	Hebrewess	Ebraia	*Hebraia*	Hebrew	Jer 34:9	n/a
Descendants	עברים	*eevriym*	Hebrews	Ebraioi	*Hebraioi*	Hebrew	Ex 2:13	2Cor 11:22
Land	n/a	n/a	n/a	n/a	n/a	n/a	n/a	n/a
Language	עברית	*eevriyt*	Hebrew	Ebraisti	*Hebraisti*	Hebrew	n/a	Jn 19:20

Table 17. Hebrew names derived from Judah

	Hebrew		Translation	Greek		Translation	OT Ref.	NT Ref.
Patriarch	יהודה	*yehudah*	Judah	Iouda	*Iouda*	Judah	Gen 29:35	Heb 8:8
Male Descendent	יהודי	*yehudiy*	Jew	Ioudaios	*Ioudaios*	Jew	Est 2:2	Act 10:28
Female Descendent	יהודיה	*yehudiyah*	Jewess	Ioudaia	*Ioudaia*	Jewess	n/a	Act 24:24
Descendants	יהודים	*yehudiym*	Jews	Ioudaioi	*Ioudaioi*	Jews	Neh 4:2	Gal 2:13
Land	יהודה	*yehudah*	Judah	Iouda, Ioudaia	*Iouda, Ioudaea*	Judah, Judaea	1Ki 1:35	Lk 1:5
Language	יהודית	*yehudiyt*	Judaean, Judaic	Ioudaisti	*Ioudaisti*	Judaean	2Ki 18:26	n/a

ABOUT THE NAME YHWH

If you have searched for the "true" pronunciation of the name of God, you probably discovered that many different theories offer different pronunciations. The reason for this is simple: there is no possible way to know with 100% accuracy how this name was originally pronounced. Let me explain.

THE FOUR HEBREW LETTERS

The name of God, often referred to as the *Tetragrammaton*[75], is written with four Hebrew letters: *Yud, Hey, Vav* and *Hey*. One of the oldest known examples of this name is found in the Temple Ostraca, written in *Paleo*-Hebrew (Figure 58).

Hey Vav Hey Yud

Figure 58. The name of God (YHWH) on the Temple Ostraca
(Image created by the author)

---

[75] A Greek word meaning "four letters."

THE YUD

This letter is pronounced with a "*y*" sound, as in the word "yellow." Most people are familiar with the transliteration of "Jehovah," which begins with the letter "J." When the letter "J" was first introduced about 500 years ago, it originally had the same "*y*" sound as the Hebrew letter *Yud*, though later, it was changed to the "*dg*" sound we are familiar with today. It should be noted that in Slavic languages, the letter "J" still retains the "*y*" sound to this day.

Two Hebrew letters, the *Yud* and the *Vav*, both of which appear in this name as discussed above, were frequently used as a consonant and a vowel. As we said previously, when this letter appears at the beginning of a word or syllable, it takes on the consonantal sound "*y*."

THE HEY

This letter, which appears twice in the name, has an "*h*" sound as in "hello."

THE VAV

In Modern Hebrew, this letter is pronounced with a "*v*" sound. However, some scholars debate this and many believe that this letter originally had a "*w*" sound. This is one of those letters that will be a consonant (*v/w*) when at the beginning of a syllable or a vowel (*o* or *u*) when at the end of a syllable.

Let's take another look at the name in the Temple Ostraca and the possible sounds for each letter.

YHVH

YHWH

YHOH

YHUH

SYLLABLE BREAKS

Where the syllable break is placed in the name determines if the letter *Vav* is used as a consonant or vowel. Because Hebrew likes to have a closed syllable (Consonant-Vowel-Consonant) at the end of a word, the letter *Vav* must be at the beginning of the syllable and therefore, it must be pronounced as a consonant (*v* or *w*). This leaves us with four possible syllable formations:

Y-H-VH

Y-H-WH

YH-VH

YH-WH

ADDED VOWEL SOUNDS

You will notice that we are still missing the implied vowels. So, our possible pronunciations for this name are many. Here are just a few of the possibilities:

Ya-Ha-VaH	Ye-He-WeH	YaH-VeH
Ye-He-VeH	Ya-He-WaH	YaH-WaH
Ya-He-VaH	YaH-VaH	YeH-WeH
Ya-Ha-WaH	YeH-VeH	YaH-WeH

THE NIKKUDOT

In the Masoretic Hebrew texts, which include the *Nikkudot*, we find six different spellings for the name of God:

יְהוָה   YeH-VaH

יְהֹוָה   YeH-o-VaH

יֱהֹוִה   YeH-o-ViH

יֱהוִה   YeH-ViH

יְהֹוִה   YeH-o-ViH

יְהוִה   YeH-ViH

Figure 59. The spellings of YHWH in the Masoretic text.
(Image created by the author)

Was the name of God pronounced these six different ways? Probably not. For over 2,000 years, Jews have forbidden the pronunciation of the name. So, rather than placing the correct *Nikkudot* into the four-letter name, they placed the *Nikkudot* from the words אֲדֹנָי (*Adonai*- Lord) or אֱלֹהִים (*Elohiym* - God) into the four letters of the name.

CONCLUSION

The bottom line is that there are many possibilities for the original pronunciation of the name, and all we can do today is make educated guesses. We must also keep in mind that the conventions of pronunciation of the Hebrew language we have been discussing are modern in nature, and we do not know with any accuracy what the conventions were for pronouncing Hebrew were in ancient times.

INCONSISTENT TRANSLATIONS OF HEBREW WORDS

When reading a Bible translation, most readers are solely dependent upon the translator and his accuracy of the translation. Unfortunately, unknown to most readers, many translations are far from consistent in their translation, such as we can see in the following examples.

A HEBREW WORD STUDY

The following verses include the translated word "heart:"

> *"And GOD saw that the wickedness of man was great in the earth, and that every imagination of the thoughts of his <u>heart</u> was only evil continually."* (Genesis 6:5, KJV)

> *"I delight to do thy will, O my God; Yea, thy law is within my <u>heart</u>."* (Psalm 40:8, KJV)

> *"You shall not oppress a stranger; you know the <u>heart</u> of a stranger, for you were strangers in the land of Egypt."* (Exodus 23:9, RSV)

> *"Their tongue is as an arrow shot out; it speaketh deceit: one speaketh peaceably to his neighbour with his mouth, but in <u>heart</u> he layeth his wait."* (Jeremiah 9:8, KJV)

> *"O let the evil of the wicked come to an end, but establish thou the righteous, thou who triest the minds and <u>hearts</u>, thou righteous God."* (Psalm 7:9, RSV)

When doing a word study such as we are doing here with the word "heart," we assume that the Hebrew word behind each word translated "heart" is the same. Simply by using *Strong's Exhaustive Concordance*, we can check each of these translations to see what Hebrew word lies behind the word "heart." What we find in Genesis 6:5 is the Hebrew word *lev*, which does mean "heart." In Psalm 40:8, we find the Hebrew word *me'ah* meaning the "gut." In Exodus 23:9 it is the word *nephesh* meaning "being," "person" or "soul." In Jeremiah 9:8 it is *qerev* meaning the "insides." In Psalm 7:9 it is *kil'yah* meaning "kidneys."

Each of these Hebrew words has a specific meaning which the bible translators have chosen to ignore. Instead, they have opted to translate all five of these Hebrew words with the English word "heart." Because the Hebrew Bible was written within a Hebraic culture, which differed greatly from our Greco-Roman culture, we do not think in Hebraic terms. Because of this difference, the translators removed the Hebraic-ness from the text, converting it to one more consistent with our Greco-Roman way of thinking. While this may seem trivial, it changes the meaning intended by the original author, making the translation incomplete or even misleading.

Now we shall use *Strong's Concordance* to reverse the process and look up verses that contain the Hebrew word *lev*, meaning "heart," to see if the translators translated this word consistently. In each of the verses below, the underlined word is the translator's choice for the Hebrew word *lev*:

> *"And Jacob stole away <u>unawares</u> to Laban the Syrian, in that he told him not that he fled."* (Genesis 31:20, KJV)

"And he that <u>regarded</u> not the word of Jehovah left his servants and his cattle in the field." (Exodus 9:21, ASV)

"And Moses said, hereby ye shall know that Jehovah hath sent me to do all these works; for I have not done them of mine own <u>mind</u>." (Numbers 16:28, ASV)

"Behold, God is mighty, and despiseth not any: He is mighty in strength of <u>understanding</u>." (Job 36:5, ASV)

"For they have consulted together with one <u>consent</u>; against thee do they make a covenant:" (Psalm 83:5, ASV)

"He that getteth <u>wisdom</u> loveth his own soul: He that keepeth understanding shall find good." (Proverbs 19:8, ASV)

Again, the translators ignored the original text, erased its original Hebraic-ness and replaced it with words that fit Greco-Roman thinking

ADDITION OF WORDS TO "FIX" THE TEXT

"...I have gotten a man <u>from</u> the LORD." (Genesis 4:1, KJV)

"...I have gotten a man with <u>the help of</u> the LORD." (Genesis 4:1, RSV)

In this verse, from two different translations, the underlined words have been added to the text and do not appear in the original Hebrew text. The literal rendering of this verse, from the Hebrew is as follows:

"I purchased a man with YHWH." (Genesis 4:1, RMT)

What exactly this passage means is uncertain, but what is clear is that the translators inserted words that are not present in the Hebrew text in order to "fix" the passage. It is this author's opinion that, at the least, the translator should inform his readers of this addition in a footnote.

GREEK INFLUENCE ON TRANSLATIONS

We are all familiar with the name "Moses." However, the pronunciation of this name comes from the Greek *Septuagint*. The correct Hebrew pronunciation is *Mosheh*. Another example of the Greek influence on Hebrew names is the name "Eve," again from the Greek *Septuagint*. The Hebrew pronunciation is *Hhawa*.

Many will be familiar with the word "*manna*," which is believed to be a Hebrew word, when in fact, it is not and never appears in the Hebrew Bible. The word *manna*, referring to the bread-like substance given by God to the Israelites while in the wilderness, is actually called *mahn*[76]. The term "manna," which appears in our English translations, comes from the Greek *Septuagint*.

This use of the Greek *Septuagint* for clarification is not limited to names only, but to the translations themselves:

---

[76] The transliteration of this Hebrew word should be *man*, but *mahn* is used so as not to confuse this Hebrew word with the English word "man."

> *"Cain said to Abel his brother, "<u>Let us go out to the</u>*
> *<u>field.</u>" And when they were in the field, Cain rose up*
> *against his brother Abel, and killed him."* (Genesis
> 4:8, RSV)

The underlined part of this verse is not found in the Hebrew Bible, but comes from the Greek *Septuagint*. In reality, the Hebrew text is missing what Cain said to his brother. Again, it is the opinion of this author that translators should, at the least, add a footnote stating that this phrase is from the *Septuagint* and is not found in the Hebrew text.

> *"When the boys grew up, Esau was a skillful hunter,*
> *a man of the field, while Jacob was a <u>quiet</u> man,*
> *dwelling in tents."* (Genesis 25:27, RSV)

> *"There was a man in the land of Uz, whose name*
> *was Job; and that man was <u>blameless</u> and upright,*
> *one who feared God, and turned away from evil."*
> (Job 1:1, RSV)

In Genesis 25:27, we read that Jacob was a "quiet" man (other translations have "simple" or "plain"). In Job 1:1, we read that Job was a "blameless" man. From this translation, we naturally would conclude that the character of Jacob is different from Job. However, the Hebrew word behind both of these words, "quiet" and "blameless," is the Hebrew word *tam*, which literally means "mature."

OTHER TRANSLATION INACCURACIES

> *"And he was there with Jehovah forty days and forty*
> *nights; he did neither eat bread, nor drink water.*

> *And he wrote upon the tables the words of the cove-*
> *nant, <u>the ten commandments</u>."* (Exodus 34:28, ASV)

The phrase "the Ten Commandments" never actually appears in the Hebrew Bible. The phrase in Hebrew is *aseret hadevariym* and literally means "the ten words" or "the ten things."

> *"You shall not make any cuttings in your flesh on*
> *account of the <u>dead</u> or tattoo any marks upon you:*
> *I am the LORD."* (Leviticus 19:28, RSV)

The Hebrew word for "dead" is *mot*, but that is not the Hebrew word used here. Instead, it is *nephesh*, meaning "being" or "person."

> *"And thou shalt make a <u>mercy-seat</u> of pure gold: two*
> *cubits and a half shall be the length thereof, and a cubit*
> *and a half the breadth thereof."* (Exodus 25:17, ASV)

The Hebrew word translated "mercy-seat" is *kaphoret*, which simply means a "covering" or "lid." By using the word "mercy-seat," the translator has interjected meaning into the text that does not exist in the original Hebrew.

> *"And he said, "Cast it on the ground." So he cast it*
> *on the ground, and it became a <u>serpent</u>; and Moses*
> *fled from it."* (Exodus 4:3, RSV)

> *"When Pharaoh says to you, `Prove yourselves by*
> *working a miracle,' then you shall say to Aaron,*
> *`Take your rod and cast it down before Pharaoh,*
> *that it may become a <u>serpent</u>.'"* (Exodus 7:9, RSV)

The Hebrew word translated as "serpent" in Exodus 4:3 is *nahhash,* but in Exodus 7:9, it is the word *taniyn.*[77] The reader is not informed that different Hebrew words are being translated as serpent. Is this significant? Maybe, maybe not. In this example it may not matter, while in others it could make a great difference.

> *"...and blessed be God Most High, who has deliv-*
> *ered your enemies into your hand!" And Abram gave*
> *him a tenth of everything."* (Genesis 14:20, RSV)

The translator has inserted the name Abram when it does not appear in the original text. The original simply states, *"and he gave him a tenth."* The "he" is not identified and may be either Melchizedek or Abram. However, the RSV translation has "fixed" this problem by telling you it is Abram. Are they correct?

These examples of translational inconsistencies should adequately demonstrate the need for Bible readers to do their own investigation, research and studies and not be completely dependent on the translators.

UNCOVERING THE ORIGINAL MEANING OF HEBREW WORDS

One of the major differences between our Greco-Roman thought and the thought of the Ancient Hebrews is that we commonly use abstract terms and thought while the Ancient Hebrews did not. Instead, the Hebrews used terms that are concrete in nature. The following verse demonstrates this difference:

---

[77] The Hebrew word *nahhash* means, according to the *Ancient Hebrew Lexicon of the Bible,* "serpent" and *taniyn* means "crocodile."

"And the LORD said unto Moses, write this for a memorial in a book, and <u>rehearse</u> it in the ears of Joshua." (Exodus 17:14, KJV)

The following is the *Mechanical Translation* from the Hebrew:

"[A]nd YHWH said to Mosheh, write this remembrance in the scroll and <u>place</u> it in the ears of Yehoshu'a..." (RMT)

Notice the difference? The Hebrew text has *Mosheh* placing the scroll into the ear of *Yeshoshu'a*. While this is not meant to be taken literally, but figuratively, it clearly demonstrates how the Ancient Hebrews thought and wrote from a concrete perspective. It is this distinction that is brought out by using the *Mechanical Translation*.

"And Jonathan rose from the table in <u>fierce anger</u>." (1 Samuel 20:34, RSV)

The RSV translation uses the abstract phrase "fierce anger," but in the *Mechanical Translation* we see the more concreteness of the passage.

"And Y'honatan rose from the table with a <u>fiery nose</u>." (Samuel 20:34, RMT)

The Hebrew word *aph* can mean a "nose," or it can be used for "anger," from the fact that one's nostrils flare when breathing heavy in anger.

METHODS FOR UNCOVERING WORD MEANINGS

While different methods are used to uncover the original concrete meaning of Hebrew words, the two major ones are to look at the *context* of the words and their the *roots*.

With context, we are looking to see how a word is used in a given passage.

> *"Look, his soul which is lifted up is not upright in him: but the just shall live by his <u>faith</u>."* (Habakkuk 2:4, KJV)

The word "faith" is an abstract word. The Hebrew behind this word is *emunah*. If we examine other passages that use *emunah* and the context in which it is used, we can find its original concrete meaning:

> *"But Moses' hands were heavy; and they took a stone, and put it under him, and he sat thereon; and Aaron and Hur stayed up his hands, the one on the one side, and the other on the other side; and his hands were <u>steady</u> until the going down of the sun."* (Exodus 17:12, KJV)

The word "steady" is the same Hebrew word *emunah*, but here, it is translated with a more concrete English word. Now let's read the Habakkuk passage through the mechanical translation.

> *"Behold, his soul is presumptuous, it is not upright in him, but the steadfast one will live with his <u>se-cureness</u>."* (Habakkuk 2:4, RMT)

The second method for uncovering the meaning of a given word is to examine the root of the word:

> *"Ye shall keep the sabbath therefore; for it is <u>holy</u> unto you."* (Exodus 31:14, KJV)

The word "holy" means "something that is religiously pure." However, the word *holy* and the idea of being "religiously pure" are abstract concepts. The Hebrew word is *qodesh* which comes from the verbal root *Q-D-Sh*. In most cases, this verb is translated as "sanctified," another abstract term. The following verse provides the more concrete meaning of the word:

> *"...And Joram brought with him articles of silver, of gold, and of bronze; these also King David <u>dedicated</u> to the LORD."* (2 Samuel 8:10-11, RSV)

Here, the verb *qadash* is translated as "dedicated," meaning to "set something aside for a special purpose or function." From this, we learn that the concrete meaning of *qodesh* is something that is "set aside for a special purpose."

IS STRONG'S DICTIONARY ENOUGH?

In preceding sections we have referred to Strong's Dictionary and Concordance as an important tool for Biblical study. For those who do not know Hebrew, this is the only tool available for studying the Hebrew text of the Bible. However, it has many limitations that need to be understood if one is going to use this resource correctly.

In the King James Version of Exodus 3:16, we read, *"The LORD God of your fathers... appeared unto me..."* A person might read this and ask, "How can the LORD 'appear' to someone when he has no form?" This person then refers to his *Strong's Exhaustive Concordance*, looks up the word "appear" from this verse, and finds it is assigned the number H7200. When he looks up this number in the Hebrew dictionary in the back of the *Exhaustive Concordance,* he finds that it is the Hebrew word ראה (*ra'ah*) and means "to see."

Armed with this bit of knowledge, the reader then retranslates this verse as, "And the LORD God of your fathers... saw me..." and then says, "Ah-ha, the LORD didn't 'appear' to him, the LORD 'saw' him."

Have you ever heard the expression, "A little knowledge is a danger-ous thing?" Well, it applies in this situation. This reader is unaware that Hebrew verbs can take on different forms, such as we discussed earlier, and these forms are not identified in Strong's dictionary. For example, in Exodus 3:4 the Hebrew verb *ra'ah* is written ירא (*yar'*), which is the simple form of the verb and means "he saw." But in Exodus 3:16 it is written as נראה (*nir'ah*), which is the passive form of the verb and means "and he was seen" or "and he appeared." According to the verb form of this Hebrew word in Exodus 3:16, the LORD is not the one "seeing," he is the one who "was seen."

THE OLD TESTAMENT

HISTORY OF THE
HEBREW BIBLE

THE ORIGINAL MANUSCRIPTS

Figure 60. Hebrew manuscript, 11th Century AD
(Image credit: Schøyen Collection)

The original manuscripts of the Hebrew Bible, which would have been handwritten on animal skins or papyrus, have long since deteriorated. What remain today are copies from these original autographs.

In this digital age, electronic copies are perfect representations of the original. However, in ancient times copying a manuscript was a much more tedious labor and not as precise, allowing for human intervention or error.

OLDEST KNOWN COPIES OF BIBLICAL TEXTS

Figure 61. Silver scroll discovered in Ketef Hinnom
(Image Credit: Tamar Hayardeni)

The oldest text of the Hebrew Bible was discovered in a tomb at Ketef Hinnom (Figure 61) in Israel in 1979. The text, inscribed on a silver scroll in a *Paleo*-Hebrew script dating to the 7th century BC, is the Aaronic blessing, which begins, *yeverekh'kha YHWH Vayishmarekha* (*May YHWH bless you and keep you*).

Figure 62. The Nash Papyrus
(Image is in the Public Domain)

Another very ancient fragment of the Hebrew Bible is the Nash Papyrus (Figure 62) discovered in Egypt in 1898. The fragment includes the Ten Commandments (Exodus 20:2-17) and the *Sh'ma* (Deuteronomy 6:4) and is dated to the 2nd century BC.

Very few ancient texts of the Hebrew Bible had been found and were very rare prior to 1947, when a depository of scrolls in the Dead Sea Caves provided us with a library of ancient manuscripts of the Hebrew Bible.

THE DEAD SEA SCROLLS

As has been mentioned before, between 1947 and 1956 ancient scrolls and fragments of the Hebrew Bible were discovered in caves near the Dead Sea dating to the 1st century BC and the 1st century AD.

The manuscripts in the form of scrolls discovered in the Dead Sea Caves included all of the canonical books of the Hebrew Bible[78], as well as non-canonical books such as Enoch, Jubilees, Tobit, Sirach and psalms that are not part of the canonical 150 Psalms. Also found among the Dead Sea Scrolls were sectarian books such as the *Community Rule*, the *War Scroll*, the *Damascus Document* and commentaries on books of the Bible.

There are several different theories as to the origin of these texts.

The predominating theory asserts that the scrolls were the work of a Jewish sect called the Essenes. It is believed that the Essenes had

---

[78] The only exception is the Book of Esther, which has not been found in any of the Dead Sea Caves.

resided in nearby Qumran, and they hid the scrolls in the near-by caves to protect them from the advancing Roman army.

Other possible theories for the creators of the scrolls include early Messianics (Christians) or Zadokite priests.

A newer theory and one ascribed to by the author is that the scrolls were old and unusable scrolls from various libraries and synagogues in Israel that were taken to the caves near Qumran for burial. In Jewish tradition, any document containing the name YHWH must be buried and may not be destroyed, burned or discarded. Supporting this theory is the fact that the only book not yet discovered in the caves is the book of Esther, which happens to be the only book of the Bible that does not contain the name YHWH, and therefore, would not be required to be buried.

THE ISAIAH SCROLL

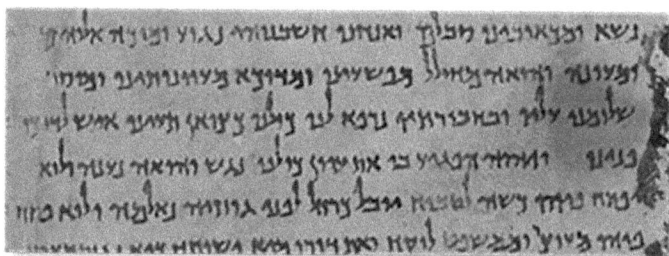

Figure 63. A section of the Isaiah Scroll
(Image is in the Public Domain)

The most famous of the scrolls found within the Dead Sea Caves is the Isaiah Scroll (Figure 63).

While most of the scrolls are fragments, deteriorating or incomplete, the Isaiah Scroll is the single complete scroll found.

The life of a scroll depends on its handling and storage, but it can be used within a community for up to several hundred years. Some *Torah* scrolls still in use in synagogues today are over 500 years old.

The Isaiah Scroll from the Dead Sea Caves has been dated to around 200 BC. Isaiah wrote his original scroll around 700 BC and it may have been in use until around 200 BC. This means that it is possible that the Isaiah Scroll from the Dead Sea Caves could easily be a copy made directly from Isaiah's original scroll.

THE ALEPPO CODEX

Figure 64. A page from the Aleppo Codex
(Image is in the Public Domain)

Until the discovery of the Dead Sea Scrolls, the oldest existing complete Hebrew Bible was the *Aleppo* Codex (Figure 64), also called the

Masoretic text, which was written in the 10ᵗʰ century AD, a thousand years after the Dead Sea Scrolls. For centuries, this text has been the foundation for Jewish and Christian translators.

The major difference between the *Aleppo* Codex and the Dead Sea Scrolls is the addition of the *nikkudot* to the Hebrew words found in the *Aleppo* Codex.

While the Masoretic text and the Dead Sea Scrolls were transcribed a thousand years apart, they are amazingly similar, proving that the copying methods employed by the Jewish scribes over the centuries were very sophisticated and successful. However, there are some differences. The majority of these differences are minor issues, such as differences in spelling and grammar, but some are much more complex.

Besides the addition of the *nikkudot*, other changes occurred in the Hebrew text after making copies of copies. One of those more dramatic changes was the accidental removal of an entire verse.

Figure 65. A portion of Psalm 145 from the Aleppo Codex
(Image is in the Public Domain)

Psalm 145 is an acrostic psalm where each verse begins with successive letters of the Hebrew alphabet. In the *Aleppo* Codex, the first verse begins with the letter *aleph*, the second with the *beyt*, the third with the *gimel*, and so on. Verse 13 begins with the letter מ (*mem*), identified with the number "1" in Figure 65 above, the 13ᵗʰ letter of the Hebrew alphabet. The next verse in the image, identified with the number "2," begins with the letter ס (*samehh)*, the 15ᵗʰ letter of the Hebrew alphabet. There is no verse beginning with the 14ᵗʰ letter נ (*nun*).

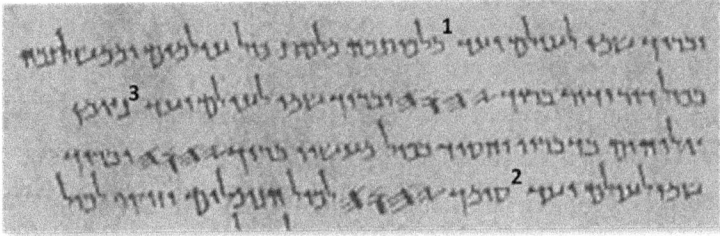

Figure 66. A portion of Psalm 145 from the Dead Sea Scrolls
(Image is in the Public Domain)

When we examine Psalm 145 from the Dead Sea Scrolls, we find between the verse beginning with the מ (*mem*), identified with a "1" in Figure 66 above, and the verse beginning with the ס (*samehh*), identified with a "2", the missing verse, beginning with the letter נ (*nun*), is present and identified with a "3" and reads as follows:

נאמן אלוהים בדבריו וחסיד בכול מעשיו

This translates as:

*"God is faithful in his words, and
gracious in all his deeds."*

This is why Psalm 145:13 reads differently in the KJV compared with modern versions such as the RSV. The KJV was written prior to discovering the Dead Sea Scrolls, while the RSV and other modern versions were written afterward and often incorporate what has been found in the Dead Sea Scrolls.

ANCIENT TRANSLATIONS

As the Jewish people began to spread beyond Israel, they adopted the language of their new neighbors. This created the need for translations of the Bible into their assimilated languages so they could continue reading the Bible. While there have been translations of the Hebrew Bible into many different languages, the three most widely used in ancient times were the Latin, Aramaic and Greek translations.

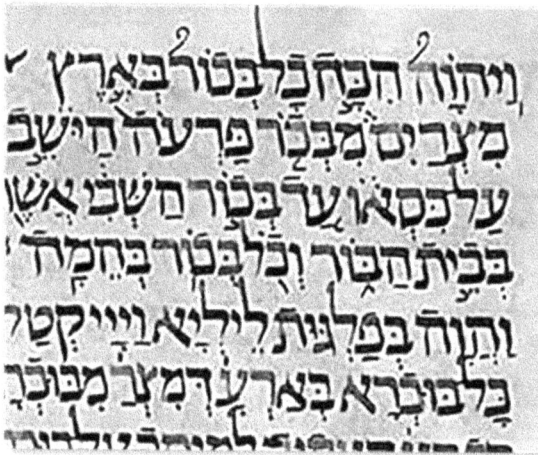

Figure 67. A portion of an Aramaic Targum
(Image credit: Schøyen Collection)

Of the many Aramaic translations of the Hebrew Bible (see Figure 67), two are principal ones. *Targum Onkelos* is an Aramaic translation of the first five books of the Bible written in the 1st century AD by Onkelos, a Roman convert to Judaism. The second is the *Targum Jonathan*, an Aramaic translation of the prophets. It was written in the 1st century BC by Jonathan Ben Uziel, a student of Hillel the Elder, a famous Jewish teacher and religious leader.

Figure 68. A portion of the Greek Septuagint
(Image is in the Public Domain)

The *Septuagint*, the Greek translation of the first five books of the Hebrew Bible (see Figure 68), was written by Jewish scholars in the 3rd century BC. The remainder of the Hebrew Bible, the writings and the prophets, was translated into Greek by unknown translators between the 2nd and 1st centuries BC.

Figure 69. A portion of the Latin Vulgate
(Image is in the Public Domain)

The *Latin Vulgate*, comprised of the Hebrew Bible as well as the New Testament (see Figure 69), was translated by Jerome, a Christian priest and apologist, in the 5th century AD.

BIBLICAL TEXTUAL CRITICISM

A process called textual criticism compares the various Hebrew, Aramaic, Greek and Latin manuscripts of the Bible. In so doing, we often find variations in how these manuscripts read.

Genesis 4:8, which we previously examined, provides a simple example of how the textual criticism process works. In the Hebrew *Aleppo* Codex, this passage reads:

> *"[A]nd Qayin said to Hevel his brother, and it came*
> *to pass in their existing in the field, and Qayin rose*
> *to Hevel his brother and he killed him,"* (RMT)

Missing from this passage is what Cain said to Abel and appears to be an accidental omission on the part of a scribe.

However, when we examine this passage in the Greek *Septuagint* translation, we find the missing words:

> *"[A]nd Qayin said to Hevel his brother, <u>let us go</u>*
> *<u>into the field</u>, and it came to pass in their existing*
> *in the field, and Qayin rose to Hevel his brother and*
> *he killed him,"* (RMT)

It appears that the *Septuagint* worked from a Hebrew manuscript that included Cain's speech, but the *Aleppo* Codex referenced a Hebrew manuscript that was missing the speech.

Another example compares different English translations of Deuteronomy 32:8, where we also find very different readings. Each of the English translations begin similarly:

> *"When the Most High gave the nations their inheritance, when He separated the sons of man, He set the boundaries of the peoples according to the number of the..."* (NASB)

However, different translations have different renderings for the end of this verse.

> *"...children of Israel"* (KJV)
> *"...sons of God"* (RSV)
> *"...angels of God"* (YLT)

These differences can be resolved by examining the different ancient texts to determine which one the translator used for this verse:

בני ישראל (*b'ney yisra'el* / children of Israel): This phrase comes from the *Aleppo* Codex and is the source for the KJV.

בני אלוהים (*b'ney elohiym* / sons of God): This phrase comes from the Dead Sea Scrolls and is the source for the RSV.

αγγελων θεου (*theou aggelon* / angels of God): This phrase comes from the Greek *Septuagint* and is the source for the YLT.

Each of these manuscripts was copied from a Hebrew source that differed from the others. The process of textual criticism compares these various texts to decide which text is the original. The consensus among scholars is that the original text is בני אל (*b'ney el* / sons of El). Notice that the letters in these two Hebrew words can be found within all three of the versions listed above; בְּנֵי יִשְׂרָאֵל (*b'ney yisra'el*), בְּנֵי אֱלוֹהִים (b'ney *elohiym*) and בְּנֵי אֵל (*b'ney el*[79]).

---

[79] A Hebrew translation of the *Septuagint.*

156

HEBREW POETRY

One often overlooked characteristic of the Bible is the poetical nature of the text. While the Psalms and Proverbs are obviously poetical, the poetry in other books is not so apparent. Let's begin by examining a few simple poetical passages from Psalms in order to understand the style of Hebrew poetry. Then we will look at some of the not-so-obvious poetical passages.

PARALLELISMS

The most common form of poetry in the Hebrew Bible is parallelism, which expresses one idea in two or more different ways:

> *"Your word is a lamp to my feet and a light for my path."* (Psalms 119:105, KJV)

The above is an example of a simple parallel, which can be written in this manner:

Your word is:

1. a lamp to my feet
2. a light for my path

Here we see that the words "lamp" and "light" are paralleled as well as the words "my feet" and "my path."

Below is another example of this style of poetry:

"My son, my teachings you shall not forget and my commands your heart shall guard." (Proverbs 3:1, KJV)

In this verse, the phrase "my teachings" is paralleled with "my commands." "You shall not forget" is paralleled with "your heart shall guard" and can be written as follows:

My son:

1. my teachings you shall not forget
2. my commands your heart shall guard

We previously learned two methods for finding the definition of a word. The first is by examining the context of how a word is used in various places in the Bible and the second was by examining the meanings of related roots and words. A third method is to look at how the word is paralleled with other words. For example, in the verse above, the word "command" is paralleled with the word "teaching." Instead of seeing God's words as "commands," such as from a general to his troops, we can better understand them as "teachings," such as from parents to their children.

Let's take a look at another passage where the poetry is a little more complex.

> *"O LORD, who shall sojourn in your tent? Who shall dwell on your holy hill? He who walks blamelessly and does what is right and speaks truth in his heart who does not slander with his tongue and does no evil to his neighbor, nor takes up a reproach against his friend."* (Psalm 15:1-3, ESV)

We can rewrite the above passage as follows:

> A1. O LORD, who shall sojourn in your tent?
> A2. Who shall dwell on your holy hill?
> B1. He who walks blamelessly
> B2. and does what is right
> C1. and speaks truth in his heart
> C2. who does not slander with his tongue
> D1. and does no evil to his neighbor
> D2. nor takes up a reproach against his friend

The letters A, B, C and D each represent one idea while the numbers 1 and 2 represent the two different ways of expressing that one idea.

Now that we've introduced the basic parallelism structures of Hebrew poetry in the Psalms and Proverbs, we shall look at the rest of the Hebrew Bible, where poetry is found throughout its pages.

> *"Lamech said to his wives, 'Adah and Zillah, listen to me; wives of Lamech, hear my words. I have*

    killed a man for wounding me and a young man for
    injuring me.'" (Genesis 4:23, KJV)

Breaking down the syntactic elements of Lamech's speech, he says first: *"Adah and Zillah, listen to me."* This phrase is a parallelism with the one that follows: *"wives of Lamech, hear my words."* Then he says that he has killed: *"a man for wounding me,"* which is parallel to: *"a young man for injuring me."* Lamech did not kill one person who wounded him and kill another who injured him (which is how most interpret this passage). Instead, he killed one person, but the act was stated it in two different ways.

Another example of Hebrew poetry can be found in Isaiah 6:10:

    "Make the heart of this people fat, and make their
    ears heavy, and shut their eyes; lest they see with
    their eyes, and hear with their ears, and understand
    with their heart, and convert, and be healed." (KJV)

We demonstrate the parallels in this passage thus:

    A^1. Make the *heart* of this people fat,
        B^1. and make their *ears* heavy,
            C^1. and shut their *eyes*;
            C^2. lest they see with their *eyes*,
        B^2. and hear with their *ears*,
    A^2. and understand with their *heart*, and convert, and be
        healed.

This format reveals that the first and last lines are paralleled, the second and second to last lines are paralleled and the two middle lines are paralleled.

Another common form of parallelism is the use of negatives where two opposing ideas are stated, as we find in Proverbs 11:19-20:

> *"Righteousness brings one to life, but the pursuit of evil brings one to his death. A twisted heart is an abomination of YHWH, but a mature path is his pleasure."* (RMT)

We show the parallels in this passage this way:

A^1. Righteousness brings one to life
   B^1. Pursuit of evil brings one to his death
   B^2. A twisted heart is an abomination of YHWH
A^2. A mature path is his pleasure

This type of parallelism is called *chiasmus* and is found throughout the Bible. In fact, the entire creation story from Genesis 1:1 to 2:3 is a chiasmus.

A. Elohiym filled the sky and the land because it was empty and it was all in chaos so the wind of Elohiym settled upon the water (1:1 to 1:2)
  A^1. Day 1 - Elohiym separates (1:3 to 1:5, day one)
    a. light
    b. dark
  A^2. Day 2 - Elohiym separates (1:6 to 1:8, day two)
    a. water
    b. sky
  A^3. Day 3 - Elohiym separates (1:9 to 1:13, day three
    a. land
    b. plants spring up from the land

B¹. Day 4 - Elohiym fills (1:14 to 1:19, day four)

    a.   the light with the sun

    b.   the dark with the moon

B². Day 5 - Elohiym fills (1:20 to 1:23, day five)

    a.   the water with fish

    b.   the sky with birds

B³. Day 6 - Elohiym fills (1:24 to 1:31, day six)

    a.   the land with animals and man

    b.   plants are given as food

B. Elohiym finishes his separating and filling of the sky and the land and rests on the seventh day (2:1 to 2:3, day seven)

Once we understand that Genesis chapter 1 is a poem that was most likely sung and not a scientific paper, we can resolve a problem that no one seems to notice.

> *"And God said, Let there be light: and there was light. And God saw the light, that it was good: and God divided the light from the darkness."* (Genesis 1:3-4, KJV)

> *"And God set [the two great lights] in the firmament of the heaven to give light upon the earth, And to rule over the day and over the night, and to divide the light from the darkness."* (Genesis 1:17-18, KJV)

If God divided the light from the darkness on day one, why is he again dividing the light from the darkness on day four? The answer is that as a poem, the days are not literal days, but a poetical convention. Day One is paralleled with Day Four and Day Two is paralleled with Day Five and Day Three is paralleled with Day Six. These are not six literal days, but six figurative days.

MISUNDERSTOOD PARALLELS

THE SMOKING FURNACE AND THE BURNING LAMP

In Genesis 15, God causes Abram to fall into a deep sleep and tells Abraham about the promises he has for him and his descendants. Then, we read:

> *"And it came to pass, that, when the sun went down,*
> *and it was dark, behold a smoking furnace, and a*
> *burning lamp that passed between those pieces."*
> (Genesis 15:17, KJV)

It is assumed by most that there are two entities passing through the pieces, a smoking furnace *and* a burning lamp. However, this is not the case. This is a parallelism and there is only one object passing through the pieces, but it is identified with two different phrases. We confirm this through examining the grammar of the passage. The verb "passed" in the Hebrew identifies the subject of the verb (what is passing through the pieces) as singular (one), not plural (two or more).

THE DONKEY AND THE COLT

> *"...thy King cometh unto thee... riding upon an*
> *ass, and upon a colt the foal of an ass."* (Zechariah
> 9:9, KJV)

Three gospels reference this passage; Mathew, Mark and Luke. Mark and Luke recognize that the "ass" and the "colt" are Hebrew parallels, one animal.

> *"Go into the village in front of you, and immediately as you enter it you will find a colt tied, on which no one has ever sat. Untie it and bring it. ... And they brought the colt to Jesus and threw their cloaks on it, and he sat on it."* (Mark 11:2-7, ESV)

> *"Go into the village in front of you, where on entering you will find a colt tied, on which no one has ever yet sat. Untie it and bring it here. ... And they brought it to Jesus, and throwing their cloaks on the colt, they set Jesus on it."* (Luke 19:30-35, ESV)

However, Matthew does not seem to understand the Hebraism here and has Yeshua riding two animals.

> *"Go into the village in front of you, and immediately you will find a donkey tied, and a colt with her. Untie them and bring them to me ... They brought the donkey and the colt and put on them their cloaks, and he sat on them."* (Matthew 21:2-7, ESV)

ABOUT BIBLE TRANSLATIONS

Historically, the purpose of a Bible translation was to bring the Bible to those who could not read the original language. However, over the centuries there has been a shift in purpose that has been fueled by the computer and digitalization of printing.

CONSUMERISM IN THE BIBLE BUSINESS

In December 2006, *"The New Yorker"* published the article *"The Good Book Business,"* which stated, *"The familiar observation that the Bible is the best-selling book of all time obscures a more startling fact: the Bible is the best-selling book of the year, every year."*[80]

In short, the translating and printing of Bibles is "Big Business." In the world of consumerism, the publisher's primary objective is to offer a product that appeals to the consumer. For this reason, a translation is required to conform to the buyer's expectations. Even if it is more accurate, a Bible that does not conform to the buyer's expectations will not sell, limiting the buyer to only those translations that have been deemed "profitable." Thus, serious students of the Bible must be willing to do their own investigation into the meaning and interpretation of the text and not be completely dependent on the translations for their total understanding of the text.

THE ORIGINAL LANGUAGE

Many theological differences, divisions and arguments are based on faulty translations and interpretations of the text that could be resolved easily by examining the original language of the Bible.

Many theological discussions, teachings and debates use phrases like "The Bible says" or "God says." From a technical point of view, that becomes problematic. These statements assume the Bible was written in English, which we know is not true.

---

[80] (Radosh, 2006)

The Bible does not say, *"In the beginning God created the heavens and the earth."* A more accurate statement would be, "The Bible says, *'bereshiyt bara elohiym et hashamayim v'et ha'arets,'* which can be translated as, *"God created the heavens and the earth...,"* but it could just as easily and correctly be translated as, *"On the summit he shaped Elohiym with the sky and the land."*

The Hebrew word ראשית (*reshiyt*) is translated as "beginning" in Genesis 1:1 in the *King James Version*. But the KJV also translates this same Hebrew word as "chief" (1 Samuel 15:21) and "principal thing" (Proverbs 4:7). The Hebrew word ראשית (*reshiyt*) may be interpreted as "beginning," but the more literal meaning is "height," as in "the height or beginning of an event," or "the height of someone in rank" or "the height of importance" or the literal height of a "summit[81]."

When we use the many tools available to examine the Hebrew behind the English translations, it quickly becomes apparent that the English translators of the text were not very consistent in their translation of Hebrew words.

Another example to consider is the Hebrew word נפש (*nephesh*). It is most frequently translated in the KJV as "soul," but in other verses this word is translated as "appetite, beast, body, breath, creature, dead, desire, ghost, heart, life, lust, man, mind, person, pleasure, self, thing and will."

---

[81] It is interesting to note that in Hebrew, every word used for space is also used for time, such as we see here where *reshiyt* can be the "height" of a time (beginning) or the height of a place (summit). Other examples are *qedem*, which can mean east (place) or ancient (time) and olam, which can mean a distant horizon or a distant time.

The Hebrew verb נתן (*N.T.N*), literally means "to give," but is translated with a wide variety of English words including: "add, aloud, apply, appoint, ascribe, assign, avenge, bestow, bring, cast, cause, charge, come, commit, consider, count, cry, deliver, direct, distribute, do, fasten, forth, frame, get, grant, hang, have, heal, heed, lay, leave, left, lend, let, lift, make, occupy, offer, ordain, over, oversight, pay, perform, place, plant, pour, present, print, pull, put, recompense, requite, restore, send, set, shoot, show, sing, sit, slander, strike, submit, suffer, take, thrust, tie, trade, turn, utter, weep, willingly, withdrew, would, yell, and yield."

These wide variation in translation should cause one to pause and wonder just how accurate are the translations we are using.

THE INADEQUACY OF A TRANSLATION

The English vocabulary and its definitions are inadequate to convey the meanings of Hebrew words. For example, in the following passages, we find the word "teach," an English word meaning "to impart knowledge or skill through instruction:"

> *"And thou shalt <u>teach</u> them ordinances and laws, and shalt shew them the way wherein they must walk, and the work that they must do."* (Exodus 18:20, KJV)

> *"And the LORD said unto Moses, come up to me into the mount, and be there: and I will give thee tables of stone, and a law, and commandments which I have written; that thou mayest <u>teach</u> them."* (Exodus 24:12, KJV)

"Now therefore hearken, O Israel, unto the statutes and unto the judgments, which I <u>teach</u> you, for to do them, that ye may live, and go in and possess the land which the LORD God of your fathers giveth you." (Deuteronomy 4:1, KJV)

"Only take heed to thyself, and keep thy soul diligently, lest thou forget the things which thine eyes have seen, and lest they depart from thy heart all the days of thy life: but <u>teach</u> them thy sons, and thy sons' sons;" (Deuteronomy 4:9, KJV)

"And thou shalt <u>teach</u> them diligently unto thy children, and shalt talk of them when thou sittest in thine house, and when thou walkest by the way, and when thou liest down, and when thou risest up." (Deuteronomy 6:7, KJV)

"If not, hearken unto me: hold thy peace, and I shall <u>teach</u> thee wisdom." (Job 33:33, KJV)

Each use of the word "teach" in these six passages is the English translation of six different Hebrew words, each having its own unique meaning:

Exodus 18:20: זהר (*zahar*) – To advise caution
Exodus 24:12: ירה (*yarah*) – To point out the direction to go
Deuteronomy 4:1: למד (*lamad*) – To urge to go in a specific direction
Deuteronomy 4:9: ידע (*yada*) – To provide experience
Deuteronomy 6:7: שמן (*shaman*) – To sharpen
Job 33:33: אלף (*alaph*) – To show through example

The original meaning of these six Hebrew words is completely erased and lost when they are simply translated as "teach." This demonstrates the need to go beyond the simple English translation to the original language to glean the actual intent of the passage.

THE MECHANICAL TRANSLATION

To resolve the issue of how to arrive at consistency in the translation of words, the author of this work developed a method of translation he calls the "mechanical translation."

The mechanical translation project began with the development of a lexicon, the *Ancient Hebrew Lexicon of the Bible* compiled by the author, where one English word was selected for each Hebrew word. The definition for each Hebrew word is based primarily on its etymology (what the word means based on its relationship to other words and roots), context (how the word is used throughout the Bible), poetry (how the word is paralleled with other words) and culture (what the word meant to those who lived within that culture).

The second part of the mechanical translation process involved replacing each Hebrew word in the Bible with its corresponding English word from the *Lexicon*.

WHAT IS THE MECHANICAL TRANSLATION?

Every Bible translation to date, including inter-linear and literal translations, translates the Hebrew text according to context. The problem with this practice is that the context can be interpreted differently based upon the translator's personal bias or opinions.

In contrast, a word for word, prefix for prefix and suffix for suffix translation is very methodical and prevents the translator from "fixing" or "interpreting" the text.

One advantage to the mechanical translation is that the reader apprehends the text in its pure and original Hebrew format. A major drawback to this method of translation, however, is Hebrew syntax (sentence structure and style), which differs greatly from English syntax. A reader who lacks a background in Hebrew syntax would be completely lost in the "mechanical translation." For example, the mechanical translation of Exodus 20:3 is as follows:

NOT *he~will~*EXIST$^{(V)}$ to~you$^{(ms)}$ Elohiym
OTHER~s UPON FACE~s~me[82] (MT)

To alleviate this problem, the "mechanical translation" is accompanied by a "revised mechanical translation" that re-arranges the words of the "mechanical translation" into a more readable and understandable English syntax. The revised mechanical translation of Exodus 20:3 reads as follows:

"Another Elohiym will not exist for you in my face."
(RMT)

There are times when the "revised mechanical translation" is difficult to read and may not make perfect sense, due to the fact that the Hebrew structure of a given sentence is sometimes difficult to

---

[82] The mechanical translation uses certain conventions to convey aspects of the Hebrew language. Words in upper case letters are Hebrew words. Words in lower case are prefixes and suffixes. Verbs are identified by the "(V)." Words in lower case and in italics are parts of the verb conjugation. Names are identified by having their first letter only in the upper case.

read itself. While most other translations "fix" the text so that it will always be read easily, this translation preserves the difficulties. It is the opinion of the *Mechanical Translation's* author that those who are interested in this translation will be willing to invest the extra effort it takes to understand a difficult passage.

To stress again, this method of translating helps immensely to eliminate personal bias on the part of the translator and maintains the intended meaning of the passage.

COMPARING TRANSLATIONS

The major advantage of the *Mechanical Translation* for the student of the Bible is that it consistently translates each Hebrew word in the exact same way every time it occurs in the text. This allows the reader, not even knowing Hebrew, to see the Hebrew text in its pure form void of any personal interpretation being interjected into the text by the translator. Below are a few examples from the book of Genesis comparing the *Mechanical Translation* (MT) and its *Revised Mechanical Translation* (RMT) with some of the more traditional translations.

GENESIS 3:15

> *"And I will put enmity between thee and the woman, and between thy seed and her seed; it shall bruise thy head, and thou shalt bruise his heel."* (KJV)

> *"I will put enmity between you and the woman, and between your seed and her seed; he shall bruise your head, and you shall bruise his heel."* (RSV)

> *"I will put enmity between you and the woman, and*
> *between your offspring and her offspring. He will*
> *pound <u>your head</u>, and you will bite <u>his heel</u>."* (SET)

These three translations completely ignore the grammar of the Hebrew text. The underlined pronouns (thy/your and his) are attached to the nouns (head and heel). But in the Hebrew, these pronouns are attached to the verbs, not the nouns, as the MT shows.

> and~HOSTILITY *I~did*~SET.DOWN[(V)]
> BETWEEN~you[(ms)] and~BETWEEN the~WOMAN
> and~BETWEEN SEED~you[(ms)] and~BETWEEN
> SEED~her HE *he~will*~FALL.UPON[(V)]~<u>you</u>[(ms)] HEAD
> and~YOU[(ms)] *you*[(ms)]~*will*~FALL.UPON[(V)]~<u>him</u>
> HEEL (MT)

> *"[A]nd I set down hostility between you and the*
> *woman, and between your seed and her seed, he will*
> *fall upon <u>you</u> a head, and you will fall upon <u>him</u> a*
> *heel[83]."* (RMT)

The YLT, like the MT, preserves the grammar of the Hebrew.

> *"and enmity I put between thee and the woman, and*
> *between thy seed and her seed; he doth bruise thee --*
> *the head, and thou dost bruise him -- the heel."* (YLT)

---

[83] In Hebrew, the word for "head" can mean "first" and the word for "heel" can mean "last," so this verse could be translated as *"[A]nd I set down hostility between you and the woman, and between your seed and her seed, he will fall upon you <u>first</u>, and you will fall upon him <u>last</u>."* This interpretation of the passage is possible with the MT and RMT, but because the KJV, RSV and SET have ignored the grammar, this interpretation is not possible.

The KJV, RSV and SET have ignored the grammar of the Hebrew verbs, which are "he will fall upon/bruise/pound you" and "you will fall upon/bruise/pound him."

GENESIS 4:7

> *"Is there not, if thou dost well, acceptance? and if thou dost not well, at the opening a <u>sin-offering</u> is crouching, and unto thee <u>its</u> desire, and thou rulest over <u>it</u>."* (YLT)

> *"If you do well, will you not be accepted? And if you do not do well, <u>sin</u> is couching at the door; <u>its</u> desire is for you, but you must master <u>it</u>."* (RSV)

> *"Surely, if you improve yourself, you will be forgiven. But if you do not improve yourself, <u>sin</u> rests at the door. <u>Its</u> desire is toward you, yet you can conquer <u>it</u>."* (SET)

In the YLT, RSV and SET, the word "it" (neutral gender) is used implying that the "it" is "sin." However, the Hebrew behind the English word "it[84]" is the masculine pronoun "him." The Hebrew word *hhatat* ("failure" in the MT) is a feminine word[85], therefore, the "him" (masculine) cannot be "sin" (feminine).

---

[84] The only gender-neutral pronouns in the Hebrew language are the first-person pronouns, "I" and "we."

[85] The *Mechanical Translation* is accompanied by a Hebrew dictionary, which will, besides defining the word, identify a noun as masculine or feminine.

?~NOT If *you*[^ms]~*will*~*make*~DO.WELL[^V] >~LIFT.
UP[^V] and~IF NOT *you*[^ms]~*will*~*make*~DO.WELL[^V]
to~OPENING <u>FAILURE</u> STRETCH.OUT[^V]~*ing*[^ms]
and~TO~you[^ms] FOLLOWING~<u>him</u> and~YOU[^ms]
you[^ms]~*will*~REGULATE[^V] in~<u>him</u> (MT)

"If you do well, will there not be a lifting up, but if
you do not do well, there will be an opening of fail-
ure stretching out, and to you is <u>his</u> following and
you will regulate in <u>him</u>." (RMT)

In this case, the KJV preserves the Hebrew grammar.

"If thou doest well, shalt thou not be accepted? and
if thou doest not well, sin lieth at the door. And unto
thee shall be his desire, and thou shalt rule over
him." (KJV)

It is not too difficult to realize, through these few examples, that translations are "open to interpretation" and it would be in the readers best interests to investigate passages in more detail. One such method is by comparing different translations allowing the reader to see how different translators interpret the text. These translations should come from both Jewish and Christian sources. If a Jewish translation agrees with a Christian one, the reader can be fairly certain that no religious bias has been interjected into the text. However, if these translations differ, it will be a clue to the reader that more investigation is required.

THE BIBLE AND OTHER SEMITIC LANGUAGES

The Bible was not written in a vacuum. It was written with a Semitic language that was very similar to other Semitic languages such as Ugarit and Eblaite, which share a great deal of their vocabulary with the Hebrew language, thus being useful in defining Hebrew words as well as shedding light on the original meanings of some passages. By studying these other languages, we can better understand Hebrew and the Bible.

UGARIT AND THE BIBLE

THE HISTORY OF UGARIT

Cuneiform[86] writing was used to write many different languages including Sumerian, Akkadian and Eblaite. It was a logogram style of writing where one cuneiform sign represented one word, similar

---

[86] The word "cuneiform" means "wedge shaped" because of the shape of the characters.

to modern-day Chinese. Many tablets containing cuneiform texts have been found throughout the Near East. It is believed by many researchers that cuneiform writing developed out of an older "pictographic" writing, similar to ancient Egyptian hieroglyphs. Over time, the pictures were replaced by the cuneiform.

In 1928, French archaeologists found an extensive collection of cuneiform tablets with a script unlike previously discovered cuneiform writing. This discovery was made at the "Ras Shamra" site near the Mediterranean coast in modern-day Syria, later identified to be the ancient Canaanite city of Ugarit.

The city of Ugarit was occupied from pre-historic times until about 1200 BC, when it was mysteriously deserted. The Ugarit cuneiform tablets were written in its later life (about 1300 to 1200 BC) and indicated that the people of the city worshipped the same Canaanite gods as their surrounding neighbors, including deities such as *El*, *Baal*, *Asherah*, and even YHWH. The culture, lifestyles and literary writings were very similar to that of the Israelites and also shed much light on the Biblical text.

Ugarit cuneiform script was a phonogram or alphabetic character, where each cuneiform sign represented one letter of an alphabet. The Ugarit alphabet was Semitic, just like Hebrew, and some have even called this alphabet "Hebrew cuneiform." In addition, the Ugarit language was also Semitic, nearly identical to Hebrew. This was an excellent discovery for Biblical Hebrew scholars, as the Ugarit language shed light on some Hebrew words with uncertain meanings.

The origins of Ugarit cuneiform script are unknown. Still, it can be assumed it was derived from the same pictographic script used to write Hebrew. The fact that the Sumerian cuneiform also evolved out of a pictographic script adds to the evidence that the Semitic/Hebrew script is older than previously thought.

THE UGARIT ALPHABET

Figure 70. An Ugarit Abecedary
(Image is in the Public Domain)

Figure 70 is an Ugarit inscription called an abecedary, an alphabetical list of the letters in the Ugarit alphabet (like Hebrew, Ugarit is read from right to left). The Ugarit alphabet has eight more letters than the Hebrew alphabet, two of which are vowels. It may be possible that these letters were originally in the Hebrew alphabet, as we speculated previously, but were dropped later (not an uncommon occurrence in the evolution of alphabets around the world).

When comparing the pictographic Hebrew script with the Ugarit cuneiform, such as we can see in Table 18 below, we find that several letters are virtually identical, supporting the idea that this cuneiform was derived from the older pictographic script.

Hebrew	Cuneiform	Note
ט	𒌋	
ם	 𒌍	Upside Down
ץ	𒂊	Turned sideways
ן	 �	Turned sideways
ש	𒂍	Turned sideways
 ך	 𒈦	
ת	𒅁	
ק	𒈠	Turned sideways
ן	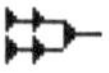 𒐕	Turned sideways

Table 18. Hebrew letters compared to Ugarit

UGARIT AND THE BIBLE

שויתי עֵזֶר על גבור הרימותי בחור מעם

The Hebrew passage above is from Psalm 89:20[19] and can be literally translated as follows:

> *"I placed help upon the warrior, I lifted up the chosen one from the people."* (RMT)

This verse is written as a parallel, where the first half is paralleled with the second half, as demonstrated below:

I placed = I lifted

help = chosen one

over the warrior = from the people

The problem here is that the word "help" is not a parallel with "chosen one." The Hebrew word for "help" is עזר (*ezer*), underlined in the Hebrew verse above. The first letter in this word is an "*ayin*," which can be silent or have a "*g*" sound, as we learned when we investigated the history of the *ghayin* and *ayin*.

In Ugarit, the word 𐎂𐎇𐎗 (*gezer*, spelled with a *gimel*) means "young man." It is possible that a scribe copying Psalm 89 inadvertently wrote an *ayin* instead of a *gimel*, both having a "*g*" sound. If we replace the word עזר (*ezer*) with the word גזר (*gezer*), we now have a more likely parallelism for this verse:

I placed = I lifted

young man = chosen one

over the mighty = from the people

For another example demonstrating the advantages of investigating the Ugarit language, let's look at Amos 1:1.

דברי עמוס אשר היה בַּנֹקְדִים

"The words of Amos who was a [?]..." (RMT)

The Hebrew word in question is the word נקד (*noqed*), underlined in the Hebrew passage above. This word is only used twice, here and in 2 Kings 3:4, where it is applied to Mesha, king of Moab. This word

179

is usually translated as "shepherd," but the common Hebrew word for a shepherd is רעה (*ro'eh*).

We have previously learned three methods that can be used to define Hebrew words: context, cognates and poetry. A fourth method, which we are doing here, is to turn to other Semitic languages where the meaning of some words can be found, such as is the case with this word.

The Ugarit word ⚋⚋— ⟨⟨ 𒑐 (*neqed*), a closely-related word to the Hebrew נקד (*noqed*), is used for one who is in the sheep business. This is not just a simple shepherd, but one who owns or manages a large operation. Thanks to the discovered Ugarit tablets, we can understand with more clarity the Biblical text. Amos was not a "shepherd," he was the employer of shepherds.

EBLAITE AND THE BIBLE

Previously, we discussed that studying extra-Biblical works was beneficial in helping to understand the Bible. The same is true with the study of other Semitic languages, as well. Take the following passage as an example:

> *"Lord of heaven and earth: the earth was not, you*
> *created it, the light of the day was not, you created*
> *it, the morning light you had not yet made exist."*

The above quotation may sound like a passage from the Bible, but it was found in three literary texts inscribed on clay tablets discovered in the Royal Library of the ancient city of Ebla.

A HISTORY OF THE DISCOVERY OF EBLA

Figure 71. Statue of Ibbit-Lim
(Image is in the Public Domain)

In 1964, the Italian Archeological Mission led by Paolo Matthiae began a dig at Tel Mardikh in Syria. In 1968, the team uncovered a statue of Ibbit-Lim, King of Ebla, which included an Akkadian (an eastern Semitic language) inscription that detailed Ibbit-Lim's bringing an offering to the goddess Ishtar. Until this time, the existence of the ancient city of Ebla was known only from the writings in other ancient near-eastern texts. However, its location was unknown. With the discovery of the statue, students suspected this might be the elusive Ebla. During future excavations, the Royal Library was discovered and it revealed and verified this was the city of Ebla. The library texts, which date to about 2500 BC, included nearly 2,000 complete tablets ranging in size from 1 inch to over a foot in length, 4,000 fragments and over 10,000 chips and small fragments, making this the most extensive library ever discovered from the 3ʳᵈ millennium BC.

The tablets were written with a cuneiform script like Ugarit in a Semitic language related to Hebrew, Ugarit, Canaanite and Phoenician. The language, as discovered by Giovanni Pettinato, the chief epigrapher for the Ebla excavation, came to be called Eblaite.

Figure 72. A tablet from the Eblaite archives
(Image is in the Public Domain)

The study of the tablets and artifacts uncovered by the excavation of Ebla revealed that the city was a major economic power, a cultural center of the land of Canaan and a large metropolis of 260,000 people. Therefore, most of the texts in the Royal Library are related to the economic and administrative details of Ebla. In addition, the texts include historical information, religious texts, academic texts, agricultural information, laws and treatises. Of most interest to the study of Semitic languages are the dictionaries (monolingual and bilingual) and encyclopedias, history's oldest dictionaries and encyclopedias to date.

Until the discovery of the Eblaite tablets, the only Semitic language known to exist in the 3rd millennium BC was Akkadian. With this discovery, another Semitic language known to be in use during that era has a very close relationship to the Hebrew language of the Bible.

EBLAITE GODS AND THE BIBLE

For the most part, the gods of Ebla were the same gods worshiped by the Canaanites and other Semitic peoples of the area. The principal god of Ebla was *Dagan,* who is referred to in the Eblaite texts as "Lord of Canaan," "Lord of the land" and "Lord of the gods." He is also mentioned several times in the Hebrew Bible (see Judges 16:23), where it is spelled דגון (*dagon, Strong's* #H1712). Other gods worshiped in Ebla that can also be found in the Hebrew Bible include *Baal* (בעל *ba'al)*, (see Numbers 22:41) and *Astarte* (עשתרת *ashtoret)*, (see Deuteronomy 1:4).

For an example of the usefulness of the Ebla texts to assist with Biblical interpretation, let's look at the following verse:

> *"And they have not cried unto me with their heart,*
> *but they howl upon their beds: they assemble them-*
> *selves for grain and new wine; they rebel against*
> *me."* (Hosea 7:14, ASV)

In the above passage, the Hebrew word for "grain" is דגן (*dagan, Strong's* #H1715). While this noun does mean "grain," it is also the name of the Canaanite god "Dagan," who was considered the "god of grain." The Hebrew word for "wine" is תירוש (*tirosh, Strong's* #H8492) and does mean "wine," but is also documented in the Eblaite tablets to be the name of the Canaanite goddess *"Tirosh,"* the "goddess of wine." With this new understanding of these words, we can read the end of the above verse as, *"they assemble themselves to Dagan and Tirosh; they rebel against me."*

Clarifying the meaning of these names in the Hebrew passage with the discovery of the Eblaite archives, we now know about the gods *Dagan* and *Tirosh.*

Following is yet another example:

> *"Before him went the pestilence, and burning coals went forth at his feet."* (Habakkuk 3:5, KJV)

The Hebrew word for "burning coals," רשף (*resheph, Strong's* #H7565), is a noun meaning "flame," but is also the name of a Canaanite god found in Ugarit as well as the Eblaite texts. The Hebrew word for "pestilence" is דבר (*daber, Strong's* #H1698). It was not until the discovery in the Eblaite texts that *daber/dabir* was identified to be one of the gods of Ebla. Knowing that these two words, in fact, are the names of Canaanite gods, the text can be translated as, *"Before him went Daber, and Resheph went forth at his feet."*

EL AND YAH IN THE EBLA TABLETS

Many names in the Hebrew Bible include the words *El* and *Yah* within them. Examples of this are the names מיכאל (*mika'el / Michael,*

Strong's #H4317) meaning "Who is like El," and מיכיה (*mika'yah /
Michaiah, Strong's* #H4320) meaning "Who is like Yah."

The use of the Semitic words *El* (also *il* in some Semitic languages) and *Yah* (also *ya* in some Semitic languages) in names is
not unique to Hebrew. The very same names, *mika'el* and *mika'ya*,
are found in the texts of Ebla. Other examples from the texts of
Ebla are the name *eb-du-il* (Servant of Il) and *eb-du-ya* (Servant
of Ya).

HEBREW NAMES IN THE EBLA TABLETS

Many other names found in the Hebrew Bible are also found in the
archives of Ebla:

Hebrew	Eblaite
Adam	*A-da-mu*
Avi'melekh (Abimelek)	*Abu-malik*
Ever (Eber)	*Ebrium*
K'na'an (Canaan)	*Ka-na-na*
Yish'ma'el (Ishmael)	*Ish-ma-il*
Yitro (Jethro)	*Wa-ti-ru*
Yonah (Jonah)	*Wa-na*

Table 19. Names found in Ebla tablets

SIMILARITIES BETWEEN HEBREW AND EBLAITE

The Eblaite language shares many similarities with the Hebrew
language including: a three-letter root system of words, the perfect
and imperfect tense of verbs, the use of the *yim* suffix for double

plurals, and a very limited use of adjectives. Eblaite uses many of the same letters as Hebrew for prefixes and suffixes to words. Like Hebrew, the letter ו (*vav*) is used as a prefix to words and means "and." The letter י (*yud*) is used as a prefix to verbs and means "he." The letter י (*yud*) is also used as a suffix to words and means "my." The letter כ (*kaph*) is used as a prefix to words and means "like." The letter כ (*kaph*) is also used as a suffix to words and means "you." Besides these similarities between the two languages, the Eblaite language shares many words with the Hebrew language:

Hebrew	Strong's	Eblaite	Translation
ab	1	*ab*	Father
ak'lah	402	*akalu*	Food
aniy	589	*an-na*	I
atah	859	*anta*	You
ayin	5869	*in*	Eye
ebed	5650	*eb'du*	Servant
hhanan	2603	*en-na*	Show favor
katab	3789	*katab*	To write
mal'kah	4436	*maliktum*	Queen
natan	5414	*natan*	To give
nephesh	5315	*nupushtum*	Soul
tehom	8415	*ti-emu*	Depth
tob	2898	*tub*	Good
iyr	5892	*ar*	City
yad	3027	*iad*	Hand
yada	3045	*yada*	To know
yalad	3205	*walad*	To give birth

Table 20. Hebrew and Eblaite words

DEFINING HEBREW WORDS
THROUGH THE EBLA TABLETS

> *"And he made him to ride in the second chariot*
> *which he had; and they cried before him, Bow the*
> *knee: and he set him over all the land of Egypt."*
> (Genesis 41:43, ASV)

The Hebrew word translated as "bow the knee" is אברך (*ab'rek*), a word of uncertain meaning and origin. However, if this is a Semitic word, it is clear that it is derived from and related in meaning to the root ברך (*barak*, *Strong's* #H1288), meaning "to bend the knee." In the Eblaite dictionaries found in the archives is the Eblaite word *a-ba-ra-gu-um*, meaning "superintendent." As the Eblaite letter "g" is often the equivalent of the Hebrew letter "k," we can read this word as *a-ba-ra-ku-um*, which is identical to the Hebrew word *ab-rek*. From this, we can conclude that the Hebrew word *ab-rek* means "superintendent," one to whom others "bend the knee."

> *"then shall they give every man a ransom for his*
> *soul unto the LORD ."* (Exodus 30:12, KJV)

> *"My beloved is unto me as a cluster of camphire*
> *in the vineyards of Engedi."* (Song of Solomon
> 1:14, KJV)

In the two passages above, the Hebrew word כפר (*kopher*, *Strong's* #H3724) is translated as "ransom" in the first verse and "camphire" (also known as "henna") in the second. The meaning of this word has been deduced from the Aramaic and Syriac languages, but can now be defined from Eblaite, where *kopher* is the Eblaite word for "copper." This fits the context of our two passages where a "ransom" is paid with "copper" and "camphire/henna" is a copper-colored dye.

> *"Three <u>pounds</u> of gold…"* (1 Kings 10:17, ASV)

The Hebrew word for "pound" is מנה (*maneh, Strong's* #H4488) and is thought to be the Aramaic word *minah*, a Babylonian unit of measurement from the first millennium BC. However, the Eblaite dictionaries reveal that this word is of Canaanite origin from at least the third millennium BC and is the origin of the Aramaic word *minah*.

Yet another word of particular interest is the Eblaite word *nabiu*, which the texts refer to as "holy men" who traveled from region to region announcing the divine message; in other words, they were "prophets." This word is derived from the Eblaite verb *naba*. The Hebrew word for a prophet is נביא (*nabi', Strong's* #H5030), a derivative from the Hebrew verb נבא (*naba, Strong's* #H5012). Because this verb is used in the Hebrew Bible only in the context of prophesying, its literal meaning was uncertain, but was thought to mean "to announce." Now, thanks to the dictionaries found in Ebla, it has been confirmed that the verb נבא (*naba*) did mean "to announce" in ancient times.

The common Hebrew word for a "child" is ילד (*yeled, Strong's* #H3206), but the cognate ולד (*walad, Strong's* #H2056) appears once in the Hebrew Bible (Genesis 11:30). It has been proposed that the word ולד (*walad*) was a defective spelling and should instead be read as ילד (*yeled*). However, the Eblaite text reveals that the Semitic word ולד (*walad*) was the original spelling. The word *walad*, found in Genesis 11:30, is not a defective spelling; rather, it preserves the more ancient spelling.

In the Hebrew language, the word בכור (*bekor, Strong's* #H1060) means "firstborn." In the Eblaite language, the word for "firstborn" is *bukalu*, almost identical to the Hebrew *bekor*, except that the Eblaite word is spelled with the letter "L" rather than with an "R."

EBLAITE AND THE BOOK OF JOB

The Eblaite language has shed much light on the Hebrew language of the Bible. For instance, the Hebrew word for water is מים (*mayim, Strong's* #H4325), but written as מי (*mey*) when in the possessive form (*water of...*). The phrase "water of snow" is found in Job 9:30. Instead of using the word מי (*mey*), the word מו (*maw*) is written. The Masoretes assumed that this was a defective spelling and in the margins of their Masoretic Hebrew text they wrote the word מי as a correction. What the Masoretes did not know, and that we only recently learned through the study of the Eblaite language, is that the ancient Semitic word for water was *mw*, and Job was preserving this more ancient spelling for "water."

The Eblaite language has also revealed the meaning of many other Biblical words that until now were uncertain or unknown. An example is the word מנלם (*min'lam, Strong's* #H4512), which is translated as "possessions" in the following passage:

> *"He shall not be rich, neither shall his substance continue, Neither shall their <u>possessions</u> be extended on the earth."* (Job 15:29, ASV)

Because the word *min'lam* appears this one time in the Hebrew Bible and was not found in any other Semitic language, the meaning of this word was completely unknown. The only clue to its meaning was that this word was being paralleled with "rich" and "substance" and therefore, we know this word had some meaning related to the idea of "wealth." In the Eblaite language, the word *ma-ni-lum* meant "cow," but could also mean "property," thereby providing us the true meaning of the word.

Most scholars date the book of Job to between the 7th and 4th centuries BC, but through research done by the author of this work into the style of language used in the book of Job, concludes that the book of Job was most likely composed in the 3rd millennium BC. These studies into the words *mw* and *min'lam* found in the book of Job are additional evidences to support this hypothesis.

BIBLICAL INTERPRETATION

The authors of the Bible wrote as they were inspired, but how we read and interpret their words influences whether we receive the same meaning intended by the writers.

How would you interpret the following passage from the book of Psalms?

> *"The LORD sitteth upon the flood; yea, the LORD sitteth King forever."* (Psalm 29:10, KJV)

Because our Western view of floods is equated with death and destruction, many people would read this and see YHWH sitting on a flood as it wipes out all the evil from the land.

If we use this interpretation of a flood in Psalm 29:10, we will never understand what the psalmist was trying to tell us. In Ancient Hebrew thought, a flood always brought to mind life and prosperity, not death and destruction. In a desert region, such as exists in the land of Israel, water is scarce, and floods coming down from the mountains bring much-needed water which also deposits nutrient-rich soil on the land to make possible the growing of crops.

If we revisit Psalm 29:10 using the *Mechanical Translation* and interpret it from a Hebraic perspective, we have the following understanding:

> *"YHWH dwells as the flood that covers all the land, spreading water and nutrients; and YHWH is the king that spreads life and prosperity through all the land as far as one can see."*

THEOLOGICAL FILTERS

A filter, such as the air filter in your car, blocks unwanted debris, yet allows clean air to continue through to the engine. A theological filter works in much the same way. It is a mental filter that blocks unwanted information, yet allows desirable information to continue through to the interpretative process. The final filtered interpretation of any given Biblical passage then confirms to the individual or group their already-formulated doctrine. Many scholars and Bible readers use these "theological filters" when reading and studying the Bible, but are not even aware that they are doing so. A more common term for this is 'bias.'

An example of a theological filter at work can be found in the various interpretations of Genesis 1:26, which states, "Let us make man." When one person reads this, he says automatically without any investigation, "The 'us' is the Trinity." Another person will say, "The 'us' are the angels." Both of these interpretations are created out of accepted doctrines, but there is no textual or cultural evidence to support either interpretation.

Even translators of the Bible employ filters for you. A good example of this is found in Exodus 33:9, which literally reads from the Hebrew:

> *"[A]nd it will come to pass, when Mosheh is about to come unto the tent, the pillar of the cloud will go down, and he will stand at the opening of the tent, and he will speak with Mosheh,"* (RMT)

According to this verse, the cloud spoke with Moses, but the translators did not like what the verse was implying, so they added the words "the LORD" to this verse to "fix" it, giving us the following translation:

> *And it came to pass, as Moses entered into the tabernacle, the cloudy pillar descended, and stood at the door of the tabernacle, and <u>the LORD</u> talked with Moses.* (KJV)

It is entirely possible that this is the original wording of the text, as it does make more sense, and somewhere along the way a scribe made a mistake. However, it is the opinion of this author that this type of "change" in the text at the least should be footnoted by the translator.

If you want to experience the Bible from a whole new perspective, be aware of your filters and remove them; do not come to the text with any preconceived ideas. Challenge your beliefs by reading the text for what it says and do not just assume you know what a particular passage is saying. Take the time to study the passage and ask questions.

WHY STUDY THE HEBREW LANGUAGE AND CULTURE?

When we read the Bible as 20th century Westerners, our culture and lifestyle influences our interpretation of the words and phrases of the Bible. "Rain" is "the coming down of water from the clouds in the sky," but our interpretation of the word "rain" will be influenced by our culture and our expectations. If the local weather station forecasts an unexpected "rain" shower for tomorrow, the bride and groom who have prepared for an outdoor wedding on that day find this is very bad news. On the other hand, it is very good news for the farmer in the middle of a drought season. To the Ancient Hebrew nomads, the word "rain" was usually equated with "life," since their very existence would not be possible without it.

In the same way, we must draw our definitions of the words in the Bible from their original cultural and linguistic context and not from our own modern perspectives.

When the Bible uses the words "keep" and "break," they are usually incorrectly interpreted as "obedience" and "disobedience."

The Hebrew word for "keep" is שמר (*shamar*, *Strong's* #H8104) and literally means "to guard, protect, and cherish," while the Hebrew word for "break" is פרר (*parar*, *Strong's* #H6565) and literally means "to trample underfoot." The Ancient Hebrew understanding of these words is not about obedience and disobedience of his commands, but of one's attitude toward them. Will we protect and cherish his teachings or throw them on the ground and trample on them as we would garbage?

A people's language is very closely related to their culture, and without an understanding of the Hebrew culture, we cannot fully understand their language. To cross this cultural bridge, we need to have a foundational understanding of the Ancient Hebrew culture, lifestyle and language.

HOW DO WE STUDY THE LANGUAGE AND CULTURE?

Archaeology uncovers ancient tools, household objects, texts and inscriptions. *Anthropology* studies ancient cultures and lifestyles. *Linguistics* study alphabets and languages. Each of these disciplines of science must be employed in order to learn as much as we can about the people of the Bible. In turn, we are then better able to interpret the Bible from their perspectives. We shall look next at certain words and their meanings based on the findings of these three disciplines.

WORD STUDIES

TORAH

The Hebrew word תורה (*torah*, Strong's #H8451) is usually translated into the English word "law." Because of this translation, there is a great misunderstanding of what "*torah*" truly is. *Torah* is not law, though there are laws in *torah*. When we use the word "law," we are assuming a meaning and concept that is not present in the Hebrew Scriptures.

Let us start by looking at the etymology of the Hebrew word *torah* to better understand its true definition. The word *torah* comes from the Hebrew root word ירה (*Y.R.H*, Strong's #H3384), a verb that means "to flow or throw something."

This can be a flowing of an arrow from an archer's bow or the flowing of a finger to point out a direction. A noun derivative of this root is the noun מורה (*moreh, Strong's* #H4175) and means "one who does the flowing."

This can be an archer who flows an arrow or a teacher who flows his finger to point out the way in which the student is to go in the walk of life. Another noun derivative of the root ירה (*Y.R.H*) is our word *torah*. *Torah* is "what is flowed by the *moreh*." This can be "the arrow from the archer" or "the teachings and instructions from the teacher."

A Hebraic definition of *torah* is "a set of instructions from a father to his children; violation of these instructions is met with the parent's discipline to foster obedience and train his children." Notice how the word *torah* is translated in the NIV translation in the following passages:

> *"Listen, my son, to your father's instruction and do not forsake your mother's* <u>teaching</u> *[torah]."* (Proverbs 1:8, NIV)

> *"My son, do not forget my* <u>teaching</u> *[torah], but keep my commands in your heart."* (Proverbs 3:1, NIV)

The purpose of a parent's *torah* is to teach and bring the children to maturity. The child is disciplined if *torah* is violated out of disrespect or defiance. However, if the child desires to follow the instructions out of loving obedience, but falls short of the expectations, the child is commended for the effort and counseled on how to perform the instructions better the next time.

Unlike *torah*, law is a set of rules from a government and is binding on a community. Violation of the rules requires punishment. With this type of law, there is no room for teaching. Either the law was broken, requiring the penalty of punishment, or it was not broken and no punishment ensues. As our heavenly Father, God gives his children his *torah* in the same manner parents give their *torah* to their children, not in the way a government enforces the law on its citizens:

> *"Happy is the warrior who you correct Yah, and from your <u>teachings</u> you teach."* (Psalms 94:12, RMT)

THE AARONIC BLESSING

Most people are familiar with the English translation of the Aaronic blessing:

> *"The LORD bless you and keep you: The LORD make his face to* shin*e upon you, and be gracious to you: The LORD lift up his countenance upon you, and give you peace."* (Numbers 6:24-26, RSV)

Notice that many of the words in this translation are abstract words, including: *bless, keep, gracious, countenance* and *peace*. Each of the Hebrew words behind the English in this passage is filled with images that are lost when translated into English. When we examine each of these words from their original cultural and linguistic perspectives, the message in this passage comes alive.

BLESS

The Hebrew verb ברך (*B.R.K, Strong's* #H1288) means "to kneel," as seen in Genesis 24:11. However, when written in the *piel* form, such as it is in the Aaronic blessing, it means "to show respect" (usually translated as "bless"). However, as "respect" is an abstract word, we need to uncover its original concrete meaning, which we can do by examining other words related to this verb. One such related word is the noun ברך (*berekh, Strong's* #H1290) meaning "knee." Another related Hebrew word is ברכה (*berakhah, Strong's* #H1293) meaning "a gift" or "present." Now we can see the concrete meaning behind the *piel* form of the verb *barak*. It is "to bring a gift to another while kneeling out of respect." The extended meaning of this word is "to do" or "give something of value to another." *Elohiym* "respects" his people by providing for their needs, and they, in turn, "respect" *Elohiym* by giving themselves to him as his servants.

KEEP

The Hebrews were a nomadic people raising livestock. It would not be uncommon for a shepherd to be out with his flock away from the camp overnight and would construct a corral of thorn bushes to surround and protect the flock; a hedge of protection around them. The Hebrew word for a thorn is שמיר (*shamiyr, Strong's* #H8068), derived from the verb שמר (*shamar, Strong's* #H8104), which literally means "to guard and protect" and is the word used in the Aaronic blessing.

FACE

The face reflects the many different moods, emotions, and thoughts of a person. The Hebrew word פנים (*paniym, Strong's* #H6440), means "face," but is always written in the plural form, reflecting this idea of multiple faces of each person such as a happy, sad or angry face. This word can also mean "presence" in the sense of the face representing the individual.

SHINE

The word אור (*owr*), as a noun (*Strong's* #H0216), means "light." When used as a verb (*Strong's* #H0215), as it is here, it means to "give light" or "shine" and is equated with bringing about order, as light illuminates or reveals what has been dark.

GRACIOUS

Most theologians define "grace" as "unmerited favor," but notice the abstractness of these words. The Hebrew verb translated as "gracious" in the Aaronic blessing is the verb חנן (*hhanan, Strong's* #H2603), often paralleled with other Hebrew words including: *healing, help, being lifted up, finding refuge, strength* and *rescue*. From a concrete Hebraic perspective, this verb means to "provide protection." Where does one run for protection? The camp, which in Hebrew is חנה (*hhanah, Strong's* #H2583), a word related to חנן (*hhanan*).

GRANT

The Hebrew verb שים (*siym, Strong's* #H7760) literally means to "set down in a fixed and arranged place."

PEACE

When we hear the word "peace," we usually associate this with the absence of war or strife. However, the Hebrew word שלום (*shalom, Strong's* #H7965) has a very different meaning. The root of this word is שלם (*Sh.L.M, Strong's* #H7999) and is usually used in the context of making restitution. When a person has caused another to become deficient in some way, such as a loss of livestock, the person who created the deficiency is responsible for restoring or replacing what has been taken, lost or stolen. The verb *Sh.L.M* literally means "to make whole or complete." The noun *shalom* has the more literal meaning of "being in a state of wholeness" or "being without deficiency."

A HEBRAIC INTERPRETATION OF THE AARONIC BLESSING

Having the Hebraic understanding of each of these Hebrew words, we now can better understand the true meaning of the Aaronic blessing as the Ancient Hebrews understood it:

> *YHWH will kneel before you[87] presenting gifts and will guard you with a hedge of protection.*

> *YHWH will illuminate his presence toward you, bringing order, and he will give you comfort and sustenance.*

> *YHWH will lift up his presence and look upon you and he will set in place all you need to be whole and complete.*

---

[87] Some may be concerned about the phrase "kneel before you" as they cannot perceive of God kneeling before us. We too often see God as the judge and ruler who sits high on the throne above us. However, from a Hebraic perspective, it is more of a familial type relationship with God, rather than a governmental type relationship. God is the father of us all, agreed? If a young son comes to his father with a request, will the father tower over him and look down on him? Or will he get down on his son's level by "kneeling" down and getting eye to eye with him and say, "What is it my son, what can I do for you?" It should be noted that this is not a literal kneeling down, but a figurative one; the common Hebrew way of expressing an abstract thought through concrete means.

When the Bible is interpreted from its original cultural concrete context, the text comes to life in ways never seen when viewed from a Western perspective.

WISDOM, KNOWLEDGE AND UNDERSTANDING

WISDOM

The parent root חם (*hham, Strong's* #H2525), meaning "heat," is the root of the adopted root חכם (*hhakham, Strong's* #H2449) which means "wisdom."

The word *hham* appears as ᎷᎸ in its original pictographic script. The letter Ꮋ is a picture of a wall which "separates" one side from another. And the letter ᎷᎷ is a picture of "water." Combined, these two letters literally mean "separate water." When "heat" (*hham*) is applied to water, we have evaporation or a "separating of water."

The following Hebrew words are all derived from the parent root חם (*hham*).

חמת	*hheymet*	skin-bag
חמה	*hheymah*	cheese
חמה	*hhammah*	sun
חמס	*hhamas*	to shake
חמד	*hhamad*	to crave/desire
חמץ	*hhamats*	to sour

Table 21. Hebrew words from the parent root חם

202

While we can plainly see the root חם (*hham*)[88] at the beginning of each of these words, what may not be as obvious is how the meanings of each of these words are so closely related:

Soured (חמץ) milk was placed in a skin-bag (חמת) that was set out in the heat (חם) of the sun (חמה) and shaken (חמס). The natural enzymes in the skin-bag caused the "water to separate" (חם) from the milk, forming the delicacy (חמד), cheese (חמה).

So, what does all of this have to do with wisdom? חכם (*hhakham*) is related to the idea of "separating," as this word means "one who is able to separate between what is good and bad." This Hebrew word can be translated as either "skill," when applied to a craftsman or "wise," when applied to a leader or counselor.

A verse found in the book of Isaiah has a fascinating connection between חמה (*hheymah*), meaning "cheese" and a חכם (*hhakham*) meaning "wisdom."

> *"And he will eat cheese (hheymah) and honey to know to reject the bad and choose the good."* (Isaiah 7:15, RMT)

According to this passage, there is a physical connection between cheese and wisdom, as it indicates that eating cheese will allow one to know the difference between bad and good, an aspect of wisdom.

---

[88] When the letter *mem* appears at the end of a word, the form ם is used. When this letter appears anywhere else in the word, the form מ is used.

KNOWLEDGE

The Hebrew word for "knowledge" is דעת (*da'at*), derived from the parent root דע (*da*). The first letter in this parent root is the letter ד, which is called *dalet* from the Hebrew word דלת (*delet*) meaning "door." This letter was originally written as ◻ in the ancient pictographic script and is a picture of the tent door. It can mean "back and forth," the idea of going "in and out" through the tent door. The name of the Hebrew letter ע is *ayin*, from the Hebrew word עין (*ayin*) meaning "eye." This letter was originally written as ◉ in the ancient pictographic script and is a picture of an eye. When *dalet* and *ayin* are combined, the Hebrew parent root ◉◻ (*dea*) is formed, meaning "the back-and-forth movement of the eye." When something is carefully examined, one moves the eyes back and forth to take in the whole of what is being studied. In the Ancient Hebrew mind, this careful examination is understood as "knowledge," not on a casual level, but on an intimate one:

> *"Do you <u>know</u> (Y.D.H) the balancings of the clouds,*
> *the wonderous works of complete <u>knowledge</u> (dea)?"*
> (Job 37:16, ESV)

The verb ידה (*Y.D.H*) is derived from the parent root דע (*da*) and carries this same meaning of "intimate knowledge." This verb is commonly used in reference to the marital relations of a husband and wife:

> *"And Adam <u>knew</u> Eve his wife; and she conceived,*
> *and bare Cain..."* (Genesis 4:1, KJV)

"And they will cling with you knowing your title, given that you will not leave the ones seeking you YHWH." (Psalm 9:11, RMT)

"Will not Elohiym examine this, given that he knows the hidden parts of the heart." (Psalm 44:22 [21], RMT)

"And by this we may be sure that we know him, if we keep his commandments." (1 John 2:3, RSV)

This last verse is translated from a Western perspective, but if we translate it through the mind of the Hebrews, we get a slightly different perspective:

"And by this we may be sure that we have an intimate relationship with him, if we preserve his directions." (RMT)

Frequently, when we use the word "know," such as in "I know him," what we really mean is I "know" of his existence. However, in Hebrew thought one can only "know" someone if theirs is a personal and intimate relationship. In Genesis 18:19 God says about Abraham, *"I know him"* meaning he has a very close relationship with Abraham.

Knowledge is "the intimate ability to perform a specific task or function." This is seen in Exodus chapter 31, where God gave men the ability to build the various furnishings of the Tabernacle.

Jeff A. Benner

UNDERSTANDING

The Hebrew word for "understanding" is תבון (*tavun*), and comes from the verbal root בין (*B.Y.N*), meaning to "understand." The deeper meaning of this word can be found in a related verbal root בנה (*B.N.H*), which means to "build." To build or construct something, one must have the ability to plan and understand the processes needed. This is the idea behind the verb בין (*biyn*) and its derivative noun תבון (*tavun*), namely, "to be able to discern the processes of construction."

IN SUMMARY

When we are reading a translation, it may seem natural to define the words of the text through the language of the translation. However, this erases the words true meaning and only through the context of the original language can they be accurately defined. This will also be evident in the following study.

GETTING TO THE HEART AND SOUL OF THE MATTER

> *"You shall love the LORD your God with all your heart and with all your soul and with all your might."* (Deuteronomy 6:5, ESV)

HEART

Let's start this study with the word "heart," which, in the verse above, is the Hebrew word לבב (*levav, Strong's* #H3824). A second

206

Hebrew word meaning "heart" is the word לב (*lev, Strong's* #H3820), which is the root of לבב (*levav*), and can be seen in the following passage:

> *"I will rejoice in doing them good, and I will plant them in this land in faithfulness, with all my <u>heart</u> and all my soul."* (Jeremiah 32:41, ESV)

While we in our modern Western world associate this word with "emotions," in the Ancient Hebrew world this word is associated with "thought," the "mind," which we can see in the following passage:

> *"The LORD saw that the wickedness of man was great in the earth, and that every intention of the thoughts of his <u>heart</u> was only evil continually."* (Genesis 6:5, ESV)

Just as our modern Western view of the "heart" is very different from that of the Ancient Hebrew, the same is true for the word "soul," a very misunderstood Hebrew concept.

SOUL

The word "soul" is defined, from a Western perspective as: *"The principle of life, feeling, thought, and action in humans, regarded as a distinct entity separate from the body, and commonly held to be separable in existence from the body; the spiritual part of humans as distinct from the physical part."*[89]

---

[89] (*Soul Definition & Meaning | Dictionary.Com*, n.d.)

This definition has no relationship to the Hebrew word נפש (*nephesh*, Strong's #H5315), which is usually translated as "soul." However, there is another definition for "soul" that does match with the meaning of the Hebrew and that is "a human being; person.[90]"

> *"All the descendants of Jacob were seventy persons; Joseph was already in Egypt."* (Exodus 1:5, ESV)

However, the word *nephesh* can also be used for a "creature:"

> *"So God created the great sea creatures and every living creature that moves, with which the waters swarm, according to their kinds, and every winged bird according to its kind. And God saw that it was good."* (Genesis 1:21, ESV)

Thus, from a Hebraic perspective, the *nephesh* is the "whole of the person or creature."

MIGHT

Next, let's take a look at the word "might." This is the Hebrew word מאד (*m'od*, Strong's #H3966). To understand this word, let's see how it is usually used:

> *"And God saw everything that he had made, and behold, it was very good. And there was evening and there was morning, the sixth day."* (Genesis 1:31, ESV)

---

[90] Ibid.

"Thus the man increased <u>greatly</u> and had large flocks, female servants and male servants, and camels and donkeys." (Genesis 30:43, ESV)

"A mixed multitude also went up with them, and very <u>much</u> livestock, both flocks and herds." (Exodus 12:38, ESV)

"Only take care, and keep your soul <u>diligently</u>, lest you forget the things that your eyes have seen, and lest they depart from your heart all the days of your life. Make them known to your children and your children's children." (Deuteronomy 4:9, ESV)

As you can see, this word is almost always used as an adverb, but, as we learned previously, Hebrew words can play double duty. The same words used as adverbs, adjectives, prepositions, conjunctions, and so on, can also be used as nouns.

The Hebrew word *m'od* can also be used as a noun meaning "muchness," for lack of a better translation, but "abundance" could also work. Muchness is all of a person's possessions, resources and abilities.

IN SUMMARY

What does it mean to *"love the LORD your God with all your <u>heart</u>, with all your <u>soul</u>, and with all your <u>might</u>?"* As mentioned, the Hebrew language loves to use parallelisms and often repeats one idea in two or more different ways. In the case of this verse, the words "heart," "soul" and "might" are being used as synonyms, but each is increasingly more inclusive. First, the heart, which is all your thoughts. Then even more with your soul, which is your whole body, and finally with even more: your muchness, meaning everything you own.

THE MEANING OF GRACE FROM A HEBREW PERSPECTIVE

The Hebrew word translated as "grace" is חן (*hhen, Strong's* #H2580), a two-letter parent root. To uncover the original meaning of this word, it is vital that we first examine each of the three-letter roots and the words that are derived from this parent root.

One of these three-letter roots is חנה (*Hh.N.H, Strong's* #H2583) and the following verse provides a good example of the meaning for this verb:

> *"And Isaac departed thence, and <u>pitched</u> his <u>tent</u> in the valley of Gerar, and dwelt there." (*Genesis 26:17, KJV)

This verb means "to pitch a tent" or "to camp." The noun that derives from this verb is מחנה (*mahhaneh, Strong's* #H4264):

> *"And it came between the <u>camp</u> of the Egyptians and the <u>camp</u> of Israel; and it was a cloud and dark-ness to them, but it gave light by night to these: so that the one came not near the other all the night."* (Exodus 14:20, KJV)

At this point, it is helpful to examine the pictographic Hebrew script that was used originally to write the word חן (*hhen*). The first letter is the letter *hhet*, written as ꟼ and is a picture of a wall with the meaning of "separation," as the wall separates the inside from the outside. The second letter is the letter *nun*, which was written as ⁔ and is a picture of a sprouting seed meaning "continue," as the seed continues a lineage to the next generation.

Figure 73. A "circle" of nomadic tents.
(Image is in the Public Domain)

When these two letters are combined, they mean "the wall that continues." The tents in the picture above are a "wall that continues" around the camp.

A second verbal root derived from the parent root חן (*hhen*) is חנן (*Hh.N.N, Strong's* #H2603). This verb is often translated as "to be gracious" or "have mercy;" however, these are abstract terms and do not help us understand the meaning of this verb from a concrete Hebraic perspective.

Let's examine some of the words with which this word is paralleled in order to discover its more concrete meaning. In the following

verses, the translation of the verb חנן (*Hh.N.N*) is underlined, and
the word that is paralleled with it is in bold:

> "*Have mercy upon me, O LORD; for I am weak: O
> LORD,* **heal** *me; for my bones are vexed.*" (Psalm
> 6:2, KJV)

> "*Hear, O LORD, and have mercy upon me: LORD,
> be thou my* **helper**." (Psalm 30:10, KJV)

> "*But thou, O LORD, be merciful unto me, and* **raise
> me up**, *that I may requite them.*" (Psalm 41:10, KJV)

> "*Be merciful unto me, O God, be merciful unto me:
> for my soul trusteth in thee: yea, in the shadow of thy
> wings will I make* **my refuge**, *until these calamities
> be overpast.*" (Psalm 57:1, KJV)

> "*O turn unto me, and have mercy upon me;* **give** *thy*
> **strength** *unto thy servant, and* **save** *the son of thine
> handmaid.*" (Psalm 86:16, KJV)

Using this process, we find that this Hebrew verb is paralleled
with such ideas as: healing, help, being lifted up, finding refuge,
strength and salvation (literally rescue). From a concrete Hebraic
perspective, חנן (*Hh.N.N*) means all of this, which we can sum up
as "providing protection." Where does one run for protection? The
camp. Now we see how חנה (*Hh.N.H*), the camp, and חנן (*Hh.N.N*),
protection, are related. How are these words then related to the
parent root חן (*hhen*)?

"A gift is as a <u>precious</u> stone in the eyes of him that hath it..." (Proverbs 17:8, KJV)

In this verse, the Hebrew word חן (*hhen*) is translated as "precious," something of beauty and value. This is precisely how the Hebrews would have seen the "camp of protection," a "graceful and precious place."

GOOD AND BAD

Very few sermons in our Western synagogues and churches would include the following passage:

"I [God] form the light and create darkness, <u>I make peace and I create evil</u>, I am the LORD who does all of these." (Isaiah 45:7, ESV)

The reason for this is that our Western mind sees these two forces, peace and evil, as opposites. However, the Eastern mind sees them as equals and necessary for perfect balance. To the Western mind, God is only good and unable to create evil. The Eastern mind sees God as a perfect balance of all things, including good (*tov* in Hebrew, *Strong's* #H2896) and bad/evil (*ra* in Hebrew, *Strong's* #H7451).

To understand the words "good" and "bad" from a more Hebraic perspective, we should understand them as meaning "functional" and "dysfunctional." God is both functional, as seen in the Creation Story of Genesis one, as well as dysfunctional, as conveyed by the destruction through the Flood.

To look at it another way, our Western mind classifies all things in two categories: either something is "good" or it is "bad." One is to be "sought," "cherished" and "protected;" the other is to be "rejected," "spurned" and "discarded." Let us take light and darkness as an example. We see light as good and darkness as bad. The idea of light brings to mind concepts like God, truth and love. Darkness, on the other hand, evokes thoughts of Satan, lies and hate.

To those of an Eastern mindset, including the Hebrews, both categories are equally necessary, as one cannot exist without the other. In the Bible God is seen as a God of light as well as of darkness:

> *"The people remained at a distance, while Moses approached the thick darkness where God was."*
> (Exodus 20:21, NIV)

What happens if you stare at the pure light of the sun? You become blind. What happens if you stand in a sealed room with no light? Again, you are blinded. Therefore, both light and darkness are bad; yet, both are good. To see, we must block out some of the light as well as some of the darkness.

From a Hebraic perspective, "good" and "bad" are not always a moral issue, but more often, they are seen like the two poles of a magnet. The two poles create balance. They are not morally good or bad, but are complimentary forces of nature.

Can "good" exist without the "bad?" Absolutely not. How can you judge something as being good if you cannot compare it to something bad? The same is true for all other concepts: "Cold" cannot exist without "heat," nor "short" without "tall," "far" without "near," or large" without "small." Our Western mind usually ignores these extremes and seeks to always find the "good" or the "bad," while the Eastern mind continually seeks both the "good" and the "bad" in order to find the balance between the two. Even Solomon recognized this when he said, *"Be not overly righteous..."* (Ecclesiastes 7:16, ESV)

This search for balance is found throughout the scriptures, yet is ignored by Westerners who do not understand the significance of balance.

COVENANTS FROM A HEBREW PERSPECTIVE

> *"They said, 'We see plainly that the Lord has been with you. So we said, let there be a sworn pact between us, between you and us, and let us <u>make a covenant</u> with you.'"* (Genesis 26:28, ESV)

The Hebrew word for "covenant" is ברית (*b'riyt, Strong's* #H1285). This noun is derived from the verb ברה (*B.R.H, Strong's* #H1262), which means "to select the best:"

> *"He stood and shouted to the ranks of Israel, 'Why have you come out to draw up for battle? Am I not a Philistine, and are you not servants of Saul? <u>Choose</u> a man for yourselves, and let him come down to me.'"* (1 Samuel 17:8, ESV)

In this passage, the Hebrew verb ברה (*B.R.H*) is used for the choosing of the best man to fight Goliath. This word can also mean "to eat," in the sense of selecting, as we see in the following verse:

> *"So Amnon lay down and pretended to be ill. And when the king came to see him, Amnon said to the king, 'Please let my sister Tamar come and make a couple of cakes in my sight, that I may <u>eat</u> from her hand.'"* (2 Samuel 13:6, ESV)

The Hebrew word ברית (*b'riyt*) is derived from the root verb ברה (*B.R.H*). Other words also derived from this verbal root are the nouns ברות (*barut, Strong's* #H1267) meaning "choice meat," and בריה (*bir'yah, Strong's* #H1274) meaning "fatten." Livestock meant for slaughter are fed special grains to make them fat, thereby making the meat of the fattened livestock the choicest.

So how is "fattened choice meat" related to the word for "covenant?" The phrase "make a covenant," such as we see in Genesis 26:28, appears eighty times in the Hebrew Bible and in every instance, it is the Hebrew phrase כרת ברית (*karat b'riyt*), which literally means "cut[91] a covenant."

A covenant was instituted by the two parties of the covenant who took a fattened animal, the best of the flock or herd, and "cut" it into two pieces. Then the two parties of the covenant walked between the pieces, symbolizing their dedication to the covenant. By this action, the two parties of the covenant were saying, "If I do not hold to the agreements of this covenant, you can do to me what we did to this animal." This methodology of "cutting" a covenant is clearly recorded in Jeremiah 34:18-20:

---

[91] This is another case of Bible translators ignoring the Hebrew and "fixing" the text for the reader by using the word "made" instead of "cut."

"And the men who transgressed my covenant and did not keep the terms of the covenant that they made before me, I will make them like the calf that they cut in two and passed between its parts — the officials of Judah, the officials of Jerusalem, the eunuchs, the priests, and all the people of the land who passed between the parts of the calf. And I will give them into the hand of their enemies and into the hand of those who seek their lives. Their dead bodies shall be food for the birds of the air and the beasts of the earth." (ESV)

With this understanding of a covenant, we can better understand the significance of what was happening in Genesis chapter 15:

"He said to him, 'Bring me a heifer three years old, a female goat three years old, a ram three years old, a turtledove, and a young pigeon.' And he brought him all these, cut them in half, and laid each half over against the other. But he did not cut the birds in half." (Genesis 15:9-10, ESV)

"When the sun had gone down and it was dark, behold, a smoking fire pot and a flaming torch passed between these pieces. On that day the LORD made (karat in Hebrew) *a covenant with Abram, saying, 'To your offspring I give this land, from the river of Egypt to the great river, the river Euphrates.'"* (Genesis 15:17-18, ESV)

Jeff A. Benner

Here YHWH is "cutting a covenant" with Abram. However, Abram does not pass between the pieces; only the pot and torch, representations of YHWH himself, pass between the pieces. Because Abram did not pass through the pieces, neither the actions of Abram or his descendants were a condition of this covenant. The only person responsible for fulfilling this covenant is YHWH and YHWH alone.

Besides this covenant, YHWH "cut" several other covenants with his people, such as the one with Noah and his descendants (Genesis 6:18, Genesis 9:9). He made another one with the Israelites at Mount Sinai:

> *"And Moses took the blood and threw it on the people and said, 'Behold the blood of the covenant that the Lord has made (cut) with you in accordance with all these words.'"* (Exodus 24:8, ESV)

Unlike the unconditional covenants that YHWH made with Noah and Abram, the following covenant would be upheld only on the condition that Israel obeyed the words of YHWH:

> *"But if you will not listen to me and will not do all these commandments, if you spurn my statutes, and if your soul abhors my rules, so that you will not do all my commandments, but break my covenant, then I will do this to you: I will visit you with panic, with wasting disease and fever that consume the eyes and make the heart ache. And you shall sow your seed in vain, for your enemies shall eat it. I will set my face against you, and you shall be struck down before your enemies. Those who hate you shall rule*

218

*over you, and you shall flee when none pursues you.
And if in spite of this you will not listen to me, then
I will discipline you again sevenfold for your sins,
and I will break the pride of your power, and I will
make your heavens like iron and your earth like
bronze. And your strength shall be spent in vain, for
your land shall not yield its increase, and the trees
of the land shall not yield their fruit."* (Leviticus
26:14-20, ESV)

And in Deuteronomy 31, YHWH foretold the day when Israel would
break this covenant by following after other gods:

*"For when I have brought them into the land flow-
ing with milk and honey, which I swore to give to
their fathers, and they have eaten and are full and
grown fat, they will turn to other gods and serve
them, and despise me and <u>break my covenant</u>."*
(Deuteronomy 31:20, ESV)

Interestingly, when Israel broke this covenant, YHWH "cut" Israel into
"two" nations, Israel to the north and Judah to the south. But YHWH
promised that he would make a new covenant with the children of
Israel, and he would unite these two nations into one nation again:

*"And I will make them one nation in the land, on the
mountains of Israel. And one king shall be king over
them all, and they shall be no longer two nations,
and no longer divided into two kingdoms."* (Ezekiel
37:22, ESV)

"Behold, the days are coming, declares the Lord, when I will make a new covenant with the house of Israel and the house of Judah, not like the covenant that I made with their fathers on the day when I took them by the hand to bring them out of the land of Egypt, my covenant that they broke, though I was their husband, declares the Lord. For this is the covenant that I will make with the house of Israel after those days, declares the Lord: I will put my law within them, and I will write it on their hearts. And I will be their God, and they shall be my people."
(Jeremiah 31:31-33, ESV)

Up to this point, the bulk of our cultural and linguistic investigations have concentrated on the Old Testament, a section of the Bible that scholars universally agree was originally written in Hebrew[92] by Hebrews. But now, we are going to venture into a section of the Bible where the culture and language are not as universally agreed upon.

---

[92] With some possible exceptions of a few passages written in Aramaic.

THE NEW TESTAMENT

THE INTERTESTAMENTAL PERIOD

Prior to the intertestamental period, the span of time between the Old and New Testaments, the kingdom of Israel had split into two kingdoms, as was mentioned previously. The southern kingdom consisted of the tribes of Judah and Benjamin and came to be known as the Kingdom of Judah. The other ten tribes of Israel (Asher, Dan, Ephraim, Gad, Issachar, Manasseh, Naphtali, Reuben, Simeon, and Zebulun) were called the Kingdom of Israel, the northern kingdom.

The Kingdom of Israel was conquered by the Neo-Assyrian Empire in 722 BC and many Hebrews were taken north as captives. They came to be known as the "lost ten tribes of Israel," but these "lost" tribes were not exactly "lost." More on that later. Those who remained in the geographic kingdom of Israel came to be known as the Samaritans, according to Samaritan tradition.

The Kingdom of Judah was conquered by the Babylonians in 586 BC and a few thousand inhabitants were taken captive to Babylon, while the rest stayed in the land.

THE BEGINNING OF JEWISH TRADITION

Those who were deported from the Kingdom of Judah to Babylon were known as *yehudiy* (belonging to Judah), the origin of the English word "Jew." During this intertestamental stay while in Babylon, the *synagogue*, *siddur* (the prayer book), *mikveh* (a ritual washing) and many other Jewish "traditions" were born as a type of replacement for those commands within the *Torah* that they could no longer observe while outside the land of Israel. It was also at this time that the Rabbis and Pharisees who developed these new traditions became the new teachers of the Jews, replacing the Levites as their roles and responsibilities became limited due to the loss of the Temple.

THE MACCABEES

Two books of the *Apocrypha*, First Maccabees and Second Maccabees, give insight about the life and times of the Jewish people during the intertestamental period.

While it is generally accepted by Christians that the Jews spoke Greek during the New Testament period, the books of the Maccabees paint a very different picture.

The Maccabees preserve the story of the Jewish revolt, about 150 years before the time of the New Testament. The Greeks, led by Antiochus Epiphanes, conquered the land of Israel and forced the

Jews to forsake their national heritage and *Torah* to begin adopting the Greek culture. Because of the Jews' hatred for all things Greek, including the culture and language, Judah Maccabee led a revolt against Antiochus Epiphanes, expelling the Greeks and slaughtering those Jews who had adopted the Greek language and culture. This revolt demonstrated the extent of the Jews' deep hatred for the Greek culture and language. Furthermore, it dispels the assumption that the Jews freely adopted the Greek language leading up to the New Testament period.

JOSEPHUS

Josephus, a 1st century Jewish historian, recorded Jewish life and sentiment during the time of the New Testament. In his work, *Antiquity of the Jews,* he writes the following:

> "*I have also taken a great deal of pains to obtain the learning of the Greeks, and understanding the elements of the Greek language, although I have so long accustomed myself to speak our own language that I cannot pronounce Greek with sufficient exactness: for our nation does not encourage those that learn the languages of many nations.*" (Josephus, Ant.20.11.2)

Josephus makes it very clear that the Jewish culture had a strong aversion to the Greek culture and language, and we learn that most Jews could not speak Greek, contradicting the notion that the Jews universally spoke Greek in the 1st century AD.

The approximate 450 years between the end of the Old Testament and the beginning of the New Testament was not void of any written texts. It is during this time that many of the Apocrypha and Pseudepigrapha were written. However, because these works are not part of most denomination's "canon" of scriptures, they are considered "extra-biblical," not biblical. Regardless of how these texts are regarded, they provide insights into the history and culture of the people of the New Testament period.

THE NEW TESTAMENT

THE HISTORY OF THE LANGUAGE

During the Old Testament period, there were many Semitic languages used in the Near East, the two most familiar to us today being Hebrew and Aramaic. While Aramaic survived as a living language into the present day, Hebrew, at some point in the past, ceased to be the language of the Hebrew people. The time of this departure has been intensely debated for many years.

The *Oxford Dictionary of the Christian Church*, in its first edition in 1958, stated that *"[Hebrew] ceased to be a spoken language around the 4th century BC."*[93]

This belief has been and still is the prevailing mainstream theory concerning when the Jews ceased using the Hebrew language. However, over the last half of the 20th century textual and archeological evidence revised this theory.

---

[93] (Cross & Livingstone, 1958)

One of the most compelling pieces of evidence for the continued use of Hebrew into the 2nd century AD is General Simon Bar Kokhba's[94] letters, which he wrote in Hebrew around 135 AD, during the second Jewish revolt against Rome, which we will look at again later.

Because of this and other evidence, the 1997 third edition of *Oxford Dictionary of the Christian Church* now states: *"[Hebrew] continued to be used as a spoken and written language in the New Testament period."*[95]

The Hebrew language continued to function as the Jewish people's native tongue until their removal from the land after the Bar Kokhba revolt ended in failure in 136 AD. Though the Jewish people continued to use the Hebrew language from then until now, it was used exclusively in synagogues and *yeshivas* for the teaching and learning of the *Torah* and the *Talmud*.

THE REVIVAL OF HEBREW

Figure 74. Eliezer Ben-Yehuda, c. 1912
(Image is in the Public Domain)

---

[94] This is his Aramaic name. In Hebrew, it is Shimon Ben Kosiba.
[95] (Cross & Livingstone, 1997)

In the late 19th century AD, Eliezer BenYehuda, a Hebrew lexicographer and newspaper editor, began a revival of the Hebrew language as a living language for the Jewish people in Israel. Then, when the state of Israel was established as an independent nation in 1948, Hebrew became the official language. Once again, it became the native language of the Hebrew people.

GREEK AND ARAMAIC MANUSCRIPTS OF THE NEW TESTAMENT

With regard to the New Testament, the question must be answered: in what language was the text originally recorded? There are three possible answers: Greek, Aramaic and Hebrew. Because most bible readers use a translation of the Bible, this may seem like an irrelevant question. But if we are going to dig deeply into the Biblical text to uncover the author's intended meanings, we must take our definitions of the words in that text from the language in which it was originally written.

Very few are aware that an Aramaic New Testament[96] exists, while most people are familiar with the Greek New Testament.

Figure 75. 4th century
Greek Manuscript

Figure 76. 5th century
Aramaic Manuscript

(Images is in the Public Domain)

---

[96] Called the *Peshitta*.

The oldest and most complete Greek manuscripts (see Figure 75) are the Codex *Sinaiticus* and the Codex *Vaticanus*. Both of these date to the 4th century AD. The oldest and most complete Aramaic manuscript (see Figure 76) is British Library, Add. 14470, which dates to the 5th century AD. Because both of these texts were scribed 300 to 400 years after the events of the New Testament, they are undoubtedly copies of previous manuscripts.

Hebrew, a sister language to Aramaic, was predominately used by Jews in the 1st century AD for religious and secular writings. This is attested to by evidence previously presented, and by the Dead Sea Scrolls, most of which were written in Hebrew. Additional evidences will be presented shortly. While no Hebrew manuscripts of the New Testament exist today, it is possible that they did exist at one time, which poses two other questions:

Was the New Testament originally written in Hebrew and then translated into Aramaic, then the Aramaic translated into Greek? Or, was the New Testament originally written in Hebrew and then translated into Aramaic and Greek?

If the New Testament was originally written in Greek, then the Greek New Testament and the translations from this Greek text will be the more reliable text. However, if the New Testament was originally written in Hebrew or Aramaic, then the Aramaic New Testament and the translations from the Aramaic will be the more reliable texts. Therefore, the answer to these questions is essential to Biblical interpretation.

The case for a Greek primacy of the New Testament versus an Aramaic primacy has been the subject of debate for a long time.

While the majority of Western Christian churches hold to a Greek primacy, the majority of Eastern Christian churches hold to an Aramaic primacy. Evidence for each argument is what we shall look at next.

TRANSLATIONS FROM THE GREEK TEXTS

A multitude of translations of the Greek New Testament exist in many different languages. Some of the more popular English translations from the Greek text include the *King James Version*, the *Revised Standard Version*, the *New International Version* and the *New American Standard Bible*. Two of the more popular Hebrew translations of the Greek New Testament are the *Salkinson-Ginsburg* and the *Delitzsch* translations.

TRANSLATIONS FROM THE ARAMAIC TEXTS

As for the Aramaic New Testament, translations are very few, but a good one is the *Aramaic English New Testament* (AENT) by Andrew Gabriel Roth. For a Hebrew translation of the Aramaic text, there is *The New Covenant Aramaic Peshitta Text with Hebrew Translation*.

We still haven't settled the question about which is the most reliable text: Greek or Aramaic? So, let us continue.

SEMITIC ORIGINS OF THE BOOK OF MATTHEW

While there are many textual pieces of evidence to show that the Book of Matthew was originally written in a Semitic language, probably Hebrew, Matthew 5:3 is a good example of this:

> *"Blessed are the <u>poor</u> in spirit: for theirs is the kingdom of heaven."* (ESV)

The Greek word for "poor" is πτωχός (*p'tochos, Strong's* #G4434), which means, "one who is destitute, afflicted, and lacking." So, what this verse literally says is, *"Blessed are the ones destitute/afflicted/ lacking in the spirit: for theirs is the kingdom of heaven."* This does not make any sense. However, if we translate the Greek word *ptochos* into Hebrew, we have the word אני (*aniy, Strong's* #H6041), which also means, "destitute, afflicted and lacking." More literally, the Hebrew word *aniy* means "bent down low," such as a poor person who is destitute. But this Hebrew word can also mean one who is humble, in the same sense of "bending down low."

Now, if we translate the Hebrew back into English, we have, *"Blessed are the humble in spirit: for theirs is the kingdom of heaven."* By understanding this passage from its Hebrew background, we can better interpret the New Testament and can reason that perhaps Matthew was written in Hebrew.

Another proof of an original Hebrew Matthew is the overwhelming number of ancient church fathers who stated that the book of Matthew was originally written in Hebrew.

Papias (150-170 AD) – *"Matthew composed the words in the Hebrew dialect, and each translated as he was able."* [A quote by Eusebius: *Eccl. Hist. 3:39*]

Ireneus (170 AD) – *"Matthew also issued a written Gospel among the Hebrews in their own dialect."* [*Against Heresies 3:1*]

Origen (210 AD) – *"The first [Gospel] is written according to Matthew, the same that was once a tax collector, but afterwards an apostle of Jesus Christ, who having published it for the Jewish believers, wrote it in Hebrew."* [A quote by Eusebius: *Eccl. Hist. 6:25*]

Eusebius (315 AD) – *"Matthew also, having first proclaimed the Gospel in Hebrew, when on the point of going also to the other nations, committed it to writing in his native tongue, and thus supplied the want of his presence to them by his writings."* [*Eccl. Hist. 3:24*]

Epiphanius (370 AD) – *"They [The Nazarenes] have the Gospel according to Matthew quite complete in Hebrew, for this Gospel is certainly still preserved among them as it was first written, in Hebrew letters."* [*Panarion 29:9:4*]

Jerome (382 AD) – *"Matthew, who is also Levi, and from a tax collector came to be an Apostle first of all evangelists composed a Gospel of Christ in Judea in the Hebrew language and letters, for the benefit of those of the circumcision who had believed; who translated it into Greek is not sufficiently ascertained. Furthermore, the Hebrew itself is preserved to this day in the library at Caesarea, which the martyr Pamphilus so diligently collected. I also was allowed by the Nazarenes who use this volume in the Syrian city of Borea to copy it. In which is to be remarked that, wherever the evangelist.... makes use of the testimonies of the Old Scripture, he does not follow the authority of the seventy translators, but that of the Hebrew."* [*Lives of Illustrious Men, Book 5*]

Isho'dad (850 AD) – *"His [Matthew's] book was in existence in Caesarea of Palestine, and everyone acknowledges that he wrote it with his hands in Hebrew."* [*Isho'dad Commentary on the Gospels*]

Jeff A. Benner

The evidence presented here does not prove that the New Testament was originally written in Hebrew, but it does suggest that at least the Book of Matthew was.

SEMITIC ORIGINS OF THE NEW TESTAMENT

Martin Luther, the Protestant Reformer from the 16th century, had this to say about Hebrew and the New Testament.

> *"The Hebrew language is the best language of all... If I were younger, I would want to learn this language, because no one can really understand the Scriptures without it. For although the New Testament is written in Greek, it is full of Hebraisms and Hebrew expressions. It has therefore been aptly said that the Hebrews drink from the spring, the Greeks from the stream that flows from it, and the Latins from a downstream pool."[97]*

AND

> *"In the beginning God created the heaven and the earth. <u>And</u> the earth was without form, and void; <u>and</u> darkness was upon the face of the deep. <u>And</u> the Spirit of God moved upon the face of the waters. <u>And</u> God said, Let there be light: <u>and</u> there was light. <u>And</u> God saw the light, that it was good: <u>and</u> God divided the light from the darkness. <u>And</u> God called the light Day, <u>and</u> the darkness he called*

---

[97] (Lapide, 1984)

234

Night. And the evening and the morning were the first day." (Genesis 1:1-5, KJV)

Hebrew, for the most part, begins a sentence with the word "and," as you can see in the passage above. Although the Greek language does not follow this convention, we do find the same sentence structure occurring in the Greek New Testament, as we can see in the passage below.

> *"And again he entered into Capernaum, after some days; and it was noised that he was in the house. And straightway many were gathered together, insomuch that there was no room to receive them, no, not so much as about the door: and he preached the word unto them. And they come unto him, bringing one sick of the palsy, which was borne of four. And when they could not come nigh unto him for the press, they uncovered the roof where he was: and when they had broken it up, they let down the bed wherein the sick of the palsy lay. When[98] Jesus saw their faith, he said unto the sick of the palsy, Son, thy sins be forgiven thee." (Mark 2:1-5, KJV)*

This and other Hebrew styles of writing found in non-Hebrew texts is called a Hebraism and the New Testament is filled with them.

IDIOMS

We all use idioms on a daily basis, but we really don't think about it. Some common idioms include; "break the ice," "beat around the

---

[98] The Greek uses the word *kai* (and), but is translated as "when" in this passage.

bush," "cut corners," "burn bridges" and "fish out of water." Every
language uses its own idioms, but you have to be familiar with the
idiom or you might take it literally. For example, if you were in Italy
and someone told you that they had "a dog in the church," you might
wonder why. You would never guess that this was an idiom meaning
they had "unwanted guests in the house."

Hebrew idioms in the Greek New Testament texts are another form
of Hebraism, and the Greek text is replete with them. As you read,
if you are not familiar with these idioms, you will interpret them
literally and miss the intended meaning.

> *"Think not that I am come to <u>destroy</u> the law, or the*
> *prophets: I am not come to destroy, but to <u>fulfil</u>."*
> (Matthew 5:17, KJV)

The words "destroy" and "fulfil" are 1st century AD rabbinic terms
that were used in reference to interpretations of the *Torah*. If a rabbi
was debating another rabbi on a particular passage of the *Torah,*
and if one of the rabbis believed that the other was incorrectly interpreting the passage, he would say, *"You have destroyed the Torah!"*
Conversely, if he believed that he had correctly interpreted it, he
would say, *"You have fulfilled the Torah!"* Unfortunately, because
Christians are unfamiliar with these idioms, they have interpreted
these passages to mean something never intended by the author.

> *"The light of the body is the eye: if therefore thine*
> *<u>eye be single</u>, thy whole body shall be full of light.*
> *But if thine <u>eye be evil</u>, thy whole body shall be full*
> *of darkness..."* (Matthew 6:22-23, KJV)

An "evil eye" is a Hebrew idiom meaning "stingy" or "greedy." This idiom is also found in the Old Testament where the KJV translates the idiom literally, while the more modern NIV translates the meaning of the idiom:

> *"Eat thou not the bread of him that hath an evil eye..."* (Proverbs 23:6, KJV)

> *"Do not eat the food of a begrudging host..."* (Proverbs 23:6, NIV)

A "good eye[99]" is a Hebrew idiom meaning "generous" and is also found in the Old Testament where again, the KJV translates the idiom literally, but the NIV uses the meaning of the idiom:

> *"He that hath a bountiful[100] eye shall be blessed..."* (Proverbs 22:9, KJV)

> *"The generous will themselves be blessed..."* (Proverbs 22:9, NIV)

As has been demonstrated, an idiom is a phrase that has no real relationship to the actual meaning of the idiom. Because of this, the author of this work is of the opinion that many phrases in the Bible we take literally are, in fact, idioms. For example, in Exodus 33:18, Moses asks God, *"Please show me your glory."* God tells him in

---

[99] When Yeshua used this idiom in Matthew 6:22, he slightly changed the idiom from "good eye" to "single eye." The late Dr. William Bean of the *Centre for the Study of Biblical Research* (CSBR) proposed that he was combining this idiom with the idiom "single of heart" found in the Testament of the Twelve Patriarchs (Testament of Reuben 4:1).

[100] The Hebrew word means "good."

verse 23, *"you shall see my back."* Is this phrase to be taken literally? Or is it an idiom? Because there is no way to resurrect a dead idiom, we will never know with certainty.

WORD PUNS

Word puns are another Hebraism found in the New Testament. These puns are a style of poetry that uses similar sounding words together. Here are two examples of word puns found in the Book of Genesis:

> *"[A]nd YHWH the Elohiym molded the <u>human</u> (<u>adam</u>) of dirt from the <u>ground</u> (<u>adamah</u>)..."* (Genesis 2:7, RMT)

In this verse, the Hebrew word puns are *adam* and *adamah*.

> *"[A]nd he said, what did you do, the voice of the <u>bloodshed</u> (<u>dam</u>) of your brother is crying out to me from the <u>ground</u> (<u>adamah</u>)."* (Genesis 4:10, RMT)

In this verse, the Hebrew word puns are *dam* and *adamah*.

These word puns can be found throughout the Hebrew text of the Old Testament, but they can also be found in the New Testament, but only if the Greek is translated back into Hebrew. One of these many word puns is found in Matthew 3:9:

> *"God is able of these <u>stones</u> (<u>ebeniym</u>) to raise up <u>children</u> (<u>beniym</u>) unto Abraham."* (KJV)

The Greek word for stones in this passage is λίθων (*lithon, Strong's* #G3037) and the word for children is τέκνα (*tekna, Strong's* #G5043).

However, when these two words are translated into Hebrew, we have אבנים (*ebeniym*, *Strong's* #H0068) for stones and בנים (*beniym*, *Strong's* #H1121) for sons.

HEBREW WORDS IN THE GREEK NEW TESTAMENT

Contained within the Greek text of the New Testament are many Hebrew words and phrases that have been transliterated from Hebrew into the Greek language. While arguably many of these words have been described as being Aramaic in origin, they may, in fact, be Hebrew words, as the Aramaic and Hebrew languages are very similar.

In Matthew 12:5 is the word σαββατον (*sabbaton*, *Strong's* #G4521), which is a Greek transliteration of the Hebrew word שבתון (*sabbaton*, *Strong's* #H7677), a Hebrew word meaning "sabbath" or "rest."

In Mark 7:11, we find the Greek word κορβαν (*korban*, *Strong's* #G2878), which is the Greek transliteration of the Hebrew word קרבן (*qarban*, Strong's #H7133) meaning an "offering."

Below is a table of all of the Hebrew words that are transliterated into Greek in the New Testament:

Verse	Greek			Hebrew			English
Mat 4:10	σατανας	satanas	4567	שטן	satan	7854	adversary
Mat 5:18	αμην	amen	281	אמן	amen	543	amen
Mat 5:22	ρακα	raka	4469	ריק	reyq	7386	empty
Mat 5:22	γεεννα	gehenna	1067	גיא הנם	gai hinom	1516/2011	valley
Mat 6:19	σης	ses	4597	סס	sas	5580	moth
Mat 12:1	Σαββατον	sabbaton	4521	שבתון	shabbaton	7677	sabbath, rest
Mat 23:7	ραββι	rabbi	4461	רבי	rabbi	7227	master
Mat 26:2	πασχα	pascha	3957	פסח	pesach	6453	Passover
Mark 7:11	κορβαν	korban	2878	קרבן	qarban	7133	offering
Luke 1:15	οινος	oinos	3631	יין	yayin	3196	wine
Luke 1:15	σικερα	sikera	4608	שכר	shekar	7941	strong drink
Luke 10:13	σακκας	sakkos	4526	שק	saq	8242	sackcloth
Luke 13:21	σατον	saton	4568	סאה	se'ah	5429	measure
Luke 16:7	κορος	koros	2884	כר	kor	3734	measure
Luke 16:19	Βυσσος	boossos	1040	בץ	buts	948	fine linen
John 6:31	μαννα	manna	3131	מן	man	4478	manna
John 12:13	ωσαννα	hosanna	5614	הושיעה נא	hoshi'ah na	3467/4994	save now
Rom 9:29	σαβαωθ	sabaoth	4519	צבאות	tsivot	6635	hosts
2 Cor 1:22	αρραβον	arrabon	728	ערבון	erabon	6162	pledge
2 Cor 11:33	σαργανη	sargane	4553	שרג	sarag	8276	wrapped
Rev 19:1	αλληλουια	halleluia	239	הללו יה	halelu yah	1984/3050	praise Yah

Table 22. Hebrew words in the New Testament

While the great number of Hebrew words and Hebraisms found in the New Testament do not prove that the New Testament was originally written in Hebrew, it does suggest that it has a Hebraic foundation. Now, let's look at some evidence that suggests Hebrew was indeed the original language of the New Testament.

THE LANGUAGE OF 1ST CENTURY ISRAEL

For many years, scholars taught that Greek and Aramaic were the languages of Israel during the Second Temple period (530 BC to 70 AD). However, over the past fifty years, more and more evidence has surfaced to indicate that the language of the Jews in Israel during this time was Hebrew.

Figure 77. Letter by Simon Bar Kockba written in Hebrew
(Image is in the Public Domain)

In 135 AD, Simon Bar Kockba led the final revolt against the Romans. Figure 77 is a fragment of a parchment that begins, *"From Shimon Ben Kosiba to Yeshua Ben Galgoula and to the men of the fort, peace..."* This is a letter from Kockba himself to one of his leaders in the revolt, and written in Hebrew, proof that Hebrew was used in Israel into the 2nd century AD.

Figure 78. 2nd Temple period coins with Hebrew inscriptions
(Image Credit: CNGCoins.Com)

All coins minted in Israel during the 2nd Temple period (586 BC to 70 AD) and into the 2nd century AD, include inscriptions written in Hebrew (Figure 78).

Figure 79. Dead Sea Scroll fragments written in *Paleo*-Hebrew
(Image is in the Public Domain)

The many scrolls and thousands of fragments uncovered in the Dead Sea Caves were written between 100 BC and 70 AD. Some of these scrolls and fragments are parts of Biblical books, but others are works concerning day-to-day business. Of all the scrolls and fragments discovered thus far in the Dead Sea Caves, approximately 90% are written in Hebrew, while only 5% are in Aramaic and 5% in Greek. While most of the Hebrew inscriptions use the Late Hebrew script, some use the older *Paleo*-Hebrew script, such as we see in the image above (Figure 79) of fragments from the book of Leviticus.

PAUL SPOKE HEBREW

When looking for evidence that Hebrew was the language of the Jews in the 1st century AD, the New Testament itself bears witness to the fact:

> "And when he had given him permission, Paul, standing on the steps, motioned with his hand to the people. And when there was a great hush, <u>he addressed them in the Hebrew language</u>, saying: 'Brothers and fathers, hear the defense that I now make before you.' And when <u>they heard that he was addressing them in the Hebrew language</u>, they became even more quiet. And he said: '<u>I am a Jew</u>, born in Tarsus in Cilicia, but brought up in this city, educated at the feet of Gamaliel according to the strict manner of the law of our fathers, being zealous for God as all of you are this day.'" (Act 21:40-22:3, ESV)

The first thing we notice in this passage is that Paul, a Jew of the 1st century AD, was speaking to the "people" in Hebrew and they understood him.

If the author of this work is correct in believing the New Testament was originally written in Hebrew, we can conclude that the original text would not have included the phrase, *"he addressed them in the Hebrew language,"* Instead, it was inserted into the Greek manuscript for clarification when it was being translated from the Hebrew.

THE NEW TESTAMENT CULTURE

THE NEW TESTAMENT AND JUDAISM

Is there any advantage to understanding 1st century Judaism when reading the New Testament?

When we read a passage in the Bible, such as the one we will examine below, we will make assumptions about the narrative based on our own personal perspectives and experiences. However, if we understand the narrative from the perspective and experiences of one living in 1st century Judaism, we will come away from the narrative with a different and more accurate understanding of the text.

> *"And he came to Nazareth, where he had been brought up: and he entered, as his custom was, into the synagogue on the sabbath day, and <u>stood up to read</u>. And there was delivered unto him the book of the prophet Isaiah. And he opened the book, and*

> *found the place where it was written, The Spirit of*
> *the Lord is upon me, Because he anointed me to*
> *preach good tidings to the poor: He hath sent me*
> *to proclaim release to the captives, And recover-*
> *ing of sight to the blind, To set at liberty them that*
> *are bruised, To proclaim the acceptable year of the*
> *Lord. And he closed the book, and gave it back to*
> *the attendant, <u>and sat down: and the eyes of all in</u>*
> *<u>the synagogue were fastened on him</u>. And he began*
> *to say unto them, To-day hath this scripture been*
> *fulfilled in your ears."* (Luke 4:16-21, ASV)

When we read this, most envision Yeshua (Jesus) getting up from his seat in the congregation and going to the podium from which he read from the Book of Isaiah. When he finished his reading, he retook his seat in the congregation and with everyone staring at him, he spoke to them. However, if we explain just one tradition that distinguishes Judaism from Christianity, we will have a clearer understanding of this passage: Christian preachers teach from a standing position, but Jewish rabbis teach from a sitting position. With this tidbit of information, we now know that in this instance Yeshua was the rabbi, not a congregant. Once he finished reading from the scroll, which is done from a standing position, he took his seat on the *bimah*[101] and began to teach. Now, read the passage above again, but this time from this newly learned perspective and you will see more clearly what was happening.

Even more clarification exists if we are open to understanding the Jewish culture of the New Testament period. Yeshua did not just "choose" this

---

[101] A Hebrew word meaning "high place" that is used to designate an elevated platform at the front of the synagogue from which the rabbi reads and teaches.

passage in Isaiah that spoke of Himself and His ministry. This passage was that Sabbath day's scheduled *haftarah*. From ancient times to the present, each Sabbath service includes two regularly scheduled readings. The first is from the *Torah* (Genesis through Deuteronomy), which is read section by section throughout the year. The second reading is the *haftarah*, specific and regularly scheduled passages from the Writings and the Prophets of the *Tanakh* (Old Testament).

On a side note, when discussing the Old Testament, we mentioned that the Great Isaiah Scroll found in the Dead Sea Caves may have been a copy made directly from Isaiah's original scroll and that this scroll may have been used in a *synagogue*. Therefore, it is possible that the Great Isaiah Scroll could be the very same scroll from which Yeshua read in the *synagogue*.

One other thing must be pointed out. Yeshua was a devout Jew who not only obeyed and followed the commands of God as outlined in the *Torah*, but also the traditions that were developed within Judaism, as long as those traditions did not violate the commands of God. In this passage, we see that it was Yeshua's "custom" to attend synagogue. As we previously discussed, the whole concept of the synagogue was created during Israel's exile in Babylon and therefore is a tradition of Judaism, not a command of God.

BAPTISM

In the Gospels, we find John the Baptist baptizing people in the Jordan River. But where did the concept of baptism originate? Did John develop it? Was this a command from God that we are not told about? Was baptism a new practice begun in the New Testament?

Because the Bible is silent on the origin of baptism, churches have created their own doctrines concerning it. Some churches baptize only adults while others baptize infants. Some sprinkle and some immerse. Some believe baptism is a sign of one's faith, but others believe it is necessary for salvation. Is it any wonder there are so many different Christian denominations?

Baptism is an example of a New Testament teaching that has its origins in Judaism, but because Christians do not study the Jewish background of the New Testament, they are ignorant of those origins.

The word "baptism" comes from the Greek noun βαπτισμα (*baptisma, Strong's* #G0908) derived from the Greek verb βαπτιζω (*baptizo, Strong's* #G0907). This verb literally means "to wash;" therefore, the noun *baptisma* must mean "washing."

In the Hebrew Bible, the verb for "washing" is רחץ (*R.Hh.Ts, Strong's* #H7364). While this word is used for the common act of washing, such as found in Genesis 18:4 when Abraham washed the feet of the three visitors, it is also used for the ritual washing of sacrificial animals, unclean people, clothing and various other articles as commanded by God in the *Torah*.

Is there a connection between the ritual washings in the Old Testament and the baptism of the New Testament? Yes, but there was an intermediate practice that bridges the two rituals.

When Israel was taken into Babylonian captivity and no longer had access to the temple and the priesthood, the Jews developed a system of laws and customs to preserve the commandments of God they could no longer observe.

As an example, the dining table in the home became a substitute altar and fathers would teach their children about the sacrifices with what was on the table. This ensured that the people would not forget the commandments of God until the time came when they were able to return to the land, the Temple and the priesthood.

Another such custom was the *mikvah*, the process by which persons immersed themselves in a pool of water for ritual purification. Because there was no more Temple priesthood, the Jews created the *miqvah*[102] as a substitute for the ritual washings that God had commanded in the *Torah*.

As John the Baptist was a Jew who would be intimately familiar with the *miqvah*, the logical conclusion is that the "baptism" practiced by John and the others is the *miqvah*.

> *"I thank God that I baptized none of you, save Crispus and Gaius; lest any should say that I had baptized in my own name. And I baptized also the house of Stephanas. Besides, I know not whether I baptized any other."* (1 Corinthians 1:14-16, ASV)

In 1st century Israel, a rabbi or teacher would immerse his disciples or students in the *miqvah* in his name. When a disciple is immersed in the name of the rabbi, it means that he is taking on the character of that rabbi. He will follow his teachings; he will do as he does and he will imitate him in every way.

---

[102] Commonly transliterated as "*mikvah*."

Jeff A. Benner

According to the verse above, Crispus, Gaius and the household of
Stephanas were baptized by Paul in his name, and were apparently
Paul's only disciples.

> "...Be baptized every one of you in the name of
> Jesus Christ..." (Acts 2:38, KJV)

In the same way that Crispus and Gaius were baptized in their teacher's name, the disciples of Yeshua are to be baptized in his name. They
are to take on the character of their teacher and become like him.

BAPTISM IN THE JORDAN RIVER

> "And it came to pass, when the people removed from
> their tents, to pass over the Jordan, the priests that
> bare the ark of the covenant before the people."
> (Joshua 3:14, KJV)

The Old Testament Israelites stood on the east bank of the Jordan
River and passed through the river onto the west side of the Jordan.
From a Hebraic perspective, the land west of the Jordan River is the
land of Israel and was symbolic of life, whereas the land east of the
Jordan River was outside of the land of Israel and was symbolic of
death. So, when they crossed the river from the east to the west, they
passed over from death to life.

> "We know that we have passed from death to life..."
> (1 John 3:14, KJV)

In Joshua 3:14 the Hebrew word translated as "pass over" can also
mean "cross over" and is the verb עבר (Ah.B.R, Strong's #H5674).

This verb is the root of the name "Eber," the ancestor of Abraham. One who is descended from Eber is called an עברי (*eevriy, Strong's* #H5680), which is the Hebrew name for a "Hebrew."

When the Israelites, who were descendants of Eber, "crossed over" the Jordan River, they became Hebrews, ones who have "crossed over" from death (outside of the land) to life (inside the land).

John the Baptist was doing his *mikvah* in the Jordan River because this is where his ancestors "crossed over" from death to life. In essence, the very first baptism occurred in the Jordan River and is recorded in Joshua 3:14.

Now let's unearth another aspect of Biblical interpretation where understanding the Jewish background of the text is vital.

1ST CENTURY JEWISH PERSPECTIVES OF PENTECOST

When people read Acts 2:1-6, void of its Jewish background, they arrive at a multitude of interpretations, which, in turn, support a multitude of religious denominations. Looking at this passage as it appears in the KJV, let us understand it from the perspective of a Jew in 1ˢᵗ century Israel.

> *"And when the day of Pentecost was fully come, they were all with one accord in one place."* (Acts 2:1, KJV)

Pentecost is the Greek name for *Shavu'ot*, the Feast of Weeks. In Jewish tradition, God gave Moses the two tablets of the *Torah* on

Mt. Sinai on *Shavu'ot*. Therefore, in the minds of the Jewish people, this feast is closely equated with the events at Mt. Sinai.

> *"And suddenly there came a sound from heaven as of a rushing mighty wind, and it filled all the house where they were sitting."* (Acts 2:2, KJV)

The "mighty wind" is reminiscent of the "loud trumpets" on Mt. Sinai (Ex 19:16) Most people assume that the "house" means the "upper room," but it was probably the Temple, the "house" of God, as all male Jews were required to go to the Temple on *Shavu'ot*. After all, how could the "multitude" in verse 6 witness these events if they were in an "upper room?"

> *"And there appeared unto them cloven tongues like as of fire, and it sat upon each of them."* (Acts 2:3, KJV)

Just as the top (which in Hebrew is *rosh* and means "head") of Mt. Sinai was on fire (Ex 19:18), we see fire on their "heads." But who are "they?" Is it just the twelve disciples? Nowhere in the account does it say, but Yeshua had many more disciples than just the closest twelve and it is very possible that there was a very large crowd of believers present.

> *"And they were all filled with the Holy Ghost, and began to speak with other tongues, as the Spirit gave them utterance."* (Acts 2:4, KJV)

It is the opinion of the author of this work that when God brought the Israelites to Mt. Sinai, it was his intention to fill them with the

Holy Spirit right then and there, but the people were afraid. They backed off and told Moses that he should speak to God for them (Ex 20:18-19). So, God went with an alternate plan. If they could not understand what it meant for God to indwell them individually, then he would dwell with them in the camp, which he did when he had them set up the tabernacle in the center of the camp. But now, in Acts 2, God brings back his original plan to indwell them individually.

> *"And there were dwelling at Jerusalem Jews, devout men, out of every nation under heaven."* (Acts 2:5, KJV)

These Jews had come to Jerusalem for the feast as commanded in the *Torah* (Ex 23:14–17).

> *"Now when this was noised abroad, the multitude came together, and were confounded, because that every man heard them speak in his own language."* (Acts 2:6, KJV)

When Israel came out of Egypt, they came out with a "multitude" of people from other nations (Exodus 12:38). In Jewish tradition, there were seventy different nations present at Mt. Sinai. Another tradition is that when God spoke to the people gathered at Mt. Sinai, they all heard him in their native languages, which is exactly what we see happening again in Acts 2.

Now, let's jump to a verse later in the chapter for one more connection back to Mt. Sinai:

> *"Then they that gladly received his word were bap-*
> *tized: and the same day there were added unto them*
> *about three thousand souls."* (Acts 2:41, KJV)

In Exodus 32, we read that Moses took a long time on Mt. Sinai and the Israelites had lost hope in him, so they made a golden calf. When Moses came down from the mountain, he was angry and destroyed the idol. Then he instructed the Levites to kill all of those who had sinned against God and, according to verse 28, *"about three thousand"* were killed.

On *Shavu'ot* at Mt. Sinai in Exodus 32, about 3,000 were killed, but on *Shavu'ot* at the Temple in Acts 2, about 3,000 were saved.

In conclusion, when studying the New Testament, it is imperative that the Jewish culture and traditions of the people of the New Testament period be taken into consideration before attempting to interpret the text; otherwise, misinterpretations will abound.

THE WORD

> *"In the beginning was the Word, and the Word was*
> *with God, and the Word was God."* (John 1:1, KJV)

The key to understanding Yeshua's teachings is to know that whenever he used the word "I," he was not referring to himself, but to *torah*, the Word of God. In the Old Testament book of Isaiah, *torah* (law) and *devar* (word) are often paralleled with each other.

> *"Hear the **word** of the LORD, ye rulers of Sodom;*
> *give ear unto the **law** of our God, ye people of*
> *Gomorrah."* (Isaiah 1:10, KJV)

*"...for out of Zion shall go forth the **law**, and the **word** of the LORD from Jerusalem."* (Isaiah 2:3, KJV)

*"...because they have cast away the **law** of the LORD of hosts, and despised the **word** of the Holy One of Israel."* (Isaiah 5:24, KJV)

Reading on in the New Testament book of John, a few verses later we read:

"The word became flesh and dwelt among us..." (John 1:14, KJV)

According to this passage, Yeshua took on the persona of God's teachings. Yeshua emptied himself of himself and instead took on the attributes of God's teachings. Therefore, whenever Yeshua speaks, it is not Yeshua speaking, but the teachings of God.

"Jesus said to him, 'I am the way, and the truth, and the life. No one comes to the Father except through me.'" (John 14:6, ESV)

When we look at this passage with the understanding that Yeshua is the teachings of God in the flesh, we find that the Old Testament confirms this. In the following verse we are told that the ordinances and laws are "the way:"

"And thou shalt teach them ordinances and laws, and shalt shew them the way wherein they must walk, and the work that they must do." (Exodus 18:20, KJV)

In the next verse we are told that the law is "the truth:"

> *"Thy righteousness is an everlasting righteousness, and thy <u>law</u> is <u>the truth</u>."* (Psalm 119:142, KJV)

And in this verse, we see that the law is the "life:"

> *"For [the words of this <u>law</u> are] not a vain thing for you; because it is your <u>life</u>: and through this thing ye shall prolong your days in the land, whither ye go over Jordan to possess it."* (Deuteronomy 32:47, KJV)

The most important figure in the Bible is Yeshua, who was a Jew, lived as a Jew and taught as a Jew. If we ignore his Jewishness, we rob him of who he is.

THE TEACHINGS OF YESHUA

Before diving into the teachings of Yeshua, it would be helpful to understand more about Yeshua's teaching style.

> *"And they were astonished at his teaching, for he taught them as one who had authority, and not as the scribes."* (Mark 1:22, ESV)

While portions of the New Testament Gospels are written in chronological order, this is not true for all the Gospels. Because the New Testament was written by Jewish authors during the 1ˢᵗ century AD, their method for recording the life and events of Yeshua followed a more Hebraic format.

"Step logic" is a form of Greek writing where events are recorded in chronological order. Since the authors of the Gospels were Hebrews, they followed a Hebraic form of writing called "block logic," which is more related to circular thought rather than linear thought.

With block logic, the life and events of Yeshua are recorded in "blocks" of related topics. Using the Book of Matthew as an example, we find most of Yeshua's healings are recorded in Chapters 8, 9 and 12, while most of his encounters with the Pharisees and officials are found in Chapters 15, 16 and 22. Many of Yeshua's teachings to his students are recorded in Chapters 18 and 24. And finally, chapters 13 and 25 contain most of his parables.

Yeshua was known as an itinerant rabbi, meaning that he was not the rabbi of a community, but instead traveled the land with his students while teaching in the countryside and towns. We can assume that Yeshua healed, met with the Pharisees, and taught his students throughout his ministry. However, when the authors of the Gospels recorded their recollections of the events, they did not record them in linear, chronological order, but in blocks according to their relativity.

Dr. Robert L. Lindsey, the founder of the *Synoptic Gospel Researchers*, discovered Yeshua's method of teaching his students. In his book *Jesus, Rabbi and Lord: The Hebrew Story of Jesus Behind Our Gospels*, he proposes that as Yeshua traveled across the countryside, an event would occur, he then gave a teaching to his students that related to the event and after the lesson he would give them two parables to demonstrate his teaching. While the event, teaching and the two parables occurred simultaneously, they were recorded separately in various places in the Gospels and sometimes in different Gospel accounts.

WORRY

EVENT

> *"Now as they went on their way, Jesus entered a village. And a woman named Martha welcomed him into her house. And she had a sister called Mary, who sat at the Lord's feet and listened to his teaching. But Martha was distracted with much serving. And she went up to him and said, 'Lord, do you not care that my sister has left me to serve alone? Tell her then to help me.' But the Lord answered her, 'Martha, Martha, you are anxious and troubled about many things, but one thing is necessary. Mary has chosen the good portion, which will not be taken away from her.'"* (Luke 10:38-42, ESV)

TEACHING

> *"Therefore I tell you, do not be anxious about your life, what you will eat or what you will drink, nor about your body, what you will put on. Is not life more than food, and the body more than clothing? Look at the birds of the air: they neither sow nor reap nor gather into barns, and yet your heavenly Father feeds them. Are you not of more value than they? And which of you by being anxious can add a single hour to his span of life? And why are you anxious about clothing? Consider the lilies of the field, how they grow: they neither toil nor spin, yet*

I tell you, even Solomon in all his glory was not arrayed like one of these. But if God so clothes the grass of the field, which today is alive and tomorrow is thrown into the oven, will he not much more clothe you, O you of little faith? Therefore do not be anxious, saying, 'What shall we eat?' or 'What shall we drink?' or 'What shall we wear?' For the Gentiles seek after all these things, and your heavenly Father knows that you need them all. But seek first the kingdom of God and his righteousness, and all these things will be added to you. Therefore do not be anxious about tomorrow, for tomorrow will be anxious for itself. Sufficient for the day is its own trouble." (Matthew 6:25-34, ESV)

PARABLE #1

"And he told them a parable, saying, 'The land of a rich man produced plentifully, and he thought to himself, "What shall I do, for I have nowhere to store my crops?" And he said, "I will do this: I will tear down my barns and build larger ones, and there I will store all my grain and my goods. And I will say to my soul, "Soul, you have ample goods laid up for many years; relax, eat, drink, be merry" But God said to him, 'Fool! This night your soul is required of you, and the things you have prepared, whose will they be?' So is the one who lays up treasure for himself and is not rich toward God." (Luke 12:16-21, ESV)

PARABLE #2

"There was a rich man who was clothed in purple and fine linen and who feasted sumptuously every day. And at his gate was laid a poor man named Lazarus, covered with sores, who desired to be fed with what fell from the rich man's table. Moreover, even the dogs came and licked his sores. The poor man died and was carried by the angels to Abraham's side. The rich man also died and was buried, and in Hades, being in torment, he lifted up his eyes and saw Abraham far off and Lazarus at his side. And he called out, 'Father Abraham, have mercy on me, and send Lazarus to dip the end of his finger in water and cool my tongue, for I am in anguish in this flame.' But Abraham said, 'Child, remember that you in your lifetime received your good things, and Lazarus in like manner bad things; but now he is comforted here, and you are in anguish. And besides all this, between us and you a great chasm has been fixed, in order that those who would pass from here to you may not be able, and none may cross from there to us.' And he said, 'Then I beg you, father, to send him to my father's house—for I have five brothers—so that he may warn them, lest they also come into this place of torment.' But Abraham said, 'They have Moses and the Prophets; let them hear them.' And he said, 'No, father Abraham, but if someone goes to them from the dead, they will repent.' He said to him, 'If they

> *do not hear Moses and the Prophets, neither will*
> *they be convinced if someone should rise from the*
> *dead.'"* (Luke 16:19-31, ESV)

In this example, the teachings and parables of Yeshua are brought together with the event that inspired them, providing us with a glimpse into Yeshua's unique style of teaching. Let's look at a second set of incidents to further confirm Lindsey's observation.

THE FIG TREE

EVENT

> *"And seeing a fig tree by the wayside, he went to it*
> *and found nothing on it but only leaves. And he said*
> *to it, 'May no fruit ever come from you again!' And*
> *the fig tree withered at once. When the disciples*
> *saw it, they marveled, saying, 'How did the fig tree*
> *wither at once'"* (Matthew 21:19-20, ESV)

TEACHING #1

> *"And Jesus answered them, 'Truly, I say to you, if*
> *you have faith and do not doubt, you will not only*
> *do what has been done to the fig tree, but even if*
> *you say to this mountain, "Be taken up and thrown*
> *into the sea," it will happen. And whatever you*
> *ask in prayer, you will receive, if you have faith'."*
> (Matthew 21:21-22, version)

TEACHING #2

"From the fig tree learn its lesson: as soon as its branch becomes tender and puts out its leaves, you know that summer is near. So also, when you see all these things, you know that he is near, at the very gates." (Matthew 24:32-33, ESV)

PARABLE #1

"And he told them a parable: 'Look at the fig tree, and all the trees. As soon as they come out in leaf, you see for yourselves and know that the summer is already near. So also, when you see these things taking place, you know that the kingdom of God is near. Truly, I say to you, this generation will not pass away until all has taken place. Heaven and earth will pass away, but my words will not pass away. But watch yourselves lest your hearts be weighed down with dissipation and drunkenness and cares of this life, and that day come upon you suddenly like a trap. For it will come upon all who dwell on the face of the whole earth. But stay awake at all times, praying that you may have strength to escape all these things that are going to take place, and to stand before the Son of Man.'" (Luke 21:29-36, ESV)

PARABLE #2

> *"And he told this parable: 'A man had a fig tree planted in his vineyard, and he came seeking fruit on it and found none. And he said to the vinedresser, "Look, for three years now I have come seeking fruit on this fig tree, and I find none. Cut it down. Why should it use up the ground?" And he answered him, "Sir, let it alone this year also, until I dig around it and put on manure. Then if it should bear fruit next year, well and good; but if not, you can cut it down."'"* (Luke 13:6-9, ESV)

With a better understanding of the "teacher," let's now examine some of his teachings.

YESHUA, THE SON OF MAN

The phrase "son of man" appears multiple times in the Old and New Testaments.

In the Old Testament, the Hebrew phrase בן אדם (*ben adam*) translates as "son of man" and is used for any named or unnamed person.

In the Greek New Testament, the phrase "son of man" is υἱὸς τοῦ ἀνθρώπου (*huios tou anthrōpou*), but is always used in reference to Yeshua, either by himself, or by others.

If Yeshua spoke Hebrew and he used the Hebrew phrase *ben adam*, then he was simply claiming to be "a person." If, on the other hand, Yeshua spoke Greek, which is doubtful, and used the phrase *huios tou anthrōpou*, he would again, simply be claiming to be "a person."

However, there is one place in the Old Testament where a different phrase is used for "son of man:"

> "*I saw in the night visions, and, behold, one like the <u>Son of man</u> came with the clouds of heaven, and came to the Ancient of Days, and they brought him near before him.*" (Daniel 7:13, KJV)

This part of the Book of Daniel is written in Aramaic and the Aramaic for "son of man" is בר אנוש (*bar enosh*). This is the only occurrence of this Aramaic phrase in the Bible.

If Yeshua spoke Aramaic and used the phrase *bar enosh*, he would still be referring to himself as "a person." But there is an alternate interpretation. If Yeshua spoke Hebrew, which is the most likely scenario based on the evidences, yet used the Aramaic phrase *bar enosh* instead of the Hebrew phrase *ben adam* in reference to himself, his listeners would catch this change and would understand that he was calling himself the *bar enosh* from Daniel 7:13, the one who is "*coming with the clouds of heaven* (NIV)."

WHAT IS THE GREAT COMMANDMENT?

> "*Master, which is the great commandment in the law?*" (Matthew 22:36, KJV)

A Pharisee posed this question to Yeshua, but before we can understand Yeshua's answer, we must first understand the question correctly.

Whether or not Yeshua used or even knew the Greek language, the question is: What language did Yeshua and his Jewish brothers use when teaching *torah*? We know that the Hebrew language was used during the time of Yeshua and even to this day in religious settings, and we know that the *Torah* was originally written in Hebrew. It is then safe to assume that when Yeshua was teaching *torah*, he used the Hebrew language.

Here we will examine the Greek words of Matthew 22:36 and translate them into Hebrew. We can then translate the Hebrew into English to understand the text from a Hebraic perspective.

There are two methods for finding Hebrew equivalents in Greek. The first is by using simple word similarities, where both Greek and Hebrew have words that mean the same thing. The second is through a study of the *Septuagint*, the ancient Greek translation of the Tanakh, the Hebrew Bible. When we find a Greek word consistently used to translate a Hebrew word in the Hebrew Bible, we know that that Greek word is its equivalent. Below is the Greek text of Matthew 22:36 and the King James translation. We will then look at each word in the KJV, examining the meaning of the Greek word behind it and the Hebrew equivalent for that Greek word.

Διδασκαλε ποια εντολη μεγαλη εν τω νομω

Master, which is the great commandment in the law?

Master (Strong's #G1320)

The Greek word *didaskolos* means "teacher" and is the equivalent to the Hebrew word *moreh*.

Which *(Strong's #G4169)*

The Greek word here is *poios* and is usually translated as "what." This word is equivalent to the Hebrew word *mah*.

Is the

These two words are added in the English translation and are not present in the Greek. While the Greek language frequently uses words meaning "is" and "the," because they are not found here, it suggests that this sentence was written with Semitic syntax, which rarely uses words for "is" and "the."

Commandment *(Strong's #G1785)*

The Greek *entole* is equivalent to the Hebrew word *mitsvah*.

Great *(Strong's #G3173)*

The Greek word here is *megas* and is equivalent to the Hebrew word *gadolah*.

In the *(no Strong's entry)*

The Greek phrase *en to* is equivalent to the Hebrew prefix *ba* meaning "in the."

Law *(Strong's #G3551)*

The Greek word *nomos* is equivalent to *torah*.

Now that we know the Hebrew equivalents to the Greek text, we can translate it into Hebrew as follows:

מורה מה מצוה גדולה בתורה

moreh mah mitsvah gadolah batorah

Now, let's translate the Hebrew into English.

Moreh *(Strong's #H4175)*

This word means "teacher."

Mah *(Strong's #H4100)*

This word means "what."

Mitsvah *(Strong's #H4687)*

While this word is often translated as "command" or "command-ment," it also means "precept,"— "A rule or principal prescribing a particular course of action or conduct."

Gadolah *(Strong's #H1420)*

This word means "great."

Ba *(no Strong's entry)*

This prefix means "in the" or "within the."

Torah *(Strong's #H8451)*

While this word means "teachings," the context implies that this word is being used as the title of the first five books of the Bible. It is interesting to note that *moreh*, the word with which this sentence begins, and *torah*, the word with which this sentence ends, are both derived from the root "*yarah*" meaning "to point [out the way]." They are also word puns, another Hebraism found in this passage.

The Greek and English translations of this verse imply that the speaker is asking for one command found in the *Torah* that is above all the others; but, when we translate the Greek back to Hebrew and then into English, we find a slightly different question:

> "*Teacher, what is the great precept within the Torah?*"

The question posed to Yeshua is, "*What is the summary of all of the Torah*"? And Yeshua responded with:

> "*You shall love YHWH your God with all your heart and with all your being and with all your belongings, this is the beginning and great precept, and another like it is You shall love your companions as yourself. Within these two precepts hang all of the Tanakh.*" (Matthew 22:37-40, RMT)

YESHUA AND THE PHARISEES

> "*Then Jesus spoke to the multitudes and to His disciples, saying, 'The scribes and the Pharisees have seated themselves in the chair of Moses; therefore, all that they tell you, do and observe, but do not do according to their deeds; for they say things, and do not do them.'*" (Matthew 23:1-4, NASB)

The first thing we will be looking at in this verse is another Hebraism. The English language implies that the phrase, *"to the multitudes and to His disciples,"* says that there were present a large crowd *plus* his disciples. However, this is another parallelism. This is not speaking about two different groups of people, but one group. Identifying it with two different phrases, a "multitude" and "disciples," this means that the multitude were the disciples of Yeshua.

Now to the real issue with this passage. It appears to say that Yeshua is commanding his disciples to do and observe all that the Pharisees command to do and observe.

This passage creates a serious problem. The *Torah* commands that no one should add to or take away from the commands of God, yet the Pharisees had added many commands to the *Torah*. Just as one example, two candles were lit before the Sabbath began and the following prayer was said: *"Blessed are you, O Lord our God, King of the universe who has commanded us to kindle the Sabbath lights."* Nowhere in the *Torah* is this commanded, but it was commanded by the Pharisees. According to them, the command comes from God. Yeshua seems to instruct his followers to follow these commands of the Pharisees.

Yeshua also seems to contradict himself in this passage when, at first, he tells his followers to do what the Pharisees say, but in the following verses, he condemns the commands and practices of the scribes and Pharisees and calls them hypocrites.

A Hebrew Matthew exists today called the "*Shem Tov Matthew*." The actual origins of this book are obscure, but it is known to have existed since the 15th century AD and is claimed to be much older than that. Below is Matthew 23:2, 3 from the "*Shem Tov Matthew*:"

לאמר על כסא משה ישבו הפירושים

והחכמים ועתה כל אשר <u>יאמר</u> לכם שמרו

ועשו ובתקנותיהם ומעשיהם אל תעשו שהם

אומרים והם אינם עושים

The underlined word in this passage is the Hebrew word יאמר (*yomer*), meaning "he says," or "he tells." The difference between this Hebrew passage and the Greek is that in the Greek it says "they tell," which in Hebrew would be יאמרו (*yom'ru*). If we replace "they tell" with "he tells" in the Greek version, we now have:

> "*The scribes and the Pharisees have seated themselves in the chair of Moses; therefore, all that <u>he tells</u> you, do and observe, but do not do according to their deeds; for they say things, and do not do them.*"

Yeshua is telling his disciples that while the scribes and Pharisees are seated in the chair of Moses, they are to do what Moses tells them to do, meaning, "You do what the *Torah* says, regardless of what the Pharisees say."

THE MISUNDERSTOOD PARABLE
OF THE UNJUST STEWARD

In his Gospel, Luke narrates one of Yeshua's parables that has left many people scratching their heads, wondering what this parable is trying to teach:

> *"And he said also unto the disciples, 'There was a certain rich man, who had a steward; and the same was accused unto him that he was wasting his goods. And he called him, and said unto him, "What is this that I hear of thee? render the account of thy stewardship; for thou canst be no longer steward." And the steward said within himself, "What shall I do, seeing that my lord taketh away the stewardship from me? I have not strength to dig; to beg I am ashamed. I am resolved what to do, that, when I am put out of the stewardship, they may receive me into their houses." And calling to him each one of his lord's debtors, he said to the first, "How much owest thou unto my lord"? And he said, "A hundred measures of oil." And he said unto him, "Take thy bond, and sit down quickly and write fifty." Then said he to another, "And how much owest thou"? And he said, "A hundred measures of wheat." He saith unto him, "Take thy bond, and write fourscore." And his lord commended the unrighteous steward because he had done wisely: for the sons of this world are for their own generation wiser than the sons of the light.'" (Luke 16:1-8, ASV)*

To summarize this parable: A rich man is about to fire his steward, the manager of his affairs. The steward is worried that after he is fired, he will have no way to make an income. So he goes to the people that owe his master money and reduces their bills, apparently in hopes of currying their favor so that after he loses his job, one of them may hire him. For his actions, his master commends him and says that he has acted wisely.

At first glance, we might conclude that the steward was cheating his master by reducing the money owed by his master's debtors. But, if this were true, why would the master commend him? This apparent conundrum has spawned many theories about what this parable teaches.

In our culture, a manager keeps track of the money owed to his employer by his customers. In return, the employer pays the manager a wage. If that manager were to reduce the bills that his employer's customers owed him and was caught, he would most likely be fired on the spot and might even find himself in jail. Is Yeshua commending this behavior? Not at all. The parable perfectly identifies a problem: When we read the Bible, we project our own cultural perspectives on the text, and that often causes serious issues with our interpretation of it.

According to the late Dr. William Bean, founder of the *Centre for the Study of Biblical Research* (CSBR), it was discovered that in the first century, the master (the employer) did not pay the steward (the manager) a wage. Instead, a steward made his money by adding his fees onto the bills of his master's debtors (the customers). When the debtor received the bill from the steward, he did not know what amount on the bill belonged to the master and what amount belonged to the steward. Only the steward would know that. When a debtor paid their bill to the steward, the steward pocketed his portion of the bill and forwarded the remaining money to his master.

As this steward is called "unrighteous," we can assume that he was placing an extraordinarily high amount on the bills for his fee. He intended to make large amounts of money at the expense of his master and his master's debtors. However, when he found out he was going to be fired, he took the debtors' bills and reduced or eliminated the amount owed to him. In so doing, he curried favor with these debtors in hopes that one of them may hire him due to his perceived "generosity."

Furthermore, the "parable" of this parable sums up this entire work: If you want to interpret the Bible correctly, you must read it from the perspective of the people who lived at that time.

CONCLUSIONS

When you open your Bible, recognize that it has a long and complicated history. Do we all need to be Hebrew and Greek scholars to read and interpret the Bible correctly? Absolutely not. However, as this narrative has disclosed, some independent study is required to read and understand the Biblical text according to the culture and philosophy of the original authors. The good news is that there are many great resources available today that can help with that education, including the lexicon and translations created by this author to assist Bible students with proper Biblical interpretation.

It is now time to immerse yourself in the culture, lifestyle, language and philosophy of the people of the Bible. The more you read and learn about them, the more you will think like them and will begin to see things from their perspective rather than from your own, bringing the Bible and its message into much clearer focus.

Lastly, it is the author's hope that *A Cultural and Linguistic Excavation of the Bible* has given you the tools you need to mine nuggets of wisdom, knowledge and understanding for yourself. Happy digging.

TIMELINE

A timeline of events as revealed in this work.

3rd millennium BC: The only Semitic languages known to exist at this time were Akkadian and Eblaite.

26th century BC: Tablets written in Eblaite are deposited in the Royal Archives in Ebla.

2nd millennium BC: Abraham and his family live as nomads in the wilderness.

20th century BC: The Wadi El-Hhol inscription is written in pictographic script.

16th century BC: Phoenicians lived north of the land of Israel.

15th century BC: Sinaitic inscriptions from the Sinai Peninsula are written in pictographic script.

14th century BC: Tablets written in Ugarit cuneiform are written.

13th century BC: The City of Ugarit, which had been occupied since pre-historic times, is no longer inhabited.

12ᵗʰ century BC: Oldest Phoenician and *Paleo*-Hebrew inscriptions are made.

12ᵗʰ century BC: The *Paleo*-Hebrew alphabet is adopted by the Greeks.

8ᵗʰ century BC: The book of Isaiah is written.

722 BC: Northern Kingdom of Israel is taken into Assyrian captivity.

7ᵗʰ century BC: A silver scroll with the Aaronic blessing written in *Paleo*-Hebrew is deposited in Ketef Hinnom in Israel.

6ᵗʰ century BC: Western philosophy has its beginnings in Greece.

530 BC: Second Temple is built.

586 BC: Kingdom of Judah is conquered by the Babylonians.

420 BC: The book of Malachi is written, beginning the intertestamental period.

4ᵗʰ century BC: The *Paleo*-Hebrew alphabet is replaced by the Aramaic square script for general use.

3ʳᵈ century BC: Phoenicians cease to live north of the land of Israel.

3ʳᵈ century BC: The *Torah* is translated by Jewish scholars into Greek, later becoming part of the *Septuagint*.

2ⁿᵈ century BC: The *Isaiah Scroll* from the Dead Sea Caves was written.

2nd century BC: The Maccabees revolt against the Greeks.

2nd century BC: The Nash Papyrus, with the *Sh'ma* and the Ten Commandments, was written in *Paleo*-Hebrew.

1st century BC: Jonathan Ben Uziel writes an Aramaic translation of the Prophets.

1st century BC: *The Hebrew Bible* is translated into Greek and titled the *Septuagint*.

1st century AD: Onkelos, a Roman convert to Judaism, writes an Aramaic translation of the *Torah*.

1st century AD: *Paleo*-Hebrew is no longer used.

70 AD: Second Temple is destroyed by the Romans.

132 AD: The second Jewish revolt, led by Simon Bar Kockba, begins.

136 AD: The second Jewish revolt ends.

4th century AD: Codex *Sinaiticus* and the Codex *Vaticanus* are written.

5th century AD: The Aramaic *Peshitta* is written.

5th century AD: The *New Testament* is translated by Jerome into Latin.

11th century AD: The *Leningrad* Codex is written.

10ᵗʰ century AD: The *Aleppo* Codex is written.

15ᵗʰ century AD: *Shem Tov Matthew* is discovered.

16ᵗʰ century AD: The letter "J" is first introduced into the Latin alphabet.

1691 AD: Henry Dodwell makes a connection between the Samaritan and Old Hebrew letters.

1799 AD: Humphrey Prideaux connects the Phoenician and Samaritan letters to the Old Hebrew letters used before the Babylonian captivity.

19ᵗʰ century AD: Eliezer Ben-Yehuda revives the Hebrew language in Israel.

1810 AD: William Gesenius publishes his Hebrew Lexicon.

1813 AD: William Gesenius publishes his Hebrew Grammar.

1831 AD: The *Encyclopedia Americana* states that the older Hebrew alphabet was replaced by the square letters of the Aramaic alphabet.

1838 AD: *Foreign Quarterly Review* writes that the Phoenician language was identical to the Hebrew.

1854 AD: Thomas Hartwell identifies twenty-two Hebrew letters of a square form.

1855 AD: Turkish laborers accidentally uncover an ancient sarcophagus in the Phoenician city of Sidon.

1868 AD: The Mesha Stele, written in *Paleo*-Hebrew, is discovered in the Biblical city of Dibon.

1880 AD: The Siloam Inscription, written in *Paleo*-Hebrew, is discovered on the wall of Hezekiah's tunnel.

1890 AD: James Strong publishes his *Exhaustive Concordance of the Bible*.

1898 AD: The Nash Papyrus is discovered in Egypt.

1905 AD: Flinders Petrie discovers the Semitic pictographic inscriptions at Serabit el-Khadim.

1908 AD: The Gezer Calendar, written in *Paleo*-Hebrew, is discovered during the excavation of the ancient city of Gezer.

1916 AD: Dr. Gardiner deciphers the *l'balt* pictographic inscription.

1922 AD: The *New Larned History for Ready Reference, Reading and Research*, in its entry for the letter "A," denotes the suspected pictographic origins of the Hebrew alphabet.

1928 AD: French archaeologists discover the Royal Library in Ugarit with an extensive collection of cuneiform tablets.

1935 AD: Eighteen ostraca, written in *Paleo*-Hebrew, are discovered in the ancient city of Lachish.

1947 AD: First Dead Sea Scroll discovered in the Dead Sea Caves.

1948 AD: Israel became a Jewish state.

1956 AD: The last of the Dead Sea Scrolls were discovered in the Dead Sea Caves.

1958 AD: The *Oxford Dictionary of the Christian Church* states in its first edition that Hebrew ceased to be a spoken language around the 4th century BC.

1966 AD: An Ammonite inscription is found in Jordan whose alphabet is the same as *Paleo*-Hebrew.

1968 AD: The Italian Archeological Mission uncovered the statue of Ibbit-Lim, King of Ebla, with an Akkadian inscription.

1993 AD: The Tel Dan Stele, written in *Paleo*-Hebrew, is discovered in northern Israel.

1997 AD: The *Oxford Dictionary of the Christian Church* states, in its third edition, that Hebrew continued to be used as a spoken and written language in the New Testament period.

2005 AD: Jeff A. Benner publishes the *Ancient Hebrew Lexicon of the Bible*.

2019 AD: Jeff A. Benner publishes *The Torah: A Mechanical Translation*.

BIBLIOGRAPHY

The American Journal of Semitic Languages and Literatures. (1919). University of Chicago.

Anati, E. (1963). *Palestine Before the Hebrews.* Alfred A. Knopf.

Barday, B. J., & Pazzini, M. (2005). *The New Covenant Aramaic Peshitta Text with Hebrew Translation.* The Bible Society.

Beegle, D. M. (1960). *God's Word into English.* Harper & Brothers.

Benner, J. A. (2005). *The Ancient Hebrew Lexicon of the Bible.* Virtual Bookworm.

Benner, J. A. (2019). *The Torah: A Mechanical Translation.* Virtual Bookworm.

Ben-Yehuda, E., & Weinstein, D. (1961). *Ben-Yehuda's Pocket English-Hebrew, Hebrew-English Dictionary.* Washington Square Press.

Boman, T. (1960). *Hebrew Thought Compared with Greek.* W. W. Norton & Company.

Brown, F., Driver, S. R., Briggs, C. A., & Gesenius, W. (1979). *The New Brown-Driver-Briggs-Gesenius Hebrew-English Lexicon.* Hendrickson Publishers.

Budge, E. A. W. (1967). *The Egyptian Book of the Dead.* Dover Publications.

Butler, T. C. (1991). *Holman Bible Dictionary.* B&H Publishing Group.

Capt, E. R. (1985). *Missing Links Discovered in Assyrian Tablets.* Artisan Pub.

Chase, M. E. (1962). *Life and Language in the Old Testament.* W. W. Norton and Company Inc.

Clark, M., & Hirsch, S. R. (1999). *Etymological Dictionary of Biblical Hebrew.* Feldheim Publishers.

Clifford, Cutri, R. M., Goslin, N., & Montero, F. (2016). *Understanding the Whole Student.* Rowman & Littlefield.

Cohane, J. P. (1969). *The Key.* Crown Publishers.

Cole, D. P. (1975). *Nomads of the Nomads.* Harlan Davidson Inc.

Cross, F. L., & Livingstone, E. A. (1958). *The Oxford Dictionary of the Christian Church.* Oxford University Press.

Cross, F. L., & Livingstone, E. A. (1997). *The Oxford Dictionary of the Christian Church.* Oxford University Press.

Davidson, B. (1848). *The Analytical Hebrew and Chaldee Lexicon.* Samuel Bagster.

Davies, B., & Mitchel, E. C. (1886). *A Compendious and Complete Hebrew and Chaldee Lexicon to the Old Testament.*

Doblhofer, E. (1961). *Voices in Stone.* Viking Press.

Dodwell, H. (1691). *A Discourse Concerning Sanchoniathon's Phoenician History.*

Douglas, J. D., Tenney, M. C., & Goodrick, E. W. (1999). *NIV Compact Dictionary of the Bible.*

Edersheim, A. (1997). *The Life and Times of Jesus the Messiah.* Hendrickson.

The Encyclopedia Americana. (1831).

Fano, G. (1992). *The Origins and Nature of Language.* Indiana University Press.

The Foreign Quarterly Review. (1838).

Gehman, H. S. (1970). *The New Westminster Dictionary of the Bible.* Philadelphia : Westminster Press.

Gesenius, W. (1893). *Gesenius' Hebrew Grammar.* Oxford Press.

Halley, H. H. (1978). *Halley's Bible Handbook.* Zondervan.

Harper, D. (n.d.). *Online Etymology Dictionary*. Retrieved June 22, 2023, from http://etymonline.com

Harper, W. R. (1895). *Elements of Hebrew*. Charles Scribner's Sons.

Hartwell, T. (1840). *An Introduction to the Critical Study and Knowledge of the Holy Scriptures* (p. 190).

Heaton, E. W. (1956). *Everyday Life in Old Testament Times*. Charles Scribner's Sons.

Horowitz, E. (1960). *How the Hebrew Language Grew*. KTAV.

Laird, C. (1953). *The Miracle of Language*. Fawcett.

Lapide, P. (1984). *Hebrew in the Church*. William B. Eerdmans Publishing Company.

Larned, J. N. (1922). *The New Larned History for Ready Reference, Reading and Research*.

Lindsey, R. L. (1989). *Jesus, Rabbi and Lord*. Cornerstone Pub.

The Lion Encyclopedia of the Bible. (1986). Lion.

Matthews, V. H. (1991). *Manners and Customs in the Bible*. Hendrickson Publishers.

Miller, M. S., & Miller, J. L. (1973). *Harper's Bible Dictionary*. Harper Collins.

Mozeson, I. (2000). *The Word*. SP Books.

Mumford, S. (2012, March 6). *Art versus Science? - Arts Matters.* Arts Matters. http://blogs.nottingham.ac.uk/artsmatters/2012/03/ 06/ art-versus-science/

Muraoka, T. (1998). *Hebrew/Aramaic Index to the Septuagint.* Continuum.

Nelson, S. L., & Strong, J. (1996). *The New Strong's Concise Concordance of the Bible.* Thomas Nelson.

Packer, J. I., Tenney, M. C., & White, W., Jr. (1995). *Nelson's Illustrated Encyclopedia of Bible Facts.* Thomas Nelson.

Pilch, J. J. (1999). *The Cultural Dictionary of the Bible.* Liturgical Press.

Prideaux, H. (1719). *The Old and New Testament Connected in the History of the Jews and Neighbouring Nations.*

Radosh, D. (2006, December 10). *The Good Book Business | The New Yorker.* The New Yorker; The New Yorker. https://www.newyorker.com/magazine/2006/12/18/the-good-book-business.

Skeat, W. W. (1895). *A Concise Etymological Dictionary of the English Language.* Capricorn Books.

Smith, G. A. (1944). *The Hebrew Genius as Exhibited in the Old Testament.*

Smith, W. (1878). *Smith's Bible Dictionary.*

Soul Definition & Meaning | Dictionary.com. (n.d.). Dictionary. Com. Retrieved June 22, 2023, from https://www.dictionary.com/browse/soul.

The Analytical Greek Lexicon (n.d.). Harper & Brothers.

Unger, M. F. (1969). *Unger's Bible Dictionary*. Moody.

Vermeule, E. (1964). *Greece in the Bronze Age*. The University of Chicago Press.

Vine, W. E. (1996). *Vine's Expository Dictionary of Old and New Testament Words*. Thomas Nelson.

Wight, F. (1983). *Manners and Customs of Bible Lands*. Moody.

INDEX

A

Aaronic Blessing 146, 198

Abecedary 177

Abel 154

Abraham 9, 20, 32, 33, 163, 205,
    248, 251, 277

Abram 138, 218

Abstract 31, 33, 141, 199, 211

Abundant 116

Acronyms 49

Acrostic 150

Adam 95

Adjectives 36, 111, 186, 209

Adonai 131

Adopted Root 107, 108, 109

Adverb 111, 209

Affix 111

Afflicted 232

Africa 29

Akkadian 175, 183

Aleph (Arabic Letter) 71

Aleph (Hebrew Letter) 44, 45, 61,
    65, 70, 98, 100

Alphabet 53
    Arabic 89
    Aramaic 62, 63, 278
    English 62
    Greek 62
    Hebrew 55, 56, 61, 63, 92, 177
    Latin 62
    Paleo-Hebrew 278, 279, 280
    Phoenician 55, 56
    Samaritan 53, 55, 280
    Semitic 63, 64, 65, 66, 67,
        92, 106
    Sinaitic 65
    Ugarit 89, 176, 177

Alpha (Greek Letter) 61, 71

Amazon 29, 31

America 29, 30, 40

Americans 40

Amman 59

Amos 180

Ancient Hebrew 30, 35, 40, 42, 53, 98, 191, 195, 207
Ancient Hebrews 30, 31, 40, 138
And 114, 234
Angel 3
Anger 139
Anna 16
Announce 188
Anthropology 195
Antiseptic 22
Ape 86
Apocrypha 1, 2, 224
Apologist 154
Appearance 24, 35, 36
Arabic 96, 98
Aram 123
Aramaic 124
Aramaic Primacy 230
Aramean 15, 62, 123
Aramitess 123
Archaeology 64, 195
Archer 196
Aristotle 33
Arm 79
Arrow 197
Asher 16, 223
Asherah 176
Assimilation 30
Assyria 223
Assyrian 16, 53
Astarte 183
Aunts 21
Authority 51, 106

Autographs 146
Ayin (Hebrew Letter) 65, 66, 70, 84, 90, 94, 96
Azazel 2, 3

B

Baal 176, 183
Babylon 33, 54, 62, 224, 247
Bad 203, 213, 215
Balance 213, 215
Baptism 248, 249, 251
Barley 22
Basket 79
Bean, Dr. William 273
Because 111
Bedouin 32, 33
Beginning 166
Behold 75
Being 133, 137, 208
Bend the Knee 187
Benjamin 223
Benner, Jeff A. 282
Ben-Yehuda, Eliezer 280
Beta (Greek Letter) 61, 72
Bethlehem 7
Beyt (Arabic Letter) 72
Beyt (Hebrew Letter) 21, 44, 45, 55, 61, 66, 72, 116, 150
Bible 30, 34, 36, 147, 154, 165, 166, 183, 195
Biliteral Root. *See* Parent Root; *See* Parent Root

Bladders 21
Blameless 136
Bless 198, 199
Block Logic 257
Blossom xxi, 41
Boman, Thorleif 34
Book of
Acts 4
Daniel 265
Deuteronomy 8, 11
Enoch 2, 3
Genesis 238
Isaiah 203, 246, 254, 278
Job 189, 190
Leviticus 243
Malachi xx, 278
Matthew xx, 231, 232,
234, 258
Psalms 191
Revelation 4
Border xviii
Bow and Arrow 22
Bowls 22
Bread 22
Break 107, 194
Breaking 105
British Library 230
Buck 106
Build 206
Burning Coals 184

C

Cain 136, 154
Cake 22
Camp 21, 23, 210, 212, 253
Camphire 187
Canaan 92, 182
Canaanite 15, 176, 182, 183, 188
Canon 2, 4, 147
Captivity 62, 67
Catholic 1, 4
Chaldean 54
Chaldeans 62
Character 249, 250
Cheese 22, 203
Cherish 194
Chiasmus 161
Chief 20, 44, 166
Child 188
Children 21, 24
Child Root 106, 107, 109
China 33
Chinese 176
Choice 216
Christian 4, 5, 148, 224, 248
Christianity 246
Clan 15, 21, 23
Clark, Matityahu 104
Clay 79
Clothing 23
Cloud 193
Codex
Aleppo 54, 149, 150, 154, 280

Leningrad 99, 118
   Sinaiticus 230
   Vaticanus 230, 279
Coins 53, 242
Cold 26
Cole, Donald P. 32
Colt 164
Columbus, Christopher 29
Command 41, 268
Commandment 40, 268
Community Rule 147
Complex 28, 29, 30
Concordance xviii, 133
Concrete 31, 33, 48, 138, 139, 141, 199, 211
Congeal 86
Conjunctions 111, 209
Consonant 106, 117, 129, 130
Consumer 165
Consumerism 165
Container 79
Containers 21
Continue 50, 83, 211
Continuing 50
Cooking 22
Copper 188
Corner xix, xx
Costume 14
Covenant 215, 216
Covering 137
Cow 190
Craftsman 203
Crispus 250

Crooked Ones 31
Crops 22
Cross Over 250
Culture 18, 25, 29, 30, 31, 33, 34, 39, 120, 169, 176, 195, 225, 246, 254, 273, 275
Cuneiform 176, 177, 182, 277
Curse 48
Curtain 24
Custom 14, 17
Cut 106

D

Dagan 183
Dal (Arabic Letter) 74
Dalet (Hebrew Letter) 24, 61, 74
Damascus Document 147
Dan 223
Darkness 94, 214
Dates 22
David 20, 45, 100
Dead 137
Dead Sea Caves 67, 100, 147, 148, 149, 243, 278, 281, 282
Dead Sea Scrolls 99, 118, 149, 150, 151, 281, 282
Death 250
Dedicated 141
Deer 36
Delicacy 203
Delitzsch 231
Delta (Greek Letter) 61, 74

Demon 3

Dental 120, 121

Descendant 123, 126

Desert 27, 31

Destitute 232

Destroy 236

Deuteronomist 11

Dibon 57

Dictionary xviii, 116, 142, 182, 187, 188

Digging 105

Disciples 16, 249, 252, 270

Doctrine 41, 193, 248

Documentary Hypothesis 6, 11

Dodwell, Henry 53, 280

Dominion 104

Door 24, 25, 26, 46, 74, 204

Drink 73

Drool 48

Dry 108

Dysfunctional 213

E

Eastern Orthodox Church 1

Eastern Thought 213

Eat 215

Eating 23

Eber 251

Ebla 180, 181, 182, 183, 185, 188

Eblaite 175, 182, 183, 184, 185, 187, 188

Edenics 119

Edge xviii

Egypt 43, 147, 253

Egyptian 15, 176

El 176, 184

Elohist 11

Elohiym 11, 131, 199

Emotion 207

Encyclopedia 183

Encyclopedia Americana 280

Enoch 147

Entertainment 23

Entrance 24

Ephraim 223

Ephrath 7

Epiphanes, Antiochus 224

Epiphanius 233

Epistles 4

Epsilon (Greek Letter) 61, 75

Essenes 147

Eternity 102

Etymology 119, 120, 169, 196

Europe 30

Europeans 29, 30

Eusebius 233

Eve 135

Evil 213

Evil Eye 237

Exodus 43

Extra-Biblical 60

Eye 69, 204

Ezra 54

F

Fabric 26
Face 199
Faith 140
Family 20, 21, 25, 26
Far East 33
Fat 22
Father 24, 25, 44, 45, 49, 111, 123
Fatten 216
Feast of Weeks 251
Filter 192
Fire 26
Firstborn 189
Flame 184
Flock 20, 21, 22
Flood 21, 191, 213
Floorplan 24
Flour 22
Flow 48, 107
Food 22, 23
Foot 73
Forcing 104
Foreigner 14
Fringe xviii, xx, 41
Fruit xxi, 22, 119, 120
Fulfil 236
Function 24, 35, 36
Functional 213
Furnace 163

G

G0907 248
G0908 248
G1320 266
G1484 15
G1672 17
G1675 17
G1785 267
G2878 239
G2899 xviii
G3037 238
G3173 267
G3551 267
G4169 267
G4339 18
G4434 232
G4521 239
G5043 238
Gad 223
Gaius 250
Gamma (Greek Letter) 61, 73, 90, 96
Gardiner, Alan 65, 66, 281
Garment xviii, xix, xx
Gather 73, 87
Gaze 121
Geem (Arabic Letter) 73
Gender 113, 173
Generous 237
Gentile 15, 17, 19
Gesenius, William 41, 48, 105, 280
Gezer 58, 281
Gezer Calendar 67, 281
Ghayin (Arabic Letter) 89

Ghayin (Hebrew Letter) 84, 89, 92, 94, 96

Gift 199

Gihon Spring 58

Gimel (Hebrew Letter) 61, 73, 179

Giovanni Pettinato 182

Give 167

Glottal Stop 117

Glue 51

Goat 3, 22

Goat Hair 25, 26, 27

God 23, 26, 51, 106, 131, 213, 247, 251, 253

Gods 176, 183

Gold 95

Golden Calf 254

Goliath 215

Good 203, 213, 215

Good Eye 237

Gospel 4, 17, 164, 247, 257, 258

Grace 200, 210

Gracious 211

Gradational Variants 104

Grain 22, 116, 117, 120, 183

Grammar 163

Grandparents 21

Grapes 22

Greco-Roman 133, 134, 138

Greece 33

Greedy 237

Greek Primacy 230

Greeks 29

Grimm's Law 120

Guard 194, 199

Gut 133

Guttural 120, 121

H

H0019 108

H0068 239

H0215 200

H0216 200

H0249 13

H1060 189

H1121 239

H1262 215

H1267 216

H1274 216

H1285 215

H1288 187, 198

H1290 199

H1293 199

H1420 268

H1471 15

H1481 14

H1616 14

H1698 184

H1712 183

H1715 183

H2056 188

H2091 95

H2101 95

H2114 13

H2224 13

H2449 202

H2525 202
H2580 210
H2583 200, 210
H2603 200, 211
H2896 213
H3206 188
H3276 93
H3277 93
H3384 196
H3394 103
H3724 187
H3820 207
H3824 206
H3842 103
H3966 208
H4100 268
H4175 196, 268
H4264 210
H4317 185
H4325 189
H4488 188
H4512 189
H4687 268
H5012 188
H5030 188
H5234 14
H5236 14
H5237 14
H5315 208
H5584 94
H5674 250
H5680 251
H5764 93

H5766 93
H5785 93
H5786 93
H5888 93
H5890 93
H5892 93
H5895 93
H6030 93
H6031 93
H6041 232
H6148 93
H6150 93
H6174 93
H6175 93
H6201 93
H6202 93
H6440 199
H6565 194
H6632 95
H6669 95
H6731 xxi
H6734 xviii
H7133 239
H7200 142
H7364 248
H7451 93, 213
H7453 93
H7565 184
H7677 239
H7760 200
H7965 200
H7999 200
H8068 199

H8104 194, 199
H8163 93
H8175 93
H8451 196, 268
H8492 184
Haftarah 247
Hair 21
Hand 79
Hang 24
Hartwell, Thomas 52, 280
Head 87
Heart 133, 206, 209
Heat 26, 202, 203
Hebraism 164, 235, 236, 241
Hebrew Bible 30, 32, 41, 47, 68,
        95, 99, 102, 116, 123, 133,
        135, 136, 137, 146, 147, 149,
        152, 153, 154, 189, 266
Hebrews 34, 40, 48, 227
Hebrew Studies 43
Heifer 63
Height 166
Heir 83
Hellenist 15, 17, 18
Help 179
Henna 187
Herds 20, 21
Hey (Hebrew Letter) 61, 75, 100,
        117, 128, 129
Hezekiah's Tunnel 58
Hhawa 135
Hhhet (Hebrew Letter) 78
Hieroglyphs 176

Hillel the Elder 153
Hiphil 115
Hitpael 115
Hobab 10
Holy 41, 141, 188
Holy Spirit 253
Home 24
Hook 76
Hophal 115
Hopi 40
Horeb 9
Horizon 87, 103, 108
Horns 21
Horowitz, Edward 97, 98
Hospitality 23
House 21, 44, 49, 72, 106, 252
House of David 60
Humbling 105

I

Ibbit-Lim 181
Idiom 236, 237
Immigrant 14
India 33
Indigenous 29
Infix 111
Inscription
    Akkadian 181
    Ammonite 59, 282
    Hebrew 58, 243
    Lachish 67
    Moabite 58

Paleo-Hebrew 278
Phoenician 58
Semitic 67
Siloam 281
Sinaitic 65, 67
Wadi El-Hhol 277
Insides 133
Interlinear 169
Interpretation xvii, 30, 34,
    113, 165
Intertestamental Period 2,
    223, 224
Ireneus 232
Iron 29
Isaac 20
Isaiah 149
Isaiah Scroll 148, 149
Isho'dad 233
Ishtar 181
Israel 7, 8, 10, 13, 15, 16, 17, 19,
    21, 33, 40, 41, 53, 60, 99,
    146, 148, 152, 176, 192, 219,
    223, 224, 229, 241, 249, 250,
    251, 277, 280, 281, 282
Israelites 63, 218
Israel, Kingdom of 278
Issachar 223

J

Jacob 20, 136
James 16
Japan 33

Jehovah 129
Jerome 154, 233, 279
Jerusalem 58, 253
Jethro 10
Jew 224
Jewish Life 4
Jewish Tradition 3
Jews 4, 5, 15, 17, 18, 30, 40,
    224, 225
Job 136
John the Baptist 247, 249, 251
Jonathan, Targum 152
Jordan 59, 282
Jordan River 247, 250, 251
Josephus 225
Joshua 139
Journey 106
Jubilees 147
Judah 223, 224
Judah, Kingdom of 278
Judaism 245, 246, 247, 248
Justice 23

K

Kaph (Hebrew Letter) 80, 116
Keep 194, 198
Ketef Hinnom 146, 278
Ketuvim 1
Kidneys 133
King 25, 60
Kingdom 102
Knee 199

Kneel 198

Knife 22, 108

Knowledge 28, 167, 204, 205

Kockba, Simon Bar 40, 228,
    242, 279

Kohen 41

L

Labials 120

Lachish 281

Lam (Arabic Letter) 81

Lamda (Greek Letter) 81

Lamed (Hebrew Letter) 66, 81

Lamp 158, 163

Landmarks 20

Language 14, 18, 28, 31, 120
    Akkadian 277, 282
    Aramaic 239
    Eblaite 190, 277
    English 40, 93, 113, 116
    Greek 17
    Hebrew 31, 41, 42, 44, 47, 48,
        49, 92, 101, 131, 183,
        209, 227, 229, 280
    Phoenician 280
    Semitic 180, 183, 189,
        231, 277
    Sinaitic 277
    Slavic 129
    Syriac 124, 187
    Ugarit 179, 277
Latin 152, 154

Latin Vulgate 154

Law 14, 196, 254

Leader 35, 36, 203

Learn 71

Lebanon 55

Levi 21

Levites 254

Leviticus Scroll 68

Lexicon 43, 116, 169

Libraries 148

Lid 137

Life 250, 256

Lifestyle xvii, 20, 31, 32

Light 26, 108, 111, 158, 200, 214

Lightning 8

Lindsey, Robert L. 258

Linguistics 28, 44, 48, 111, 195

Linguists 31, 103

Lip 112

Liquids 120

Livestock 20

Logogram 175

Lord 131

Lost Ten Tribes 223

Love 23

Luke 164, 272

Luther, Martin 234

M

Maccabees 224

Maiden 102

Manasseh 223

Manna 135

Mannerisms 14

Manuscripts 146, 154

Mark 88, 164

Masoretes 32, 189

Masoretic 68, 99, 100, 118, 131,
    150, 189

Mat 25

Matthew 164, 271

Matthews, Victor H. 34

Matthiae, Paolo 181

Mattock 77

Mattocks 22

Mature 136

Meat 21, 22, 216

Mechanical Translation xiv, 169,
    170, 171

Medicine 22

Melchizedek 138

Mem (Hebrew Letter) 82

Mercy 23, 211

Mercy-Seat 137

Mesha 179

Mesha Stele 57, 67, 281

Messiah 4

Messianics 148

Middle East 33

Might 208, 209

Mikvah 249, 251

Milk 21, 22, 203

Mill 22

Mitsvah 267

Moab 179

Moabite 57

Moabites 15, 57

Moabite Stone. *See* Mesha Stele;
    See Mesha Stele

Modern Greek 61

Modern Hebrew 41, 54, 69, 92, 94,
    98, 113, 129

Mood 113, 114

Moon 103

Moreh 197

Morphology 111

Moses 5, 6, 7, 10, 20, 21, 135, 139,
    251, 253, 271

Mosheh. *See* Moses; *See* Moses

Mother 51

Mouth 69

Mud 79

Multitude 253

N

Name 123, 124, 130, 135, 250

Name of God 128, 131

Naphtali 223

Nasals 120

Nash Papyrus 147, 279, 281

Nation 15, 16, 17, 253

Nation of Israel 60

Native 13, 14, 40

Native-born 14

Near East xxi, 27, 33

Nevi'im 1

New Testament xviii, 2, 4, 15, 16, 18, 124, 154, 224, 225, 230, 239, 241, 254, 257

New Testament period 282

Nikkud 32, 75, 100, 116, 118, 131, 150

nikkudot. *See* Nikkud; *See* Nikkud

Niphal 115

Noah 218

Nomad 20, 21, 23, 32, 194

Nose 139

Noun 110, 112

Number 113

Nun (Hebrew Letter) 82

O

Oak 35, 36

Oasis 20

Offering 239

Offspring 83

Old Testament 1, 4, 12, 99, 227, 238, 247

Olives 22

Omega (Greek Letter) 84

Omicron (Greek Letter) 84

Onkelos 279

Open 110

Oppressing 104

Origen 233

Original Authors 34

Orthodox 41

Ostraca 59

Ox 49, 50, 51, 63, 71

P

Pa'al 115

Paleo-Hebrew 45, 53, 57, 58, 59, 60, 62, 65, 67, 128, 146, 243

Palm 80

Panels 25

Papias 232

Papyrus 146

Parable 262, 272

Parallel 178, 179, 190, 211

Parallelism 157, 160, 161, 163, 209, 270

Parent Root 104, 107, 108, 109, 110, 119, 210, 212

Parents 21

Pass Over 250

Pasture 20, 21

Path 103

Patriarch 123, 126

Paul 17, 244, 250

Peace 198, 200

Peg 76

Pegs 27

Peh (Hebrew Letter) 69, 85, 116

Pencil 36

Pentateuch 1, 5, 53, 54

Pentecost 251

Perish 115

Person 113, 133, 137, 208, 265

Peshitta 279

Pestilence 184

Petrie, Flinders 64, 281

Pettinato, Giovanni 182

Pharisee 258, 265, 270, 271

Philology 42, 43

Philosophers 33

Philosophy 28, 29, 30, 31, 33,
    35, 275

Phoenician 53, 57, 59, 182

Phoenicians 55, 277, 278

Phonogram 176

Pictograph 24, 25, 44, 45, 176,
    177, 210

Piel 115, 198, 199

Pi (Greek Letter) 85

Pine 36

Pirahã 31

Plain 136

Plato 33

Plow 77

Plural 110

Poetry 158, 238

Point 108, 196

Poles 27

Pomegranates 22

Pool of Siloam 58

Poor 232

Possessions 189

Power 71

Prayer 23

Preach 17

Precept 268

Precious 213

Prefix 111, 170

Prepositions 111, 209

Presence 199

Prideaux, Humphrey 53, 55, 280

Priest 41, 154

Priesthood 249

Principal 166, 268

Pronoun 113

Pronunciation 116, 128, 131

Property 190

Prophet 153, 188

Proselytes 15

Protect 194, 199

Protection 23, 212, 213

Protestant 1, 2, 4

Proverbs 157

Psalms 147, 157

Pseudepigrapha 2

Pual 115

Pure 141

Pus 95

Q

Qal 115

Queen 102

Quiet 136

Qumran 148

Quph (Hebrew Letter) 86

R

Rabbi 236, 249, 258

Rachel 7

Rain 20, 21, 23, 26, 194

Rank 166

Ransom 187

Ras Shamra 176

Redactor 8, 11

Reeds 73

Religion 23

Respect 198

Rest 239

Restitution 201

Reuben 223

Revolt 224, 228

Rho (Greek Letter) 87

Rich 190

Right 31

Ritual 248, 249

River 20

Road 121

Roman 30

Roman Army 148

Roof 26

Root System 109, 119

Ropes 23, 27

Rot 108

Roth, Andrew Gabriel 231

Royal Archives 184, 185

Royalty 102

Rule 268

Ruling 104

S

Sabbath 17, 239

Said 114

Sails 29

Salkinson-Ginsburg 231

Samaritan 53

Samaritans 53, 54, 223

Samehh (Hebrew Letter) 83

Sanctified 141

San (Greek Letter) 86

Sarah 33

Sarcophagus 56, 67

Satan 214

Scapegoat 2, 3

Science 28, 29, 44, 195

Scribe 150, 179

Scroll 146

Second Temple 278, 279

Secret 102, 103

Seed 50, 83

Semitic People 62

Senses 34

Separating 203

Separation 211

Septuagint xviii, 15, 123, 124, 135,
        136, 153, 154, 155, 156, 266,
        278, 279

Serabit el-Khadim 65, 281

Serpent 138

Shaken 203

Shavu'ot 251, 252, 254

Sheep 22

Shelter 23
Shem Tov Matthew 271, 280
Shepherd 180, 199
Shine 200
Shin (Hebrew Letter) 88, 98
Sh'ma 147
Sickles 22
Siddur 224
Side 86
Sidon 55, 56, 280
Siloam Inscription 67
Simeon 223
Simple 28, 29, 30, 136
Sin 173
Sinai 8, 9, 64, 67, 218, 252,
        253, 254
Sirach 147
Skill 167, 203
Skin 21, 22, 146
Skin-Bag 203
Sky 26
Slaughter 109
Smith, George Adam 35
Snow 189
Soap 22
Socrates 33
Solomon 215
Son 50, 106
Son Of Man 264
Soul 166, 207, 209
South 30
Spears 22
Special 22, 41, 141

Spirant 72, 80, 85
Spirants 116
Spit 48
Spittle 48
Spoons 22
Staff 51, 81
Stag 35
Stars 26
Steady 140
Stephanas 250
Step Logic 257
Stingy 237
Stink 108
Stomach 22
Stone Age 30
Stops 116
Storytelling 23
Straight Ones 31
Stranger 13, 18
Strength 50, 51, 71, 106
Striking 105
String 78
Stronghold 86
Strong, James xviii
Strong's Concordance 133
Strong's Dictionary 141
Students 258
Subject 114
Substance 190
Suffix 111, 112, 170
Sumerian 175
Sun 203
Sunrise 87

Sunset 87

Superintendent 187

Sword 108

Syllable 117, 129, 130

Synagogue 17, 148, 149, 224, 228, 247

Synonyms 209

Syntax 170

Syria 33, 123, 176, 181

Syrian 123

T

Tabernacle 205, 253

Tablet 58, 176, 182, 183, 251

Talmud 68, 228

Tanakh 1, 247

Targum Onkelos 152

Tav (Arabic Letter) 89

Tav (Hebrew Letter) 66, 88

Taw (Greek Letter) 89

Teach 167, 168

Teacher 197, 266, 268

Teaching 41, 262

Teeth 88

Tel Dan Stele 60, 282

Tel Mardikh 181

Temple 241, 242, 249, 252, 254

Temple Ostraca 128, 129

Ten Commandments 137, 147

Ten Lost Tribes 16

Tenses, Verb 40, 113, 114

Tent 21, 23, 25, 26, 27, 32, 72, 78, 204, 210

Tent Poles 22

Ten Words 137

Tet (Hebrew Letter) 79

Tetragrammaton 128

Textual Criticism 154, 156

Theta (Greek Letter) 79

Thorn 83

Thousand 44

Throne 25

Thunder 8

Timbers 29

Time 39, 40

Tirosh 184

Tobit 147

Torah 1, 5, 7, 11, 14, 18, 41, 53, 54, 196, 224, 228, 247, 249, 251, 254, 266, 267, 269, 271

Torah Scroll 149

Track 121

Tradition xvii, 224, 247, 251, 253, 254

Trample 195

Translation 155, 156, 164, 165, 166, 212

Translators 31, 133, 135, 150, 153

Transliteration 129

Tribe 15, 21, 23, 31

Trumpets 21, 252

Truth 256

Tsade (Hebrew Letter) 85

Tsiytsiyt 40, 41

Twelve Tribes 16
Twisted rope 89
Tyre 55

U

Ugarit 277, 281
Uncles 21
Understanding 206
United States 40
Upper Room 252
Utensils 22
Uziel, Jonathan Ben 153, 279

V

Vav (Hebrew Letter) 76, 114, 117, 128, 129, 130
Verb 36, 40, 113, 142
Verbs 173
Vocabulary 48, 167
Voice 113, 114
Vowel 106, 117, 120, 129, 130

W

Wadi El-Hhol 67
Walk 106
Wall 25, 46, 78, 95, 211
War Scroll 147
Wash 248
Washing 22, 248
Water 20, 21, 50, 82, 108, 189, 202
Watering hole 73
Waw. *See* Vav; *See* Vav

Wealth 190
Weapons 22
Western Thought 213
Wheat 22
Whistling Fricative 120, 121
White 103
Whole 201
Whorf, Benjamin Lee 39
Whorf Hypothesis 39
Wickedness 94
Wicker 79
Wilderness 3, 10, 20
Wind 27, 252
Wine 184
Wing xix
Wisdom 202, 203
Wise 203
Word 254
Word Puns 238
Working 23
Wounds 22
Writing 11, 153, 175

X

Xsi (Greek Letter) 83

Y

Yah 184
Yahwist 11
Yehuda, Eliezer Ben 229
Yellow 95
Yeshivas 228

Yeshua xx, 4, 16, 17, 164, 246,
        250, 252, 254, 256, 258,
        264, 265, 269, 272
YHWH 3, 9, 11, 16, 19, 130, 146,
        176, 218
Yoke 63, 71
Young Man 179
Young Woman 103
Yud (Hebrew Letter) 65, 79, 100,
        117, 128, 129

Z

Zadokite Priests 148
Zayin (Hebrew Letter) 77
Zebulun 223
Zeta (Greek Letter) 77

www.ingramcontent.com/pod-product-compliance
Lightning Source LLC
Chambersburg PA
CBHW060246100426
42742CB00011B/1651